To

KT-221-349

Fiona x
2018

Little Oxford Dictionary of
Quotations

Little Oxford Dictionary of ✳

Quotations

FIFTH EDITION

Edited by
Susan Ratcliffe

OXFORD
UNIVERSITY PRESS

OXFORD
UNIVERSITY PRESS

Great Clarendon Street, Oxford, OX2 6DP,
United Kingdom

Oxford University Press is a department of the University of Oxford.
It furthers the University's objective of excellence in research, scholarship,
and education by publishing worldwide. Oxford is a registered trade mark of
Oxford University Press in the UK and in certain other countries

First Edition published in 1994
Second Edition published in 2001
Third edition published in 2005
Fourth edition published in 2008
Fifth edition published in 2012

Impression: 6

British Library Cataloguing in Publication Data

Data available

Library of Congress Cataloging in Publication Data

Data available

ISBN 978–0–19–965450–5

Printed in India by Replika Press Pvt Ltd

❋ Contents

Foreword ✳

An English proverb has it that 'The best things come in small packages', and if that is true then this is the best dictionary of quotations. While the comprehensive *Oxford Dictionary of Quotations* includes over 20,000 quotations, here the essence of that volume is distilled into 4,000 of the most famous and most useful sayings in the English language. The words of the great and the good, or sometimes the bad but witty, are gathered together to enable the user to add colour to a speech or offer support for a point of view.

The quotations are arranged by subject, so that a variety of angles on the same topic can be found together: on **Weather**, you can choose to quote Jerome K. Jerome: 'The weather is like the Government, always in the wrong' or St Teresa of Ávila: 'There is no such thing as bad weather. All weather is good because it is God's'. Some themes encompass special events such as **Birthdays** ('But after all, what *are* birthdays? Here today and gone tomorrow' A. A. Milne), some cover interests such as **Music** ('Music is a higher revelation than all wisdom and philosophy' Beethoven), while others are more abstract such as **Happiness** ('Happiness is a how, not a what; a talent, not an object' Hermann Hesse) or **Old Age** ('Age is whatever you think it is. You are as old as you think you are' Muhammad Ali). New themes in this edition include **Facts**, **India**, **Kissing**, and **Wisdom** ('The fool wonders, the wise man asks', said Disraeli).

Within each theme the quotations are arranged in alphabetical order of author's name, and a brief description is given for each author. Where a little more background information is necessary to understand the quotation, this

Foreword

is supplied after the author details. An index is provided to help readers seeking a quotation from a particular author.

Oxford continues to collect and authenticate new quotations as it has for over seventy years. Some of these quotations are by current authors, such as the writer Maya Angelou: 'You may not control all the events that happen to you but you can decide not to be reduced by them' or, on a more modern topic, the novelist Terry Pratchett: 'One of the universal rules of happiness is: always be wary of any helpful item that weighs less than its operating manual'. Others may go back more than two thousand years, but still resonate today: it was the Greek philosopher Plato who said: 'Of all animals the boy is the most unmanageable'. Perhaps that was what Willa Cather had in mind when she said 'The dead might as well try to speak to the living as the old to the young'. But the dead do speak to us: why else would we continue to quote the inventor Thomas Alva Edison 'The value of an idea lies in the using of it'. Perhaps the French moralist Montaigne has the answer: 'I quote others only the better to express myself'.

St Ambrose wrote more than 1500 years ago that 'No duty is more urgent than that of returning thanks'. It is not a duty but a pleasure to thank the many people who have contributed to this book, in particular Joanna Harris, Commissioning Editor for Quotations, Susanne Charlett, Jean Harker, and Verity Mason for their contributions to the Quotations Reading Programme, Ralph Bates for library research, and Kim Allen for proofreading. And it is perhaps appropriate to conclude with the words of E. F. Schumacher and Mies van der Rohe: 'Small is beautiful' and 'Less is more'.

SUSAN RATCLIFFE

Oxford 2012

List of Subjects ❋

List of Subjects

List of Subjects

The Law
Leadership
Leisure
Letters
Liberty
Libraries
Lies
Life
Life Sciences
Lifestyles
Literature
London
Love
Lovers
Luck

M

Madness
Management
Manners
Marriage
Mathematics
Meaning
Medicine
Meeting
Memory
Men
Men and Women
Middle Age
The Mind
Misfortune
Mistakes
Moderation
Money
Morality
Mothers
Mountains

Murder
Music

N

Names
Nature
News
Night

O

Old Age
Opinion
Optimism
Originality

P

Painting
Parents
Parties
Parting
The Past
Patience
Patriotism
Peace
Perfection
Persistence
Pessimism
Philosophy
Photography
Planning
Pleasure
Poetry
Politicians
Politics

Pollution
Poverty
Power
Practicality
Praise
Prayer
Prejudice
The Present
The Presidency
Pride
Progress
Promises
Protest
Punctuality
Punishment

Q

Quotations

R

Race
Railways
Reading
Reality
Relationships
Religion
Retirement
Revenge
Revolution
Royalty

S

Satisfaction
Science

List of Subjects

Ability

Natural abilities are like natural plants, that need pruning by study.
> **Francis Bacon** 1561–1626 English courtier

If a man write a better book, preach a better sermon, or make a better mouse-trap than his neighbour, tho' he build his house in the woods, the world will make a beaten path to his door.
> **Ralph Waldo Emerson** 1803–82 American writer

DUMBLEDORE: It is our choices, Harry, that show what we truly are, far more than our abilities.
> **J. K. Rowling** 1965– English novelist

MARLON BRANDO: I could have had class. I could have been a contender.
> **Budd Schulberg** 1914–2009 American writer, *in the film* On the Waterfront

Non omnia possumus omnes.

We can't all do everything.
> **Virgil** 70–19 BC Roman poet

Intelligence is quickness to apprehend as distinct from ability, which is capacity to act wisely on the thing apprehended.
> **Alfred North Whitehead** 1861–1947 English philosopher

Absence

The Lord watch between me and thee, when we are absent one from another.
> **Bible**

The heart may think it knows better: the senses know that absence blots people out. We have really no absent friends.
> **Elizabeth Bowen** 1899–1973 Anglo-Irish novelist

Achievement

The absent are always in the wrong.
Philippe Néricault Destouches 1680–1754 French dramatist

Absence diminishes commonplace passions and increases great ones, as the wind extinguishes candles and kindles fire.
Duc de la Rochefoucauld 1613–80 French moralist

Absence makes the heart grow fonder.
Proverb

Most of what matters in your life takes place in your absence.
Salman Rushdie 1947– Indian-born British novelist

 # Achievement see also **Ambition**, **Effort**

That's one small step for a man, one giant leap for mankind.
Neil Armstrong 1930–2012 American astronaut, *stepping onto the moon*

We can lift ourselves out of ignorance, we can find ourselves as creatures of excellence and intelligence and skill.
Richard Bach 1936– American novelist

The desire accomplished is sweet to the soul.
Bible

Give us the tools and we will finish the job.
Winston Churchill 1874–1965 British statesman

None climbs so high as he who knows not whither he is going.
Oliver Cromwell 1599–1658 English statesman

The distance is nothing; it is only the first step that is difficult.
Mme Du Deffand 1697–1780 French literary hostess, *commenting on the legend that St Denis, carrying his head in his hands, walked two leagues*

The reward of a thing well done, is to have done it.
Ralph Waldo Emerson 1803–82 American writer

Those who believe that they are exclusively in the right are generally those who achieve something.
Aldous Huxley 1894–1963 English novelist

Being the richest man in the cemetery doesn't matter to me…Going to bed at night saying we've done something wonderful…that's what matters to me.
Steve Jobs 1955–2011 American computer executive

He has, indeed, done it very well; but it is a foolish thing well done.
Samuel Johnson 1709–84 English lexicographer

It is sobering to consider that when Mozart was my age he had already been dead for a year.
Tom Lehrer 1928– American humorist

He who does *something* at the head of one regiment, will eclipse him who does *nothing* at the head of a hundred.
Abraham Lincoln 1809–65 American statesman

Fame is an accident; merit a thing absolute.
Herman Melville 1819–91 American novelist

So little done, so much to do.
Cecil Rhodes 1853–1902 South African statesman

Acting see also **Cinema**, **Theatre**

To grasp the full significance of life is the actor's duty, to interpret it is his problem, and to express it his dedication.
Marlon Brando 1924–2004 American actor

Just say the lines and don't trip over the furniture.
Noël Coward 1899–1973 English dramatist

Action

Actors are cattle.
Alfred Hitchcock 1899–1980 British-born film director

Acting is a masochistic form of exhibitionism. It is not quite the occupation of an adult.
Laurence Olivier 1907–89 English actor

She ran the whole gamut of the emotions from A to B.
Dorothy Parker 1893–1967 American critic

Acting is merely the art of keeping a large group of people from coughing.
Ralph Richardson 1902–83 English actor

Suit the action to the word, the word to the action.
William Shakespeare 1564–1616 English dramatist

They say an actor is only as good as his parts. Well, my parts have done me pretty well, darling.
Barbara Windsor 1937– English actress

 # Action

But men must know, that in this theatre of man's life it is reserved only for God and angels to be lookers on.
Francis Bacon 1561–1626 English courtier

Vision without action is merely a dream. Action without vision just passes the time. Vision with action can change the world.
Joel Arthur Barker American futurist

Let's roll.
Todd Beamer 1968–2001, *as Beamer and other passengers were planning to storm the cockpit of the hijacked United Airlines Flight 93, 11 September 2001*

Better to light a candle than curse the darkness.
Peter Benenson 1921–2005 English lawyer

Advertising

The world can only be grasped by action, not by contemplation…The hand is the cutting edge of the mind.
Jacob Bronowski 1908–74 Polish-born scientist

Action is consolatory. It is the enemy of thought and the friend of flattering illusions.
Joseph Conrad 1857–1924 Polish-born English novelist

Think nothing done while aught remains to do.
Samuel Rogers 1763–1855 English poet

If it were done when 'tis done, then 'twere well
It were done quickly.
William Shakespeare 1564–1616 English dramatist

Advertising

Word of mouth is the best medium of all.
Bill Bernbach 1911–82 American advertising executive

Advertising is the most fun you can have with your clothes on.
Jerry Della Femina 1936–   American advertising executive

Promise, large promise, is the soul of an advertisement.
Samuel Johnson 1709–84 English lexicographer

Society drives people crazy with lust and calls it advertising.
John Lahr 1941–   American critic

Advertising may be described as the science of arresting human intelligence long enough to get money from it.
Stephen Leacock 1869–1944 Canadian humorist

Half the money I spend on advertising is wasted, and the trouble is I don't know which half.
Lord Leverhulme 1851–1925 English industrialist

Advice

The consumer isn't a moron; she is your wife.
David Ogilvy 1911–99 British-born advertising executive

Advertising is the rattling of a stick inside a swill bucket.
George Orwell 1903–50 English novelist

Good wine needs no bush.
Proverb

Advice

Books will speak plain when counsellors blanch.
Francis Bacon 1561–1626 English courtier

Well, if you knows of a better 'ole, go to it.
Bruce Bairnsfather 1888–1959 British cartoonist

A word spoken in due season, how good is it!
Bible

Advice is seldom welcome; and those who want it the most always like it the least.
Lord Chesterfield 1694–1773 English writer

Fools need advice most, but wise men only are the better for it.
Benjamin Franklin 1706–90 American statesman and scientist

Get the advice of everybody whose advice is worth having—they are very few—and then do what you think best yourself.
Charles Stewart Parnell 1846–91 Irish nationalist leader

After all, when you seek advice from someone it's certainly not because you want them to give it. You just want them to be there while you talk to yourself.
Terry Pratchett 1948–2015 English novelist

Look for what's missing. Many advisers can tell a president how to improve what's proposed, or what's gone amiss. Few are able to see what isn't there.

Donald Rumsfeld 1932– American politician

I always pass on good advice. It is the only thing to do with it. It is never of any use to oneself.

Oscar Wilde 1854–1900 Irish dramatist

Africa ✤

The state of Africa is a scar on the conscience of the world.

Tony Blair 1953– British Labour statesman

We have Africa in our blood and Africa has our bones. We are all Africans.

Richard Dawkins 1941– English biologist

We are…a nation of dancers, singers and poets.

Olaudah Equiano c.1745–c.97 African writer and former slave, *of the Ibo people*

The shape of Africa resembles a revolver, and the Congo is the trigger.

Frantz Fanon 1925–61 French West Indian psychoanalyst

In Africa a thing is true at first light and a lie by noon.

Ernest Hemingway 1899–1961 American novelist

The wind of change is blowing through this continent.

Harold Macmillan 1894–1986 British Conservative statesman

I have dedicated my life to this struggle of the African people. I have fought against white domination, and I have fought against black domination. I have cherished the ideal of a democratic and free society in which all persons live together in harmony with equal opportunities.

Nelson Mandela 1918–2013 South African statesman

Ambition

Semper aliquid novi Africam adferre.
Africa always brings [us] something new.
   Pliny the Elder AD 23-79 Roman senator

 Ambition see also **Achievement**, **Effort**

No bird soars too high, if he soars with his own wings.
   William Blake 1757-1827 English poet

Aut Caesar, aut nihil.
Caesar or nothing.
   Cesare Borgia 1476-1507 Italian statesman

Ah, but a man's reach should exceed his grasp,
Or what's a heaven for?
   Robert Browning 1812-89 English poet

Well is it known that ambition can creep as well as soar.
   Edmund Burke 1729-97 Irish-born politician

[I] had rather be first in a village than second at Rome.
   Julius Caesar 100-44 BC Roman statesman

Ambition leads me not only farther than any other man
has been before me, but as far as I think it possible for man
to go.
   James Cook 1728-79 English explorer

At the age of six I wanted to be a cook. At seven I wanted to
be Napoleon. And my ambition has been growing steadily
ever since.
   Salvador Dali 1904-89 Spanish painter

Hitch your wagon to a star.
   Ralph Waldo Emerson 1803-82 American writer

Better to reign in hell, than serve in heaven.
   John Milton 1608-74 English poet

Fain would I climb, yet fear I to fall.
>**Walter Ralegh** c.1552–1618 English courtier, *line written on a window-pane; Queen Elizabeth I (1533–1603) replied 'If thy heart fails thee, climb not at all'*

When that the poor have cried, Caesar hath wept;
Ambition should be made of sterner stuff.
>**William Shakespeare** 1564–1616 English dramatist

The world continues to offer glittering prizes to those who have stout hearts and sharp swords.
>**F. E. Smith** 1872–1930 British lawyer

There is always room at the top.
>**Daniel Webster** 1782–1852 American politician

America

Good Americans, when they die, go to Paris.
>**Thomas Gold Appleton** 1812–84 American epigrammatist

America! America!
God shed His grace on thee
And crown thy good with brotherhood
From sea to shining sea!
>**Katherine Lee Bates** 1859–1929 American writer

God bless America,
Land that I love,
Stand beside her and guide her
Thru the night with a light from above.
>**Irving Berlin** 1888–1989 American songwriter

We are a nation of communities…a brilliant diversity spread like stars, like a thousand points of light in a broad and peaceful sky.
>**George Bush** 1924– American statesman

America

There is nothing wrong with America that cannot be fixed by what is right with America.
Bill Clinton 1946– American statesman

Isn't this a billion dollar country?
Charles Foster 1828–1904 American politician, *responding to a Democratic gibe about a 'million dollar Congress'*

Yes, America is gigantic, but a gigantic mistake.
Sigmund Freud 1856–1939 Austrian psychoanalyst

Go West, young man, and grow up with the country.
Horace Greeley 1811–72 American journalist

America is not a lie, it is a disappointment. But it can be a disappointment only because it is also a hope.
Samuel Huntington 1927–2008 American political scientist

Give me your tired, your poor,
Your huddled masses yearning to breathe free.
Emma Lazarus 1849–87 American poet

There is not a black America and a white America and Latino America and Asian America; there's the United States of America.
Barack Obama 1961– American statesman

I like to be in America!
OK by me in America!
Ev'rything free in America
For a small fee in America!
Stephen Sondheim 1930– American songwriter

Overpaid, overfed, oversexed, and over here.
Tommy Trinder 1909–89 British comedian, *of American troops in Britain during the Second World War*

America is a vast conspiracy to make you happy.
John Updike 1932–2009 American writer

The United States themselves are essentially the greatest poem.

Walt Whitman 1819–92 American poet

America is God's Crucible, the great Melting-Pot where all the races of Europe are melting and re-forming!

Israel Zangwill 1864–1926 Jewish writer

Anger

An angry look on the face is wholly against nature.

Marcus Aurelius AD 121–180 Roman emperor

Anger makes dull men witty, but it keeps them poor.

Francis Bacon 1561–1626 English courtier

A soft answer turneth away wrath.

Bible

Anger is never without an argument, but seldom with a good one.

Lord Halifax 1633–95 English politician

Anger is a short madness.

Horace 65–8 BC Roman poet

When angry, count ten before you speak; if very angry a hundred.

Thomas Jefferson 1743–1826 American statesman

Usually, when people are sad, they don't do anything.
They just cry over their condition. But when they get angry, they bring about a change.

Malcolm X 1925–65 American civil rights campaigner

Never let the sun go down on your anger.

Proverb

Animals

When angry, count four; when very angry, swear.
Mark Twain 1835–1910 American writer

 # Animals see also **Cats**, **Dogs**

All things bright and beautiful,
All creatures great and small,
All things wise and wonderful,
The Lord God made them all.
Cecil Frances Alexander 1818–95 Irish poet

The question is not, Can they reason? nor, Can they talk?
but, Can they suffer?
Jeremy Bentham 1748–1832 English philosopher

A righteous man regardeth the life of his beast: but the
tender mercies of the wicked are cruel.
Bible

Tiger Tiger, burning bright,
In the forests of the night;
What immortal hand or eye,
Could frame thy fearful symmetry?
William Blake 1757–1827 English poet

A four-legged friend, a four-legged friend,
He'll never let you down.
J. Brooks

Wee, sleekit, cow'rin', tim'rous beastie,
O what a panic's in thy breastie!
Robert Burns 1759–96 Scottish poet, *on a mouse*

Wherever there is animal worship, there is human
sacrifice.
G. K. Chesterton 1874–1936 English writer

I am fond of pigs. Dogs look up to us. Cats look down on us. Pigs treat us as equals.

Winston Churchill 1874–1965 British statesman

Animals, whom we have made our slaves, we do not like to consider our equal.

Charles Darwin 1809–82 English naturalist

Where in this wide world can man find nobility without pride,
Friendship without envy, or beauty without vanity?

Ronald Duncan 1914–82 English dramatist, *on the horse*

Animals are such agreeable friends—they ask no questions, they pass no criticism.

George Eliot 1819–80 English novelist

I hate a word like 'pets': it sounds so much
Like something with no living of its own.

Elizabeth Jennings 1926–2001 English poet

Anxiety

What's the use of worrying?
It never was worth while,
So, pack up your troubles in your old kit-bag,
And smile, smile, smile.

George Asaf 1880–1951 British songwriter

A ruffled mind makes a restless pillow.

Charlotte Brontë 1816–55 English novelist

In trouble to be troubled
Is to have your trouble doubled.

Daniel Defoe 1660–1731 English novelist

Apology

Anxiety is love's greatest killer.

Anaïs Nin 1903–77 American writer

O polished perturbation! golden care!

William Shakespeare 1564–1616 English dramatist

What though care killed a cat, thou hast mettle enough in thee to kill care.

William Shakespeare 1564–1616 English dramatist

Neurosis is the way of avoiding non-being by avoiding being.

Paul Tillich 1886–1965 German-born theologian

Apology

If you have to eat crow, eat it while it's hot.

Alben W. Barkley 1877–1956 American politician

Very sorry can't come. Lie follows by post.

Lord Charles Beresford 1846–1919 British politician, *telegraphed message to the Prince of Wales, on being summoned to dine at the eleventh hour*

Never make a defence or apology before you be accused.

Charles I 1600–49 British monarch

Never complain and never explain.

Benjamin Disraeli 1804–81 British statesman

Several excuses are always less convincing than one.

Aldous Huxley 1894–1963 English novelist

It is a good rule in life never to apologize. The right sort of people do not want apologies, and the wrong sort take a mean advantage of them.

P. G. Wodehouse 1881–1975 English writer

Appearance see also **Body**

For the Lord seeth not as man seeth: for man looketh on
the outward appearance, but the Lord looketh on the heart.
>   **Bible**

Even I don't wake up looking like Cindy Crawford.
>   **Cindy Crawford** 1966– American model

If everyone were cast in the same mould, there would be no
such thing as beauty.
>   **Charles Darwin** 1809–82 English naturalist

I am the family face;
Flesh perishes, I live on.
>   **Thomas Hardy** 1840–1928 English novelist

At 50, everyone has the face he deserves.
>   **George Orwell** 1903–50 English novelist

Men seldom make passes
At girls who wear glasses.
>   **Dorothy Parker** 1893–1967 American critic

It costs a lot of money to look this cheap.
>   **Dolly Parton** 1946– American singer

Had Cleopatra's nose been shorter, the whole face of the
world would have changed.
>   **Blaise Pascal** 1623–62 French scientist and philosopher

There's no art
To find the mind's construction in the face.
>   **William Shakespeare** 1564–1616 English dramatist

It is only shallow people who do not judge by appearances.
>   **Oscar Wilde** 1854–1900 Irish dramatist

✳ Architecture

A monstrous carbuncle on the face of a much-loved and elegant friend.

> **Charles, Prince of Wales** 1948– , *on the proposed extension to the National Gallery, London*

We shape our buildings, and afterwards our buildings shape us.

> **Winston Churchill** 1874–1965 British statesman

Light (God's eldest daughter) is a principal beauty in a building.

> **Thomas Fuller** 1608–61 English preacher

Less is more.

> **Ludwig Mies van der Rohe** 1886–1969 German-born architect

God is in the details.

> **Ludwig Mies van der Rohe** 1886–1969 German-born architect

When we build, let us think that we build for ever.

> **John Ruskin** 1819–1900 English critic

Architecture in general is frozen music.

> **Friedrich von Schelling** 1775–1854 German philosopher

Form follows function.

> **Louis Henri Sullivan** 1856–1924 American architect

Well building hath three conditions. Commodity, firmness, and delight.

> **Henry Wotton** 1568–1639 English diplomat

The physician can bury his mistakes, but the architect can only advise his client to plant vines—so they should go as far as possible from home to build their first buildings.

> **Frank Lloyd Wright** 1867–1959 American architect

Argument

It takes in reality only one to make a quarrel. It is useless for the sheep to pass resolutions in favour of vegetarianism, while the wolf remains of a different opinion.
> **Dean Inge** 1860–1954 English writer

There is no good in arguing with the inevitable. The only argument available with an east wind is to put on your overcoat.
> **James Russell Lowell** 1819–91 American poet

The Catholic and the Communist are alike in assuming that an opponent cannot be both honest and intelligent.
> **George Orwell** 1903–50 English novelist

Who can refute a sneer?
> **William Paley** 1743–1805 English theologian

The argument of the broken window pane is the most valuable argument in modern politics.
> **Emmeline Pankhurst** 1858–1928 English suffragette leader

I am not arguing with you—I am telling you.
> **James McNeill Whistler** 1834–1903 American-born painter

Armed Forces see also **War**

Lions led by donkeys.
> **Anonymous**, *associated with British forces during the First World War, but of earlier origin*

The sergeant is the army.
> **Dwight D. Eisenhower** 1890–1969 American statesman

Armed Forces

Old soldiers never die,
They simply fade away.
J. Foley 1906–70 British songwriter

The courage of a soldier is found to be the cheapest, and most common, quality of human nature.
Edward Gibbon 1737–94 English historian

How do you ask a man to be the last man to die in Vietnam? How do you ask a man to be the last man to die for a mistake?
John Kerry 1943– American politician

O it's Tommy this, an' Tommy that, an' 'Tommy, go away';
But it's 'Thank you, Mister Atkins,' when the band begins
    to play.
Rudyard Kipling 1865–1936 English writer

Remember that there is not one of you who does not carry in his cartridge-pouch the marshal's baton of the duke of Reggio; it is up to you to bring it forth.
Louis XVIII 1755–1824 French monarch, *to military cadets*

An army without culture is a dull-witted army, and a dull-witted army cannot defeat the enemy.
Mao Zedong 1893–1976 Chinese statesman

When I was in the military, they gave me a medal for killing two men and a discharge for loving one.
Leonard Matlovich 1943–88 American soldier

An army marches on its stomach.
Napoleon I 1769–1821 French emperor

What passing-bells for these who die as cattle?
Only the monstrous anger of the guns.
Wilfred Owen 1893–1918 English poet

Wars may be fought with weapons, but they are won by men.
George S. Patton 1885–1945 American general

A man who is good enough to shed his blood for the country is good enough to be given a square deal afterwards.
Theodore Roosevelt 1858–1919 American statesman

When the military man approaches, the world locks up its spoons and packs off its womankind.
George Bernard Shaw 1856–1950 Irish dramatist

Theirs not to make reply,
Theirs not to reason why,
Theirs but to do and die:
Into the valley of Death
Rode the six hundred.
Alfred, Lord Tennyson 1809–92 English poet, *on the charge of the Light Brigade*

Discipline is the soul of an army. It makes small numbers formidable; procures success to the weak and esteem to all.
George Washington 1732–99 American statesman

I don't know what effect these men will have upon the enemy, but, by God, they frighten me.
Duke of Wellington 1769–1852 British general, *popular version of Wellington's remark: 'As Lord Chesterfield said of the generals of his day, "I only hope that when the enemy reads the list of their names, he trembles as I do"'*

Art see also **Painting**, **Sculpture**

You don't have to like everything.
Alan Bennett 1934– English writer, *proposing a notice for the National Gallery*

Art is meant to disturb, science reassures.
Georges Braque 1882–1963 French painter

Art

A product of the untalented, sold by the unprincipled to the utterly bewildered.

Al Capp 1907–79 American cartoonist, *on abstract art*

Without tradition art is a flock of sheep without a shepherd. Without innovation it is a corpse.

Winston Churchill 1874–1965 British statesman

An artist cannot speak about his art any more than a plant can discuss horticulture.

Jean Cocteau 1889–1963 French film director

Art for art's sake, with no purpose, for any purpose perverts art. But art achieves a purpose which is not its own.

Benjamin Constant 1767–1834 French novelist

I always said God was against art and I still believe it.

Edward Elgar 1857–1934 English composer

All art is autobiographical; the pearl is the oyster's autobiography.

Federico Fellini 1920–93 Italian film director

The artist must be in his work as God is in creation, invisible and all-powerful; one must sense him everywhere but never see him.

Gustave Flaubert 1821–80 French novelist

In art one is either a plagiarist or a revolutionary.

Paul Gauguin 1848–1903 French painter, *usually quoted as 'Art is either plagiarism or revolution'*

In art the best is good enough.

Johann Wolfgang von Goethe 1749–1832 German writer

The proletarian state must bring up thousands of excellent 'mechanics of culture', 'engineers of the soul'.

Maxim Gorky 1868–1936 Russian writer

Life is short, the art long.

Hippocrates *c*.460–357 BC Greek physician, *often quoted in Latin as 'Ars longa, vita brevis [Art is long, life is short]'*

It's clever, but is it Art?

Rudyard Kipling 1865–1936 English writer

We all know that Art is not truth. Art is a lie that makes us realize truth.

Pablo Picasso 1881–1973 Spanish painter

Life without industry is guilt, and industry without art is brutality.

John Ruskin 1819–1900 English critic

Art is not a handicraft, it is the transmission of feeling the artist has experienced.

Leo Tolstoy 1828–1910 Russian novelist

Australia

Who knows but that England may revive in New South Wales when it has sunk in Europe.

Joseph Banks 1743–1820 English botanist

A nation for a continent and a continent for a nation.

Edmund Barton 1849–1920 Australian statesman, *on Australian federation*

True patriots we; for be it understood,
We left our country for our country's good.

Henry Carter d. 1806, *written for the opening of the Playhouse, Sydney, New South Wales, when the actors were principally convicts*

Australia is a lucky country run mainly by second-rate people who share its luck.

Donald Richmond Horne 1921– Australian writer

Autumn

Australia has a marvellous sky and air and blue clarity, and a hoary sort of land beneath it, like a Sleeping Princess on whom the dust of ages has settled.
D. H. Lawrence 1885–1930 English writer

In joyful strains then let us sing
Advance Australia fair.
P. D. McCormick c.1834–1916 Australian musician

What Great Britain calls the Far East is to us the near north.
Robert Gordon Menzies 1894–1978 Australian statesman

The crimson thread of kinship runs through us all.
Henry Parkes 1815–95 Australian statesman, *on Australian federation*

Above our writers—and other artists—looms the intimidating mass of Anglo-Saxon culture. Such a situation almost inevitably produces the characteristic Australian Cultural Cringe.
Arthur Angell Phillips 1900–85 Australian critic

 # Autumn

Early autumn—
rice field, ocean,
one green.
Matsuo Basho 1644–94 Japanese poet

Now is the time for the burning of the leaves.
Laurence Binyon 1869–1943 English poet

'What is autumn?' 'A second spring, where every leaf is a flower.'
Albert Camus 1913–60 French writer

It was one of those perfect English autumnal days which occur more frequently in memory than in life.
   P. D. James 1920–2014 English writer

Season of mists and mellow fruitfulness,
Close bosom-friend of the maturing sun;
Conspiring with him how to load and bless
With fruit the vines that round the thatch-eaves run.
   John Keats 1795–1821 English poet

I want to go south, where there is no autumn, where the cold doesn't crouch over one like a snow-leopard waiting to pounce.
   D. H. Lawrence 1885–1930 English writer

O wild West Wind, thou breath of Autumn's being,
Thou, from whose unseen presence the leaves dead
Are driven, like ghosts from an enchanter fleeing.
   Percy Bysshe Shelley 1792–1822 English poet

For man, autumn is a time of harvest, of gathering together. For nature, it is a time of sowing, of scattering abroad.
   Edwin Way Teale 1899–1980 American journalist

In…the fall, the whole country goes to glory.
   Frances Trollope 1780–1863 English writer, *of North America*

Babies see also **Birth**

There is no finer investment for any community than putting milk into babies.
   Winston Churchill 1874–1965 British statesman

So for the mother's sake the child was dear,
And dearer was the mother for the child.
   Samuel Taylor Coleridge 1772–1834 English poet

Baseball

It is a pleasant thing to reflect upon, and furnishes a complete answer to those who contend for the general degeneration of the human species, that every baby born into the world is a finer one than the last.
Charles Dickens 1812–70 English novelist

There never was a child so lovely but his mother was glad to get him asleep.
Ralph Waldo Emerson 1803–82 American writer

Having a baby is like getting a tattoo on your face. You really need to be certain it's what you want before you commit.
Elizabeth Gilbert 1969– American writer

A loud noise at one end and no sense of responsibility at the other.
Ronald Knox 1888–1957 English writer, *definition of a baby*

Diaper backward spells repaid. Think about it.
Marshall McLuhan 1911–80 Canadian communications scholar

A baby is God's opinion that life should go on.
Carl Sandburg 1878–1967 American poet

You know more than you think you do.
Benjamin Spock 1903–98 American paediatrician, *opening words of* Baby and Child Care

 # Baseball

Think! How the hell are you gonna think and hit at the same time?
Yogi Berra 1925–2015 American baseball player

A ball player's got to be kept hungry to become a big leaguer. That's why no boy from a rich family ever made the big leagues.
Joe DiMaggio 1914–99 American baseball player

Baseball is very big with my people. It figures. It's the only way we can get to shake a bat at a white man without starting a riot.

Dick Gregory 1932– American comedian

Take me out to the ball game,
Take me out with the crowd.
Buy me some peanuts and cracker-jack—
I don't care if I never get back.

Jack Norworth 1879–1959 American songwriter

All you have to do is keep the five players who hate your guts away from the five who are undecided.

Casey Stengel 1891–1975 American baseball player

Baseball, it is said, is only a game. True. And the Grand Canyon is only a hole in Arizona. Not all holes, or games, are created equal.

George F. Will 1941– American columnist

Beauty see also **Good Looks**

Being thought of as a beautiful woman has spared me nothing in life. No heartache, no trouble. Beauty is essentially meaningless.

Halle Berry 1968– American actress

Consider the lilies of the field, how they grow; they toil not, neither do they spin:
And yet I say unto you, That even Solomon in all his glory was not arrayed like one of these.

Bible

If you get simple beauty and naught else,
You get about the best thing God invents.

Robert Browning 1812–89 English poet

Beauty

I never saw an ugly thing in my life: for let the form of an object be what it may,—light, shade, and perspective will always make it beautiful.

John Constable 1776–1837 English painter

Beauty is mysterious as well as terrible. God and devil are fighting there, and the battlefield is the heart of man.

Fedor Dostoevsky 1821–81 Russian novelist

Beauty will save the world.

Fedor Dostoevsky 1821–81 Russian novelist

He was afflicted by the thought that where Beauty was, nothing ever ran quite straight, which, no doubt, was why so many people looked on it as immoral.

John Galsworthy 1867–1933 English novelist

All things counter, original, spare, strange;
Whatever is fickle, freckled (who knows how?)
With swift, slow; sweet, sour; adazzle, dim;
He fathers-forth whose beauty is past change:
Praise him.

Gerard Manley Hopkins 1844–89 English poet

'Beauty is truth, truth beauty,'—that is all
Ye know on earth, and all ye need to know.

John Keats 1795–1821 English poet

A thing of beauty is a joy for ever:
Its loveliness increases; it will never
Pass into nothingness.

John Keats 1795–1821 English poet

At some point in life the world's beauty becomes enough. You don't need to photograph, paint or even remember it. It is enough.

Toni Morrison 1931– American novelist

Remember that the most beautiful things in the world are the most useless; peacocks and lilies for instance.
John Ruskin 1819–1900 English critic

Beauty is all very well at first sight; but who ever looks at it when it has been in the house three days?
George Bernard Shaw 1856–1950 Irish dramatist

Beauty is no more than a promise of happiness.
Stendhal 1783–1842 French novelist

It is amazing how complete is the delusion that beauty is goodness.
Leo Tolstoy 1828–1910 Russian novelist

Beginning see also **Ending**

In the beginning God created the heaven and the earth. And the earth was without form, and void; and darkness was upon the face of the deep.
Bible

'Begin at the beginning,' the King said, gravely, 'and go on till you come to the end: then stop.'
Lewis Carroll 1832–98 English writer

What we call the beginning is often the end
And to make an end is to make a beginning.
The end is where we start from.
T. S. Eliot 1888–1965 American-born British poet

All this will not be finished in the first 100 days. Nor will it be finished in the first 1,000 days, nor in the life of this Administration, nor even perhaps in our lifetime on this planet. But let us begin.
John F. Kennedy 1917–63 American statesman

Behaviour

Are you sitting comfortably? Then I'll begin.
Julia Lang 1921– British radio presenter

A tower of nine storeys begins with a heap of earth.
The journey of a thousand *li* starts from where one stands.
Lao Tzu c.604–c.531 BC Chinese philosopher

I've started so I'll finish.
Magnus Magnusson 1929–2007 Icelandic broadcaster, *said when a contestant's time ran out while a question was being put on* Mastermind

If we wait for the moment when everything, absolutely everything, is ready, we shall never begin.
Ivan Turgenev 1818–83 Russian novelist

 Behaviour see also **Manners**

When I go to Rome, I fast on Saturday, but here [Milan] I do not. Do you also follow the custom of whatever church you attend, if you do not want to give or receive scandal.
St Ambrose c.339–397 French-born bishop of Milan, *usually quoted as 'When in Rome, do as the Romans do'*

Private faces in public places
Are wiser and nicer
Than public faces in private places.
W. H. Auden 1907–73 English poet

In necessary things, unity; in doubtful things, liberty; in all things, charity.
Richard Baxter 1615–91 English divine

When people are on their best behaviour they aren't always at their best.
Alan Bennett 1934– English writer

Caesar's wife must be above suspicion.
Julius Caesar 100–44 BC Roman statesman

He only does it to annoy,
Because he knows it teases.
Lewis Carroll 1832–98 English writer

He was a verray, parfit gentil knyght.
Geoffrey Chaucer c.1343–1400 English poet

Take the tone of the company that you are in.
Lord Chesterfield 1694–1773 English writer

O tempora, O mores!
Oh, the times! Oh, the manners!
Cicero 106–43 BC Roman statesman

I get too hungry for dinner at eight.
I like the theatre, but never come late.
I never bother with people I hate.
That's why the lady is a tramp.
Lorenz Hart 1895–1943 American songwriter

Be a good animal, true to your instincts.
D. H. Lawrence 1885–1930 English writer

Go directly—see what she's doing, and tell her she mustn't.
Punch 1841–1992 English humorous periodical

Belief ✻

For what a man would like to be true, that he more readily believes.
Francis Bacon 1561–1626 English courtier

Every time a child says 'I don't believe in fairies' there is a little fairy somewhere that falls down dead.
J. M. Barrie 1860–1937 Scottish writer

Belief

Lord, I believe; help thou mine unbelief.
Bible

Faith is the substance of things hoped for, the evidence of things not seen.
Bible

Of course not, but I am told it works even if you don't believe in it.
Niels Bohr 1885–1962 Danish physicist, *when asked whether he really believed a horseshoe hanging over his door would bring him luck*

Why, sometimes I've believed as many as six impossible things before breakfast.
Lewis Carroll 1832–98 English writer

It is wrong, always, everywhere and for any one, to believe anything upon insufficient evidence.
William Clifford 1845–79 English mathematician and philosopher

I do not believe…I know.
Carl Gustav Jung 1875–1961 Swiss psychologist

Credulity is the man's weakness, but the child's strength.
Charles Lamb 1775–1834 English writer

Nothing is so firmly believed as that which we least know.
Montaigne 1533–92 French moralist

We can believe what we choose. We are answerable for what we choose to believe.
John Henry Newman 1801–90 English theologian

What is wanted is not the will to believe, but the wish to find out, which is its exact opposite.
Bertrand Russell 1872–1970 British philosopher

There lives more faith in honest doubt,
Believe me, than in half the creeds.
Alfred, Lord Tennyson 1809–92 English poet

Certum est quia impossibile est.

It is certain because it is impossible.
Tertullian C.AD 160–C.225 Roman theologian, *often quoted as
'Credo quia impossibile [I believe because it is impossible]'*

Bereavement see also **Sorrow**

You can shed tears that she is gone or you can smile because
she has lived.
Anonymous, *preface to the Order of Service at the funeral of
Queen Elizabeth the Queen Mother, 2002*

He was my North, my South, my East and West,
My working week and my Sunday rest,
My noon, my midnight, my talk, my song;
I thought that love would last for ever: I was wrong.
W. H. Auden 1907–73 English poet

Blessed are they that mourn: for they shall be comforted.
Bible

Do not stand at my grave and weep:
I am not there. I do not sleep.
I am a thousand winds that blow.
I am the diamond glints on snow…
Do not stand at my grave and cry;
I am not there, I did not die.
Mary E. Frye 1905–2004 American poet, *quoted in letter left by
British soldier Stephen Cummins when killed by the IRA*

Bereavement

Bereavement is a universal and integral part of our experience of love. It follows marriage as normally as marriage follows courtship or as autumn follows summer.
C. S. Lewis 1898–1963 English literary scholar

A man's dying is more the survivors' affair than his own.
Thomas Mann 1875–1955 German novelist

Time does not bring relief; you all have lied
Who told me time would ease me of my pain!
Edna St Vincent Millay 1892–1950 American poet

I can't think of a more wonderful thanksgiving for the life I have had than that everyone should be jolly at my funeral.
Lord Mountbatten 1900–79 British statesman

The spring has gone out of the year.
Pericles c.495–429 BC Greek statesman, *funeral oration*

I come to bury Caesar, not to praise him.
The evil that men do lives after them,
The good is oft interrèd with their bones.
William Shakespeare 1564–1616 English dramatist

Moderate lamentation is the right of the dead, excessive grief the enemy to the living.
William Shakespeare 1564–1616 English dramatist

The bitterest tears shed over graves are for words left unsaid and deeds left undone.
Harriet Beecher Stowe 1811–96 American novelist

Even memory is not necessary for love. There is a land of the living and a land of the dead and the bridge is love, the only survival, the only meaning.
Thornton Wilder 1897–1975 American writer

But how could I forget thee? Through what power,
Even for the least division of an hour,

Have I been so beguiled as to be blind
To my most grievous loss?
   William Wordsworth 1770–1850 English poet

He first deceased; she for a little tried
To live without him: liked it not, and died.
   Henry Wotton 1568–1639 English diplomat

Biography

A well-written Life is almost as rare as a well-spent one.
   Thomas Carlyle 1795–1881 Scottish historian

An autobiography is an obituary in serial form with the last
instalment missing.
   Quentin Crisp 1908–99 English writer

There is properly no history; only biography.
   Ralph Waldo Emerson 1803–82 American writer

Nobody can write the life of a man, but those who have eat
and drunk and lived in social intercourse with him.
   Samuel Johnson 1709–84 English lexicographer

Lives of great men all remind us
We can make our lives sublime,
And, departing, leave behind us
Footprints on the sands of time.
   Henry Wadsworth Longfellow 1807–82 American poet

To write one's memoirs is to speak ill of everybody except
oneself.
   Marshal Pétain 1856–1951 French statesman

Discretion is not the better part of biography.
   Lytton Strachey 1880–1932 English biographer

Birds

Every great man nowadays has his disciples, and it is always
Judas who writes the biography.
    Oscar Wilde 1854–1900 Irish dramatist

Birds

That's the wise thrush; he sings each song twice over,
Lest you should think he never could recapture
The first fine careless rapture!
    Robert Browning 1812–89 English poet

The bisy larke, messager of day.
    Geoffrey Chaucer c.1343–1400 English poet

It was the Rainbow gave thee birth,
And left thee all her lovely hues.
    W. H. Davies 1871–1940 Welsh poet, *of the kingfisher*

I caught this morning morning's minion, kingdom of
   daylight's dauphin, dapple-dawn-drawn Falcon.
    Gerard Manley Hopkins 1844–89 English poet

Oh, a wondrous bird is the pelican!
His bill will hold more than his belican.
He can take in his beak
Enough food for a week
But I'm damned if I see how the helican.
    Dixon Lanier Merritt 1879–1972 American editor

Alone and warming his five wits,
The white owl in the belfry sits.
    Alfred, Lord Tennyson 1809–92 English poet

I once had a sparrow alight upon my shoulder for a moment
while I was hoeing in a village garden, and I felt that I was

more distinguished by that circumstance than I should have been by any epaulette I could have worn.
Henry David Thoreau 1817–62 American writer

Birth see also **Babies**

It doesn't matter about being born in a duckyard, as long as you're hatched from a swan's egg!
Hans Christian Andersen 1805–75 Danish writer

In sorrow thou shalt bring forth children.
Bible

No phallic hero, no matter what he does to himself or to another to prove his courage, ever matches the solitary, existential courage of the woman who gives birth.
Andrea Dworkin 1946–2005 American feminist

I am not yet born; O fill me
With strength against those who would freeze my humanity.
Louis MacNeice 1907–63 British poet

Death and taxes and childbirth! There's never any convenient time for any of them.
Margaret Mitchell 1900–49 American novelist

Men should be bewailed at their birth, and not at their death.
Montesquieu 1689–1755 French political philosopher

Good work, Mary. We all knew you had it in you.
Dorothy Parker 1893–1967 American critic, *telegram to Mrs Sherwood on the arrival of her baby*

Love set you going like a fat gold watch.
The midwife slapped your footsoles, and your bald cry

Birthdays

Took its place among the elements.
Sylvia Plath 1932–63 American poet

What you say of the pride of giving life to an immortal
soul is very fine, dear, but I own I can not enter into that;
I think much more of our being like a cow or a dog at such
moments; when our poor nature becomes so very animal
and unecstatic.
Queen Victoria 1819–1901 British monarch

Our birth is but a sleep and a forgetting…
Not in entire forgetfulness,
And not in utter nakedness,
But trailing clouds of glory do we come.
William Wordsworth 1770–1850 English poet

 # Birthdays

A diplomat is a man who always remembers a woman's
birthday but never remembers her age.
Robert Frost 1874–1963 American poet

You know you're getting old when the candles cost more
than the cake.
Bob Hope 1903–2003 American comedian

Do you count your birthdays thankfully?
Horace 65–8 BC Roman poet

One of the sadder things, I think,
Is how our birthdays slowly sink:
Presents and parties disappear,
The cards grow fewer year by year.
Philip Larkin 1922–85 English poet

Believing, hear, what you deserve to hear:
Your birthday as my own to me is dear…

But yours gives most; for mine did only lend
Me to the world; yours gave to me a friend.
Martial c.AD 40–c.104 Roman epigrammatist

EEYORE: But after all, what *are* birthdays? Here today and
gone tomorrow.
A. A. Milne 1882–1956 English writer

Our birthdays are feathers in the broad wing of time.
Jean Paul Richter 1763–1825 German novelist

Boats

Jolly boating weather,
And a hay harvest breeze,
Blade on the feather,
Shade off the trees
Swing, swing together
With your body between your knees.
William Cory 1823–92 English poet

A wet sheet and a flowing sea,
A wind that follows fast
And fills the white and rustling sail
And bends the gallant mast.
Allan Cunningham 1784–1842 Scottish poet

There is *nothing*—absolutely nothing—half so much worth
doing as simply messing about in boats.
Kenneth Grahame 1859–1932 Scottish-born writer

Quinquireme of Nineveh from distant Ophir
Rowing home to haven in sunny Palestine,
With a cargo of ivory,
And apes and peacocks,
Sandalwood, cedarwood, and sweet white wine.
John Masefield 1878–1967 English poet

The Body see also **Appearance**

I will give thanks unto thee, for I am fearfully and
wonderfully made.
Bible

A woman watches her body uneasily, as though it were an
unreliable ally in the battle for love.
Leonard Cohen 1934–2016 Canadian singer

i like my body when it is with your
body. It is so quite new a thing.
Muscles better and nerves more.
e. e. cummings 1894–1962 American poet

The leg, a source of much delight,
which carries weight and governs height.
Ian Dury 1942–2000 British rock singer

Anatomy is destiny.
Sigmund Freud 1856–1939 Austrian psychoanalyst

The body says what words cannot.
Martha Graham 1894–1991 American dancer

For some inexplicable reason the sense of smell does not
hold the high position it deserves among its sisters. There is
something of the fallen angel about it.
Helen Keller 1880–1968 American writer

Nothing tastes as good as skinny feels.
Kate Moss 1974– English model, *when asked for her motto*

I'm fat, but I'm thin inside. Has it ever struck you that there's
a thin man inside every fat man, just as they say there's a
statue inside every block of stone?
George Orwell 1903–50 English novelist

Our bodies are our gardens, to which our wills are gardeners.
William Shakespeare 1564–1616 English dramatist

You can never be too rich or too thin.
Wallis Simpson (Duchess of Windsor) 1896–1986

Every man is the builder of a temple, called his body.
Henry David Thoreau 1817–62 American writer

Our body is a machine for living. It is organized for that, it is its nature. Let life go on in it unhindered and let it defend itself.
Leo Tolstoy 1828–1910 Russian novelist

I sing the body electric.
Walt Whitman 1819–92 American poet

The human body is the best picture of the human soul.
Ludwig Wittgenstein 1889–1951 Austrian-born philosopher

Books see also **Libraries, Literature, Reading**

Some books are undeservedly forgotten; none are undeservedly remembered.
W. H. Auden 1907–73 English poet

Some books are to be tasted, others to be swallowed, and some few to be chewed and digested.
Francis Bacon 1561–1626 English courtier

Books say: she did this because. Life says: she did this. Books are where things are explained to you; life is where things aren't.
Julian Barnes 1946– English novelist

Of making many books there is no end; and much study is a weariness of the flesh.
Bible

Books

A great book is like great evil.
>**Callimachus** c.305–c.240 BC Greek poet

A classic is a book that has never finished saying what it has to say.
>**Italo Calvino** 1923–85 Italian writer

'What is the use of a book', thought Alice, 'without pictures or conversations?'
>**Lewis Carroll** 1832–98 English writer

I don't trust books. They're all fact, no heart.
>**Stephen Colbert** 1964– American satirist

There is more treasure in books than in all the pirates' loot on Treasure Island.
>**Walt Disney** 1901–66 American film producer

Another damned, thick, square book! Always scribble, scribble, scribble! Eh! Mr Gibbon?
>**Duke of Gloucester** 1743–1805

A book must be the axe for the frozen sea within us.
>**Franz Kafka** 1883–1924 Czech novelist

To produce a mighty book, you must choose a mighty theme.
>**Herman Melville** 1819–91 American novelist

A good book is the precious life-blood of a master spirit.
>**John Milton** 1608–74 English poet

There is no book so bad that some good cannot be got out of it.
>**Pliny the Elder** AD 23–79 Roman senator

The principle of procrastinated rape is said to be the ruling one in all the great best-sellers.
>**V. S. Pritchett** 1900–97 English writer

I hate books; they only teach us to talk about things we know nothing about.
Jean-Jacques Rousseau 1712–78 French philosopher

All books are divisible into two classes, the books of the hour, and the books of all time.
John Ruskin 1819–1900 English critic

No furniture so charming as books.
Sydney Smith 1771–1845 English essayist

A good book is the best of friends, the same to-day and for ever.
Martin Tupper 1810–89 English writer

'*Classic.*' A book which people praise and don't read.
Mark Twain 1835–1910 American writer

Publish and be damned.
Duke of Wellington 1769–1852 British general, *replying to a blackmail threat*

Boredom

Nothing happens, nobody comes, nobody goes, it's awful!
Samuel Beckett 1906–89 Irish writer

Life, friends, is boring. We must not say so…
And moreover my mother told me as a boy
(repeatingly) 'Ever to confess you're bored
means you have no
Inner Resources.'
John Berryman 1914–72 American poet

Everyone is a bore to someone. That is unimportant.
The thing to avoid is being a bore to oneself.
Gerald Brenan 1894–1987 British writer

Boxing

What's wrong with being a boring kind of guy?
George Bush 1924-   American statesman

Millions long for immortality who don't know what to do
with themselves on a rainy Sunday afternoon.
Susan Ertz 1894–1985 American writer

Nothing, like something, happens anywhere.
Philip Larkin 1922–85 English poet

We often forgive those who bore us, but we cannot forgive
those whom we bore.
Duc de la Rochefoucauld 1613–80 French moralist

Boredom is…a vital problem for the moralist, since half the
sins of mankind are caused by the fear of it.
Bertrand Russell 1872–1970 British philosopher

A healthy male adult bore consumes *each year* one and a
half times his own weight in other people's patience.
John Updike 1932–2009 American writer

The secret of being a bore…is to tell everything.
Voltaire 1694–1778 French writer

 # Boxing

Float like a butterfly, sting like a bee.
Muhammad Ali 1942–2016 American boxer, *summary of his
boxing strategy*

I'm the greatest.
Muhammad Ali 1942–2016 American boxer

Boxing's just showbusiness with blood.
Frank Bruno 1961-   English boxer

Honey, I just forgot to duck.
>**Jack Dempsey** 1895–1983 American boxer, *to his wife, on losing the World Heavyweight title*

The bigger they are, the further they have to fall.
>**Robert Fitzsimmons** 1862–1917 New Zealand boxer, *prior to a boxing match*

We was robbed!
>**Joe Jacobs** 1896–1940 American boxing manager, *after Jack Sharkey beat Max Schmeling (of whom Jacobs was manager) in a heavyweight title fight*

He can run. But he can't hide.
>**Joe Louis** 1914–81 American boxer, *of Billy Conn, his opponent*

Brevity

It is a foolish thing to make a long prologue, and to be short in the story itself.
>**Bible**

The beauty of concision…is that you can only repeat conventional thoughts.
>**Noam Chomsky** 1928– American linguist

I strive to be brief, and I become obscure.
>**Horace** 65–8 BC Roman poet

I have made this [letter] longer than usual, only because I have not had the time to make it shorter.
>**Blaise Pascal** 1623–62 French scientist and philosopher

Words are like leaves; and where they most abound,
Much fruit of sense beneath is rarely found.
>**Alexander Pope** 1688–1744 English poet

If there is anywhere a thing said in two sentences that could have been as clearly and as engagingly said in one, then it's amateur work.

Robert Louis Stevenson 1850–94 Scottish novelist

 # Britain

Great Britain has lost an empire and has not yet found a role.

Dean Acheson 1893–1971 American politician

The land of embarrassment and breakfast.

Julian Barnes 1946–   English novelist, *of Britain*

You cannot trust people who have such bad cuisine. It is the country with the worst food after Finland.

Jacques Chirac 1932–   French statesman, *on the British*

The British nation is unique in this respect. They are the only people who like to be told how bad things are, who like to be told the worst.

Winston Churchill 1874–1965 British statesman

What is our task? To make Britain a fit country for heroes to live in.

David Lloyd George 1863–1945 British statesman

Fifty years on from now, Britain will still be the country of long shadows on county [cricket] grounds, warm beer, invincible green suburbs, dog lovers, and—as George Orwell said—old maids bicycling to Holy Communion through the morning mist.

John Major 1943–   British statesman

No sex, please—we're British.

Anthony Marriott 1931–2014 and **Alistair Foot** British dramatists

Rule, Britannia, rule the waves;
Britons never will be slaves.
James Thomson 1700–48 Scottish poet

Other nations use 'force'; we Britons alone use 'Might'.
Evelyn Waugh 1903–66 English novelist

Bureaucracy see also **Management**

A memorandum is written not to inform the reader but to
protect the writer.
Dean Acheson 1893–1971 American politician

It is an inevitable defect, that bureaucrats will care more for
routine than for results.
Walter Bagehot 1826–77 English economist

Guidelines for bureaucrats: (1) When in charge, ponder.
(2) When in trouble, delegate. (3) When in doubt, mumble.
James H. Boren 1925– American bureaucrat

The Civil Service is profoundly deferential—'Yes, Minister!
No, Minister! If you wish it, Minister!'
Richard Crossman 1907–74 British politician

A desk is a dangerous place from which to watch the world.
John le Carré 1931– English novelist

The man who is denied the opportunity of taking decisions
of importance begins to regard as important the decisions
he is allowed to take.
C. Northcote Parkinson 1909–93 English writer

Back in the East you can't do much without the right papers,
but *with* the right papers you can do *anything*. They *believe*
in papers. Papers are power.
Tom Stoppard 1937– British dramatist

Business

There is nothing more requisite in business than dispatch.
Joseph Addison 1672–1719 English writer

A merchant shall hardly keep himself from doing wrong.
Bible (Apocrypha)

Rule No 1: never lose money. Rule No 2: never forget rule No 1.
Warren Buffett 1930– American businessman

They [corporations] cannot commit treason, nor be outlawed, nor excommunicate, for they have no souls.
Edward Coke 1552–1634 English jurist

Here's the rule for bargains: 'Do other men, for they would do you.' That's the true business precept.
Charles Dickens 1812–70 English novelist

Remember that time is money.
Benjamin Franklin 1706–90 American statesman and scientist

Necessity never made a good bargain.
Benjamin Franklin 1706–90 American statesman and scientist

If business always made the right decisions, business wouldn't be business.
J. Paul Getty 1892–1976 American industrialist

Only the paranoid survive.
Andrew Grove 1936–2016 American businessman

The best of all monopoly profits is a quiet life.
J. R. Hicks 1904–89 British economist

Only a fool holds out for the top dollar.
Joseph P. Kennedy 1888–1969 American financier, *selling stock before the Wall Street crash of 1929*

Never invest in any idea you can't illustrate with a crayon.
Peter Lynch 1944-   American investor

A salesman is got to dream, boy. It comes with the territory.
Arthur Miller 1915-2005 American dramatist

After a certain point money is meaningless. It ceases to be the goal. The game is what counts.
Aristotle Onassis 1906-75 Greek businessman

The customer is never wrong.
César Ritz 1850-1918 Swiss hotel proprietor

I think that business practices would improve immeasurably if they were guided by 'feminine' principles—qualities like love and care and intuition.
Anita Roddick 1942-2007 English businesswoman

People of the same trade seldom meet together, even for merriment and diversion, but the conversation ends in a conspiracy against the public, or in some contrivance to raise prices.
Adam Smith 1723-90 Scottish economist

Deals are my art form. Other people paint beautifully on canvas or write wonderful poetry. I like making deals, preferably big deals. That's how I get my kicks.
Donald Trump 1946-   American businessman

The public be damned! I'm working for my stockholders.
William H. Vanderbilt 1821-85 American railway magnate

[Commercialism is] doing well that which should not be done at all.
Gore Vidal 1925-2012 American writer

There is only one boss. The customer. And he can fire everybody in the company from the chairman on down, simply by spending his money somewhere else.
Sam Walton 1919-92 American businessman

You cannot be a success in any business without believing that it is the greatest business in the world…You have to put your heart in the business and the business in your heart.

Thomas Watson Snr. 1874–1956 American businessman

 # Canada

Americans are benevolently ignorant about Canada, while Canadians are malevolently well-informed about the United States.

John Bartlet Brebner 1895–1957 Canadian historian

Dusty, cobweb-covered, maimed, and set at naught,
Beauty crieth in an attic, and no man regardeth.
O God! O Montreal!

Samuel Butler 1835–1902 English novelist

I am rather inclined to believe that this is the land God gave to Cain.

Jacques Cartier 1491–1557 French explorer

Some say that no one ever leaves Montreal, for that city, like Canada itself, is designed to preserve the past, a past that happened somewhere else.

Leonard Cohen 1934–2016 Canadian singer

I see Canada as a country torn between a very northern, rather extraordinary, mystical spirit which it fears and its desire to present itself to the world as a Scotch banker.

Robertson Davies 1913–95 Canadian novelist

Vive Le Québec Libre.

Long Live Free Quebec.

Charles de Gaulle 1890–1970 French statesman

If some countries have too much history, we have too much geography.

William Lyon Mackenzie King 1874–1950 Canadian statesman

That's ours—lock, stock and iceberg.
Brian Mulroney 1939-   Canadian statesman, *asked about Canadian sovereignty over the Arctic*

To be Prime Minister of Canada, you need the hide of a rhinoceros, the morals of St. Francis, the patience of Job, the wisdom of Solomon, the strength of Hercules, the leadership of Napoleon, the magnetism of a Beatle and the subtlety of Machiavelli.
Lester Pearson 1897–1972 Canadian statesman

Mon pays ce n'est pas un pays, c'est l'hiver.

My country is not a country, it is winter.
Gilles Vigneault 1928-   Canadian singer

These two nations have been at war over a few acres of snow near Canada, and…they are spending on this fine struggle more than Canada itself is worth.
Voltaire 1694–1778 French writer

O Canada! Our home and native land!
True patriot love in all thy sons command.
With glowing hearts we see thee rise,
The True North strong and free!
Robert Stanley Weir 1856–1926 Canadian lawyer

Careers see also **Work**

I will undoubtedly have to seek what is happily known as gainful employment, which I am glad to say does not describe holding public office.
Dean Acheson 1893–1971 American politician

For promotion cometh neither from the east, nor from the west: nor yet from the south.
Bible

Cars

McJob: A low-pay, low-prestige, low-dignity, low benefit, no-future job in the service sector.
Douglas Coupland 1961– Canadian writer

To do nothing and get something, formed a boy's ideal of a manly career.
Benjamin Disraeli 1804–81 British statesman

By working faithfully eight hours a day, you may eventually get to be a boss and work twelve hours a day.
Robert Frost 1874–1963 American poet

It is wonderful, when a calculation is made, how little the mind is actually employed in the discharge of any profession.
Samuel Johnson 1709–84 English lexicographer

I didn't get where I am today without....
David Nobbs 1935–2015 British novelist, *catchphrase used by Reginald Perrin's manager C. J.*

Thou art not for the fashion of these times,
Where none will sweat but for promotion.
William Shakespeare 1564–1616 English dramatist

It is difficult to get a man to understand something when his salary depends on his not understanding it.
Upton Sinclair 1878–1968 American novelist

The test of a vocation is the love of the drudgery it involves.
Logan Pearsall Smith 1865–1946 American writer

 # Cars

Take it easy driving—the life you save may be mine.
James Dean 1931–55 American actor

[There are] only two classes of pedestrians in these days of reckless motor traffic—the quick, and the dead.
Lord Dewar 1864–1930 British industrialist

The horseless vehicle is the coming wonder.
Thomas Alva Edison 1847–1931 American inventor, *in 1895*

The poetry of motion! The *real* way to travel! The *only* way to travel! Here today—in next week tomorrow!
Kenneth Grahame 1859–1932 Scottish-born writer

O bliss! O poop-poop! O my!
Kenneth Grahame 1859–1932 Scottish-born writer

What good is speed if the brain has oozed out on the way?
Karl Kraus 1874–1936 Austrian satirist

The car has become an article of dress without which we feel uncertain, unclad and incomplete in the urban compound.
Marshall McLuhan 1911–80 Canadian communications scholar

Beneath this slab
John Brown is stowed.
He watched the ads,
And not the road.
Ogden Nash 1902–71 American humorist

Cats

Macavity, Macavity, there's no one like Macavity,
There never was a Cat of such deceitfulness and suavity.
He always has an alibi, and one or two to spare:
At whatever time the deed took place — MACAVITY WASN'T THERE!
T. S. Eliot 1888–1965 American-born British poet

Cats, I always think, only jump into your lap to check if you are cold enough, yet, to eat.
Anne Enright 1962– Irish writer

He walked by himself, and all places were alike to him.
Rudyard Kipling 1865–1936 English writer

Censorship

Cats seem to go on the principle that it never does any harm to ask for what you want.

Joseph Wood Krutch 1893–1970 American critic and naturalist

If a fish is the movement of water embodied, given shape, then cat is a diagram and pattern of subtle air.

Doris Lessing 1919–2013 English writer

When I play with my cat, who knows whether she isn't amusing herself with me more than I am with her?

Montaigne 1533–92 French moralist

The trouble with a kitten is
THAT
Eventually it becomes a
CAT.

Ogden Nash 1902–71 American humorist

For I will consider my Cat Jeoffry…
For he counteracts the powers of darkness by his electrical skin and glaring eyes.
For he counteracts the Devil, who is death, by brisking about the life.

Christopher Smart 1722–71 English poet

 # Censorship

Is it a book you would even wish your wife or your servants to read?

Mervyn Griffith-Jones 1909–79 British lawyer,
of D. H. Lawrence's Lady Chatterley's Lover

Wherever books will be burned, men also, in the end, are burned.

Heinrich Heine 1797–1856 German poet

Censorship

One has to multiply thoughts to the point where there aren't enough policemen to control them.
Stanislaw Lec 1909–66 Polish writer

The power of the press is very great, but not so great as the power of suppress.
Lord Northcliffe 1865–1922 British newspaper proprietor

If these writings of the Greeks agree with the book of God, they are useless and need not be preserved; if they disagree, they are pernicious and ought to be destroyed.
Caliph Omar c.581–644, *on burning the library of Alexandria*

Don't you see that the whole aim of Newspeak is to narrow the range of thought? In the end we shall make thoughtcrime literally impossible, because there will be no words in which to express it.
George Orwell 1903–50 English novelist

It is obvious that 'obscenity' is not a term capable of exact legal definition; in the practice of the Courts, it means 'anything that shocks the magistrate'.
Bertrand Russell 1872–1970 British philosopher

If decade after decade the truth cannot be told, each person's mind begins to roam irretrievably. One's fellow countrymen become harder to understand than Martians.
Alexander Solzhenitsyn 1918–2008 Russian novelist

The state has no place in the nation's bedrooms.
Pierre Trudeau 1919–2000 Canadian statesman

I disapprove of what you say, but I will defend to the death your right to say it.
Voltaire 1694–1778 French writer, *a later summary of his attitude towards Helvétius following the burning of the latter's* De l'esprit

Certainty see also **Doubt**

My mind is not a bed to be made and re-made.
James Agate 1877–1947 British writer

If a man will begin with certainties, he shall end in doubts; but if he will be content to begin with doubts, he shall end in certainties.
Francis Bacon 1561–1626 English courtier

We often call a certainty a hope, to bring it luck.
Elizabeth Bibesco 1897–1945 British writer

The archbishop is usually to be found nailing his colours to the fence.
Frank Field 1942– British politician, *of Archbishop Runcie*

What, never?
No, never!
What, *never*?
Hardly ever!
W. S. Gilbert 1836–1911 English writer

I'll give you a definite maybe.
Sam Goldwyn 1882–1974 American film producer

The answers we have found have only served to raise a whole set of new questions. In some ways we feel that we are as confused as ever, but we think we are confused on a higher level, and about more important things.
Earl C. Kelley 1895–1970 American educationist

It's one thing to be certain, but you can be certain and you can be wrong.
John Kerry 1943– American politician

I wish I was as cocksure of anything as Tom Macaulay is of everything.
Lord Melbourne 1779–1848 British statesman

Ah, what a dusty answer gets the soul
When hot for certainties in this our life!
> **George Meredith** 1828–1909 English writer

The only certainty is that nothing is certain.
> **Pliny the Elder** AD 23–79 Roman senator

Minds like beds always made up,
(more stony than a shore)
unwilling or unable.
> **William Carlos Williams** 1883–1963 American poet

Chance see also Luck

Cast thy bread upon the waters: for thou shalt find it after many days.
> **Bible**

But for the grace of God there goes John Bradford.
> **John Bradford** c.1510–55 English martyr, *on seeing a group of criminals being led to their execution; usually quoted as 'There but for the grace of God go I'*

The best laid schemes o' mice an' men
Gang aft a-gley.
> **Robert Burns** 1759–96 Scottish poet

The chapter of knowledge is a very short, but the chapter of accidents is a very long one.
> **Lord Chesterfield** 1694–1773 English writer

If there were no coincidence, it would be the greatest coincidence of all.
> **G. K. Chesterton** 1874–1936 English writer

At this moment he was unfortunately called out by a person on business from Porlock.
> **Samuel Taylor Coleridge** 1772–1834 English poet, *preliminary note to 'Kubla Khan', explaining why the poem remained unfinished*

Change

Accidents will occur in the best-regulated families.
Charles Dickens 1812–70 English novelist

If an army of monkeys were strumming on typewriters they *might* write all the books in the British Museum.
Arthur Eddington 1882–1944 British astrophysicist

I am convinced that *He* [God] does not play dice.
Albert Einstein 1879–1955 German-born theoretical physicist

Mr Bond, they have a saying in Chicago: 'Once is happenstance. Twice is coincidence. The third time it's enemy action.'
Ian Fleming 1908–64 English writer, *Goldfinger to James Bond*

Predictability: Does the flap of a butterfly's wings in Brazil set off a tornado in Texas?
Edward N. Lorenz 1917–2008 American meteorologist

O! many a shaft, at random sent,
Finds mark the archer little meant!
And many a word, at random spoken,
May soothe or wound a heart that's broken.
Sir Walter Scott 1771–1832 Scottish novelist

There is a tide in the affairs of men,
Which, taken at the flood, leads on to fortune.
William Shakespeare 1564–1616 English dramatist

 Change see also **Beginning, Ending**

He that will not apply new remedies must expect new evils; for time is the greatest innovator.
Francis Bacon 1561–1626 English courtier

Can the Ethiopian change his skin, or the leopard his spots?
Bible

Change

Variety's the very spice of life,
That gives it all its flavour.
William Cowper 1731–1800 English poet

       He not busy being born
Is busy dying.
Bob Dylan 1941– American singer

When it is not necessary to change, it is necessary not to change.
Lucius Cary, Viscount Falkland 1610–43 English politician

Most of the change we think we see in life
Is due to truths being in and out of favour.
Robert Frost 1874–1963 American poet

We must be the change we wish to see in the world.
Mahatma Gandhi 1869–1948 Indian statesman

You can't step twice into the same river.
Heraclitus c.540–c.480 BC Greek philosopher

Consistency is contrary to nature, contrary to life. The only completely consistent people are the dead.
Aldous Huxley 1894–1963 English novelist

Change is not made without inconvenience, even from worse to better.
Samuel Johnson 1709–84 English lexicographer

Plus ça change, plus c'est la même chose.
The more things change, the more they are the same.
Alphonse Karr 1808–90 French writer

If we want things to stay as they are, things will have to change.
Giuseppe di Lampedusa 1896–1957 Italian writer

Change

JUDY GARLAND: Toto, I've a feeling we're not in Kansas any more.
> **Noel Langley** 1911–80 American screenwriter, *in the film* The Wizard of Oz

It is best not to swap horses when crossing streams.
> **Abraham Lincoln** 1809–65 American statesman

Change and decay in all around I see;
O Thou, who changest not, abide with me.
> **Henry Francis Lyte** 1793–1847 English hymn-writer

Tomorrow to fresh woods, and pastures new.
> **John Milton** 1608–74 English poet

And now for something completely different.
> **Monty Python's Flying Circus** 1969–74 British television programme

Growth [is] the only evidence of life.
> **John Henry Newman** 1801–90 English theologian

God, give us the serenity to accept what cannot be changed;
Give us the courage to change what should be changed;
Give us the wisdom to distinguish one from the other.
> **Reinhold Niebuhr** 1892–1971 American theologian

Forward, forward let us range,
Let the great world spin for ever down the ringing grooves of change.
> **Alfred, Lord Tennyson** 1809–92 English poet

If we do not find anything pleasant, at least we shall find something new.
> **Voltaire** 1694–1778 French writer

All changed, changed utterly:
A terrible beauty is born.
> **W. B. Yeats** 1865–1939 Irish poet

Character

It is not in the still calm of life, or the repose of a pacific station, that great characters are formed...Great necessities call out great virtues.
Abigail Adams 1744–1818 American letter writer

A thick skin is a gift from God.
Konrad Adenauer 1876–1967 German statesman

You will never make a crab walk straight.
Aristophanes c.450–c.385 BC Greek comic dramatist

In one and the same fire, clay grows hard and wax melts.
Francis Bacon 1561–1626 English courtier

Talent develops in quiet places, character in the full current of human life.
Johann Wolfgang von Goethe 1749–1832 German writer

Those who stand for nothing fall for anything.
Alex Hamilton 1936–

A man's character is his fate.
Heraclitus c.540–c.480 BC Greek philosopher

A propensity to hope and joy is real riches: one to fear and sorrow, real poverty.
David Hume 1711–76 Scottish philosopher

Nothing gives one person so great advantage over another, as to remain always cool and unruffled under all circumstances.
Thomas Jefferson 1743–1826 American statesman

If you can fill the unforgiving minute
With sixty seconds' worth of distance run,
Yours is the Earth and everything that's in it,

Charity

And—which is more—you'll be a Man, my son!
Rudyard Kipling 1865–1936 English writer

I see the better things, and approve; I follow the worse.
Ovid 43 BC–c.AD 17 Roman poet

You can tell a lot about a fellow's character by his way of eating jellybeans.
Ronald Reagan 1911–2004 American statesman

      My nature is subdued
To what it works in, like the dyer's hand.
William Shakespeare 1564–1616 English dramatist

If you can't stand the heat, get out of the kitchen.
Harry Vaughan 1893–1981 American military aide, *associated with Harry S. Truman*

We are what we pretend to be.
Kurt Vonnegut 1922–2007 American writer

 Charity see also **Gifts**

God loveth a cheerful giver.
Bible

CHAIRMAN: What is service?
CANDIDATE: The rent we pay for our room on earth.
Tubby Clayton 1885–1972 British clergyman, *admission ceremony of Toc H*

The best form of charity I know is the art of meeting a payroll.
J. Paul Getty 1892–1976 American industrialist

Charity

You cannot feed the hungry on statistics.
David Lloyd George 1863–1945 British statesman

People often feed the hungry so that nothing may disturb their own enjoyment of a good meal.
W. Somerset Maugham 1874–1965 English novelist

Do good by stealth, and blush to find it fame.
Alexander Pope 1688–1744 English poet

He gives the poor man twice as much good who gives quickly.
Publilius Syrus fl. 1st century BC Roman writer

'Tis not enough to help the feeble up,
But to support him after.
William Shakespeare 1564–1616 English dramatist

Thy necessity is yet greater than mine.
Philip Sidney 1554–86 English writer, *on giving his water-bottle to a dying soldier on the battle-field of Zutphen; commonly quoted as 'thy need is greater than mine'*

Charity begins today. Today somebody is suffering, today somebody is in the street, today somebody is hungry.
Mother Teresa 1910–97 Roman Catholic nun

No one would remember the Good Samaritan if he'd only had good intentions. He had money as well.
Margaret Thatcher 1925–2013 British stateswoman

Friends, I have lost a day.
Titus AD 39–81 Roman emperor, *on reflecting that he had done nothing to help anybody all day*

Behold, I do not give lectures or a little charity,
When I give I give myself.
Walt Whitman 1819–92 American poet

Charm

Charm…it's a sort of bloom on a woman. If you have it, you don't need to have anything else; and if you don't have it, it doesn't much matter what else you have.
J. M. Barrie 1860–1937 Scottish writer

You know what charm is: a way of getting the answer yes without having asked any clear question.
Albert Camus 1913–60 French writer

All charming people have something to conceal, usually their total dependence on the appreciation of others.
Cyril Connolly 1903–74 English writer

Oozing charm from every pore,
He oiled his way around the floor.
Alan Jay Lerner 1918–86 American songwriter

Children see also **Babies**, **Family**, **Youth**

Children sweeten labours, but they make misfortunes more bitter.
Francis Bacon 1561–1626 English courtier

Quality time? There's always another load of washing.
Julian Barnes 1946– English novelist

Childhood is measured out by sounds and smells
And sights, before the dark of reason grows.
John Betjeman 1906–84 English poet

Suffer the little children to come unto me, and forbid them not: for of such is the kingdom of God.
Bible

When I was a child, I spake as a child, I understood as a child, I thought as a child: but when I became a man, I put away childish things.

Bible

There is no such thing as other people's children.

Hillary Rodham Clinton 1947– American lawyer

Our greatest natural resource is the minds of our children.

Walt Disney 1901–66 American film producer

Alas, regardless of their doom,
The little victims play!
No sense have they of ills to come,
Nor care beyond to-day.

Thomas Gray 1716–71 English poet

Allow them [children] to be happy their own way, for what better way will they ever find?

Samuel Johnson 1709–84 English lexicographer

If there is anything that we wish to change in the child, we should first examine it and see whether it is not something that could better be changed in ourselves.

Carl Gustav Jung 1875–1961 Swiss psychologist

A child is owed the greatest respect; if you ever have something disgraceful in mind, don't ignore your son's tender years.

Juvenal c.AD 60–c.140 Roman satirist

Literature is mostly about having sex and not much about having children. Life is the other way round.

David Lodge 1935– English novelist

It should be noted that children at play are not playing about; their games should be seen as their most serious-minded activity.

Montaigne 1533–92 French moralist

Choice

The affection you get back from children is sixpence given as change for a sovereign.
Edith Nesbit 1858–1924 English writer

Of all animals the boy is the most unmanageable.
Plato 429–347 BC Greek philosopher

Behold the child, by Nature's kindly law
Pleased with a rattle, tickled with a straw.
Alexander Pope 1688–1744 English poet

A child is not a vase to be filled, but a fire to be lit.
François Rabelais c.1494–c.1553 French humanist

Any man who hates dogs and babies can't be all bad.
Leo Rosten 1908–97 American writer, *of W. C. Fields, and often attributed to him*

Grown-ups never understand anything for themselves, and it is tiresome for children to be always and forever explaining things to them.
Antoine de Saint-Exupéry 1900–44 French novelist

The Child is father of the Man.
William Wordsworth 1770–1850 English poet

 # Choice

White shall not neutralize the black, nor good
Compensate bad in man, absolve him so:
Life's business being just the terrible choice.
Robert Browning 1812–89 English poet

The die is cast.
Julius Caesar 100–44 BC Roman statesman, *at the crossing of the Rubicon*

Any customer can have a car painted any colour that he wants so long as it is black.
Henry Ford 1863–1947 American car manufacturer, *of the Model T Ford*

Two roads diverged in a wood, and I—
I took the one less travelled by,
And that has made all the difference.
Robert Frost 1874–1963 American poet

How happy could I be with either,
Were t'other dear charmer away!
John Gay 1685–1732 English writer

Which do you want? A whipping and no turnips or turnips and no whipping?
Toni Morrison 1931– American novelist

You pays your money and you takes your choice.
Punch 1841–1992 English humorous periodical

I'll make him an offer he can't refuse.
Mario Puzo 1920–99 American novelist

To be, or not to be: that is the question.
William Shakespeare 1564–1616 English dramatist

Take care to get what you like or you will be forced to like what you get.
George Bernard Shaw 1856–1950 Irish dramatist

There is no real alternative.
Margaret Thatcher 1925–2013 British stateswoman

Between two evils, I always pick the one I never tried before.
Mae West 1892–1980 American film actress

Christmas

Christmas won't be Christmas without any presents.
>   **Louisa May Alcott** 1832–88 American novelist

I'm dreaming of a white Christmas,
Just like the ones I used to know.
>   **Irving Berlin** 1888–1989 American songwriter

And girls in slacks remember Dad,
And oafish louts remember Mum,
And sleepless children's hearts are glad,
And Christmas-morning bells say 'Come!'
>   **John Betjeman** 1906–84 English poet

She brought forth her firstborn son, and wrapped him in
swaddling clothes, and laid him in a manger; because there
was no room for them in the inn.
>   **Bible**

Yes, Virginia, there is a Santa Claus.
>   **Francis Pharcellus Church** 1839–1906 American editor,
>   *newspaper editorial replying to a letter from eight-year-old*
>   *Virginia O'Hanlon*

Christmas is the Disneyfication of Christianity.
>   **Don Cupitt** 1934–   British theologian

'Bah,' said Scrooge. 'Humbug!'
>   **Charles Dickens** 1812–70 English novelist, *responding to the*
>   *greeting 'Merry Christmas'*

A lovely thing about Christmas is that it's compulsory, like a
thunderstorm, and we all go through it together.
>   **Garrison Keillor** 1942–   American writer

'Twas the night before Christmas, when all through the house
Not a creature was stirring, not even a mouse.
>   **Clement C. Moore** 1779–1863 American writer

Be nice to yu turkeys dis Christmas
Cos' turkeys just wanna hav fun.
Benjamin Zephaniah 1958- British poet

The Church see also **Religion**

The nearer the Church the further from God.
Bishop Lancelot Andrewes 1555–1626 English preacher

He cannot have God for his father who has not the church
for his mother.
St Cyprian c.AD 200–258 Roman writer and martyr

A church is God between four walls.
Victor Hugo 1802–85 French writer

I want to throw open the windows of the Church so that we
can see out and the people can see in.
John XXIII 1881–1963 Italian pope

We are an Easter people and Alleluia is our song.
John Paul II 1920–2005 Polish pope

'The Church is an anvil which has worn out many hammers',
and the story of the first collision is, in essentials, the story
of all.
Alexander Maclaren 1826–1910 Scottish divine

The Church [of England] should go forward along the path
of progress and be no longer satisfied only to represent the
Conservative Party at prayer.
Maude Royden 1876–1956 English writer

I never saw, heard, nor read, that the clergy were beloved
in any nation where Christianity was the religion of the
country. Nothing can render them popular, but some degree
of persecution.
Jonathan Swift 1667–1745 Irish poet and satirist

The Cinema

As often as we are mown down by you, the more we grow in numbers; the blood of Christians is the seed.
>   **Tertullian** c.AD 160–c.225 Roman theologian, *traditionally*
>   'The blood of the martyrs is the seed of the Church'

I look upon all the world as my parish.
>   **John Wesley** 1703–91 English preacher

 # The Cinema see also **Acting**

WILLIAM HOLDEN: You used to be in pictures. You used to be big.
GLORIA SWANSON: I am big. It's the pictures that got small.
>   **Charles Brackett** 1892–1969 and **Billy Wilder** 1906–2002
>   American screenwriters, *in the film* Sunset Boulevard

There are no rules in film-making. Only sins. And the cardinal sin is dullness.
>   **Frank Capra** 1897–1991 American film director

All I need to make a comedy is a park, a policeman and a pretty girl.
>   **Charlie Chaplin** 1889–1977 English film actor

GEORGES FRANJU: Movies should have a beginning, a middle and an end.
GODARD: Certainly, but not necessarily in that order.
>   **Jean-Luc Godard** 1930– French film director

Photography is truth. The cinema is truth 24 times per second.
>   **Jean-Luc Godard** 1930– French film director

Nobody knows anything.
>   **William Goldman** 1931– American writer, *on the film industry*

Pictures are for entertainment, messages should be delivered by Western Union.
Sam Goldwyn 1882–1974 American film producer

Why should people go out and pay to see bad movies when they can stay at home and see bad television for nothing?
Sam Goldwyn 1882–1974 American film producer

If I made Cinderella, the audience would immediately be looking for a body in the coach.
Alfred Hitchcock 1899–1980 British-born film director

We've got more stars than there are in the heavens, all of them except for that damned Mouse over at Disney.
Louis B. Mayer 1885–1957 American film executive

The trouble, Mr Goldwyn, is that you are only interested in art and I am only interested in money.
George Bernard Shaw 1856–1950 Irish dramatist, *telegraphed version of the outcome of a conversation between Shaw and Sam Goldwyn*

This is the biggest electric train a boy ever had!
Orson Welles 1915–85 American film director, *of the RKO studios*

It is like writing history with lightning. And my only regret is that it is all so terribly true.
Woodrow Wilson 1856–1924 American statesman, *on seeing D. W. Griffith's film* The Birth of a Nation

Civilization

The three great elements of modern civilization, Gunpowder, Printing, and the Protestant Religion.
Thomas Carlyle 1795–1881 Scottish historian

Civilization and profits go hand in hand.
Calvin Coolidge 1872–1933 American statesman

Civilization

JOURNALIST: Mr Gandhi, what do you think of modern civilization?
GANDHI: That would be a good idea.

Mahatma Gandhi 1869–1948 Indian statesman

If a nation expects to be ignorant and free, in a state of civilization, it expects what never was and never will be.

Thomas Jefferson 1743–1826 American statesman

Whenever I hear the word culture…I release the safety-catch of my Browning!

Hanns Johst 1890–1978 German dramatist, *often attributed to Hermann Goering, and quoted as 'Whenever I hear the word culture, I reach for my pistol!'*

If civilization had been left in female hands, we would still be living in grass huts.

Camille Paglia 1947– American writer

You can't say civilization don't advance, however, for in every war they kill you in a new way.

Will Rogers 1879–1935 American actor

Civilization has made the peasantry its pack animal. The bourgeoisie in the long run only changed the form of the pack.

Leon Trotsky 1879–1940 Russian revolutionary

In Italy for thirty years under the Borgias they had warfare, terror, murder, bloodshed—they produced Michelangelo, Leonardo da Vinci and the Renaissance. In Switzerland they had brotherly love, five hundred years of democracy and peace and what did that produce…? The cuckoo clock.

Orson Welles 1915–85 American film director

Class

The rich man in his castle,
The poor man at his gate,
God made them, high or lowly,
And ordered their estate.
Cecil Frances Alexander 1818–95 Irish poet

Il faut épater le bourgeois.
One must astonish the bourgeois.
Charles Baudelaire 1821–67 French poet

Like many of the Upper Class
He liked the Sound of Broken Glass.
Hilaire Belloc 1870–1953 British writer

The Stately Homes of England,
How beautiful they stand,
To prove the upper classes
Have still the upper hand.
Noël Coward 1899–1973 English dramatist

O let us love our occupations,
Bless the squire and his relations,
Live upon our daily rations,
And always know our proper stations.
Charles Dickens 1812–70 English novelist

The proletarians have nothing to lose but their chains. They
have a world to win. WORKING MEN OF ALL COUNTRIES,
UNITE!
Karl Marx 1818–83 and **Friedrich Engels** 1820–95 German
philosopher and German socialist, *commonly rendered
'Workers of the world, unite!'*

Clothes

When Adam dalfe and Eve spane…
Where was than the pride of man?
Richard Rolle de Hampole *c.*1290–1349 English mystic, *taken in the form 'When Adam delved and Eve span, who was then the gentleman?' by John Ball as the text of his revolutionary sermon on the outbreak of the Peasants' Revolt, 1381*

The State is an instrument in the hands of the ruling class, used to break the resistance of the adversaries of that class.
Joseph Stalin 1879–1953 Soviet dictator

The French want no-one to be their *superior*. The English want *inferiors*. The Frenchman constantly raises his eyes above him with anxiety. The Englishman lowers his beneath him with satisfaction.
Alexis de Tocqueville 1805–59 French historian

 # Clothes

It is totally impossible to be well dressed in cheap shoes.
Hardy Amies 1909–2003 English couturier

From the cradle to the grave, underwear first, last and all the time.
Bertolt Brecht 1898–1956 German dramatist

No perfumes, but very fine linen, plenty of it, and country washing.
Beau Brummell 1778–1840 English dandy

Look for the woman in the dress. If there is no woman, there is no dress.
Coco Chanel 1883–1971 French couturière

The sense of being well-dressed gives a feeling of inward tranquillity which religion is powerless to bestow.
Miss C. F. Forbes 1817–1911 English writer

A sweet disorder in the dress
Kindles in clothes a wantonness.
> **Robert Herrick** 1591–1674 English poet

Dress cute wherever you go. Life is too short to blend in.
> **Paris Hilton** 1981– American heiress

You should never have your best trousers on when you go
out to fight for freedom and truth.
> **Henrik Ibsen** 1828–1906 Norwegian dramatist

A tie is a noose, and inverted though it is, it will hang a man
nonetheless if he's not careful.
> **Yann Martel** 1963– Canadian writer

I have often said that I wish I had invented blue jeans.
> **Yves Saint Laurent** 1936–2008 French couturier

His socks compelled one's attention without losing one's
respect.
> **Saki** 1870–1916 Scottish writer

The apparel oft proclaims the man.
> **William Shakespeare** 1564–1616 English dramatist

Beware of all enterprises that require new clothes.
> **Henry David Thoreau** 1817–62 American writer

Computers

To err is human but to really foul things up requires a
computer.
> **Anonymous**

Google is white bread for the mind.
> **Tara Brabazon** 1969– Australian academic

I like to think
(it has to be!)

Computers

of a cybernetic ecology
where we are free of our labours
and joined back to nature,
returned to our mammal
brothers and sisters,
and all watched over
by machines of loving grace.

Richard Brautigan 1935–84 American writer

The email of the species is deadlier than the mail.

Stephen Fry 1957– English comedian

I think computer viruses should count as life. Maybe it says something about human nature, that the only form of life we have created so far is purely destructive.

Stephen Hawking 1942– English theoretical physicist

The PC is the LSD of the '90s.

Timothy Leary 1920–96 American psychologist

Computer says No.

Matt Lucas 1974– and **David Walliams** 1971– British comedians

You have zero privacy anyway. Get over it.

Scott McNealy 1954– American businessman, *on the introduction of Jini networking technology*

If you have a child, you'll notice they'll have two states, asleep or online.

Eric Schmidt 1955– American computer executive

On the Internet, nobody knows you're a dog.

Peter Steiner 1940– American cartoonist

We used to have lots of questions to which there were no answers. Now with the computer there are lots of answers to which we haven't thought up the questions.

Peter Ustinov 1921–2004 British actor

We've all heard that a million monkeys banging on a million typewriters will eventually reproduce the entire works of Shakespeare. Now, thanks to the Internet, we know this is not true.

Robert Wilensky 1951– American academic

Conscience

We have erred, and strayed from thy ways like lost sheep. We have followed too much the devices and desires of our own hearts.

Book of Common Prayer 1662

Conscience is thoroughly well-bred and soon leaves off talking to those who do not wish to hear it.

Samuel Butler 1835–1902 English novelist

O dignitosa coscienza e netta,
Come t'è picciol fallo amaro morso!

O pure and noble conscience, how bitter a sting to thee is a little fault!

Dante Alighieri 1265–1321 Italian poet

In many walks of life, a conscience is a more expensive encumbrance than a wife or a carriage.

Thomas De Quincey 1785–1859 English essayist

A good conscience is a continual Christmas.

Benjamin Franklin 1706–90 American statesman and scientist

I cannot and will not cut my conscience to fit this year's fashions.

Lillian Hellman 1905–84 American dramatist

Conversation

Cowardice asks the question, 'Is it safe?' Expediency asks the question, 'Is it politic?' Vanity asks the question, 'Is it popular?' But Conscience asks the question, 'Is it right?'
Martin Luther King 1929–68 American civil rights leader

The one thing that doesn't abide by majority rule is a person's conscience.
Harper Lee 1926–2016 American novelist

Conscience: the inner voice which warns us that someone may be looking.
H. L. Mencken 1880–1956 American journalist

Thus conscience doth make cowards of us all.
William Shakespeare 1564–1616 English dramatist

Corporations have neither bodies to be punished, nor souls to be condemned, they therefore do as they like.
Edward, 1st Baron Thurlow 1731–1806 English jurist,
usually quoted as 'Did you ever expect a corporation to have a conscience, when it has no soul to be damned, and no body to be kicked?'

 # Conversation see also **Speechmaking**

On every formal visit a child ought to be of the party, by way of provision for discourse.
Jane Austen 1775–1817 English novelist

Although there exist many thousand subjects for elegant conversation, there are persons who cannot meet a cripple without talking about feet.
Ernest Bramah 1868–1942 English writer

'The time has come,' the Walrus said,
'To talk of many things:

Of shoes—and ships—and sealing wax—
Of cabbages—and kings.'
Lewis Carroll 1832–98 English writer

Religion is by no means a proper subject of conversation in a mixed company.
Lord Chesterfield 1694–1773 English writer

Too much agreement kills a chat.
Eldridge Cleaver 1935–98 American political activist

Someone to tell it to is one of the fundamental needs of human beings.
Miles Franklin 1879–1954 Australian writer

And, when you stick on conversation's burrs,
Don't strew your pathway with those dreadful *urs*.
Oliver Wendell Holmes 1809–94 American physician

A…sharp tongue is the only edged tool that grows keener with constant use.
Washington Irving 1783–1859 American writer

Questioning is not the mode of conversation among gentlemen. It is assuming a superiority.
Samuel Johnson 1709–84 English lexicographer

Must I always be a mere listener?
Juvenal c.AD 60–c.140 Roman satirist

The opposite of talking isn't listening. The opposite of talking is waiting.
Fran Lebowitz 1950– American writer

With thee conversing I forget all time.
John Milton 1608–74 English poet

A good listener is not only popular everywhere, but after a while he knows something.
Wilson Mizner 1876–1933 American dramatist

Cookery

The feast of reason and the flow of soul.
Alexander Pope 1688–1744 English poet

I am not bound to please thee with my answer.
William Shakespeare 1564–1616 English dramatist

 # Cookery see also **Eating**, **Food**

Anyone who tells a lie has not a pure heart, and cannot make a good soup.
Ludwig van Beethoven 1770–1827 German composer

Be content to remember that those who can make omelettes properly can do nothing else.
Hilaire Belloc 1870–1953 British writer

Cooking is the most ancient of the arts, for Adam was born hungry.
Anthelme Brillat-Savarin 1755–1826 French gourmet

Good food is always a trouble and its preparation should be regarded as a labour of love.
Elizabeth David 1913–92 British cook

Heaven sends us good meat, but the Devil sends cooks.
David Garrick 1717–79 English actor-manager

Kissing don't last: cookery do!
George Meredith 1828–1909 English writer

I never see any home cooking. All I get is fancy stuff.
Philip, Duke of Edinburgh 1921–   Greek-born husband of Elizabeth II

The cook was a good cook, as cooks go; and as cooks go, she went.
Saki 1870–1916 Scottish writer

Cooperation

If a house be divided against itself, that house cannot stand.
>   **Bible**

Bear ye one another's burdens.
>   **Bible**

When bad men combine, the good must associate; else they will fall, one by one, an unpitied sacrifice in a contemptible struggle.
>   **Edmund Burke** 1729–97 Irish-born politician

All for one, one for all.
>   **Alexandre Dumas** 1802–70 French novelist

We must indeed all hang together, or, most assuredly, we shall all hang separately.
>   **Benjamin Franklin** 1706–90 American statesman and scientist

If someone claps his hand a sound arises. Listen to the sound of the single hand!
>   **Hakuin** 1686–1769 Japanese monk

If we cannot end now our differences, at least we can help make the world safe for diversity.
>   **John F. Kennedy** 1917–63 American statesman

We must learn to live together as brothers or perish together as fools.
>   **Martin Luther King** 1929–68 American civil rights leader

When Hitler attacked the Jews I was not a Jew, therefore, I was not concerned. And when Hitler attacked the Catholics, I was not a Catholic, and therefore, I was not concerned. And when Hitler attacked the unions and the industrialists, I was not a member of the unions and

The Country

I was not concerned. Then, Hitler attacked me and the
Protestant church—and there was nobody left to be
concerned.

Martin Niemöller 1892–1984 German theologian

Government and cooperation are in all things the laws of
life; anarchy and competition the laws of death.

John Ruskin 1819–1900 English critic

The Country see also **Environment**

'Tis distance lends enchantment to the view,
And robes the mountain in its azure hue.

Thomas Campbell 1777–1844 Scottish poet

God made the country, and man made the town.

William Cowper 1731–1800 English poet

It is my belief, Watson, founded upon my experience, that
the lowest and vilest alleys in London do not present a more
dreadful record of sin than does the smiling and beautiful
countryside.

Arthur Conan Doyle 1859–1930 Scottish-born writer

Green belts should be the start of the countryside, not a
ditch between Subtopias.

Hugh Gaitskell 1906–63 British politician

Our salvation can only come through the farmer. Neither
the lawyers, nor the doctors, nor the rich landlords are
going to secure it.

Mahatma Gandhi 1869–1948 Indian statesman

Agriculture is the foundation of manufactures; since the
productions of nature are the materials of art.

Edward Gibbon 1737–94 English historian

There is nothing good to be had in the country, or if there is, they will not let you have it.
William Hazlitt 1778–1830 English essayist

The Farmer will never be happy again;
He carries his heart in his boots;
For either the rain is destroying his grain
Or the drought is destroying his roots.
A. P. Herbert 1890–1971 English writer

Oh, give me land, lots of land under starry skies above,
Don't fence me in.
Cole Porter 1891–1964 American songwriter

I have no relish for the country; it is a kind of healthy grave.
Sydney Smith 1771–1845 English essayist

Anybody can be good in the country.
Oscar Wilde 1854–1900 Irish dramatist

Courage

No coward soul is mine,
No trembler in the world's storm-troubled sphere:
I see Heaven's glories shine,
And faith shines equal, arming me from fear.
Emily Brontë 1818–48 English writer

Courage is rightly esteemed the first of human qualities because as has been said, it is the quality which guarantees all others.
Winston Churchill 1874–1965 British statesman

Boldness, and again boldness, and always boldness!
Georges Jacques Danton 1759–94 French revolutionary

Courage is the price that Life exacts for granting peace,
The soul that knows it not, knows no release

Courage

From little things.
Amelia Earhart 1898–1937 American aviator

What counts is not necessarily the size of the dog in the fight — it's the size of the fight in the dog.
Dwight D. Eisenhower 1890–1969 American statesman

Grace under pressure.
Ernest Hemingway 1899–1961 American novelist, *when asked what he meant by 'guts'*

Tender-handed stroke a nettle,
And it stings you for your pains;
Grasp it like a man of mettle,
And it soft as silk remains.
Aaron Hill 1685–1750 English writer

When you know you're licked before you begin but you begin anyway and you see it through no matter what. You rarely win, but sometimes you do.
Harper Lee 1926–2016 American novelist, *on 'real courage'*

Courage is not simply *one* of the virtues but the form of every virtue at the testing point.
C. S. Lewis 1898–1963 English literary scholar

As to moral courage, I have very rarely met with two o'clock in the morning courage: I mean instantaneous courage.
Napoleon I 1769–1821 French emperor

Life shrinks or expands in proportion to one's courage.
Anaïs Nin 1903–77 American writer

Cowards die many times before their deaths;
The valiant never taste of death but once.
William Shakespeare 1564–1616 English dramatist

Fortune assists the bold.
Virgil 70–19 BC Roman poet, *often quoted as 'Fortune favours the brave'*

Creativity

The more you reason, the less you create.
Raymond Chandler 1888–1959 American writer

Think before you speak is criticism's motto; speak before you think creation's.
E. M. Forster 1879–1970 English novelist

That which is creative must create itself.
John Keats 1795–1821 English poet

Poems are made by fools like me,
But only God can make a tree.
Joyce Kilmer 1886–1918 American poet

Nothing can be created out of nothing.
Lucretius c.94–55 BC Roman poet

The worst crime is to leave a man's hands empty.
Men are born makers, with that primal simplicity
In every maker since Adam.
Derek Walcott 1930–2017 West Indian writer

Urge and urge and urge,
Always the procreant urge of the world.
Walt Whitman 1819–92 American poet

Cricket

Bowl fast, bowl faster. When you play Test cricket you don't give Englishmen an inch. Play it tough, all the way. Grind them into the dust.
Don Bradman 1908–2001 Australian cricketer

Never read print, it spoils one's eye for the ball.
W. G. Grace 1848–1915 English cricketer, *habitual advice to his players*

Crime

It's more than a game. It's an institution.
Thomas Hughes 1822–96 English lawyer and writer

What do they know of cricket who only cricket know?
Cyril Lionel Robert James 1901–89 Trinidadian writer

Cricket—a game which the English, not being a spiritual people, have invented in order to give themselves some conception of eternity.
Lord Mancroft 1914–87 British politician

Cricket civilizes people and creates good gentlemen. I want everyone to play cricket in Zimbabwe; I want ours to be a nation of gentlemen.
Robert Mugabe 1924– African stateman

There's a breathless hush in the Close to-night—
Ten to make and the match to win—
A bumping pitch and a blinding light,
An hour to play and the last man in.
Henry Newbolt 1862–1938 English writer

Personally, I have always looked on cricket as organized loafing.
William Temple 1881–1944 English theologian

 Crime see also **Justice, Murder, Punishment**

Labour is the party of law and order in Britain today. Tough on crime and tough on the causes of crime.
Tony Blair 1953– British statesman

Once in the racket you're always in it.
Al Capone 1899–1947 American gangster

Crime isn't a disease, it's a symptom. Cops are like a doctor that gives you aspirin for a brain tumour.
Raymond Chandler 1888–1959 American writer

Thieves respect property. They merely wish the property to become their property that they may more perfectly respect it.
    G. K. Chesterton 1874–1936 English writer

The mood and temper of the public in regard to the treatment of crime and criminals is one of the most unfailing tests of the civilization of any country.
    Winston Churchill 1874–1965 British statesman

Thou shalt not steal; an empty feat,
When it's so lucrative to cheat.
    Arthur Hugh Clough 1819–61 English poet

Singularity is almost invariably a clue. The more featureless and commonplace a crime is, the more difficult is it to bring it home.
    Arthur Conan Doyle 1859–1930 Scottish-born writer

For de little stealin' dey gits you in jail soon or late. For de big stealin' dey makes you Emperor and puts you in de Hall o' Fame when you croaks.
    Eugene O'Neill 1888–1953 American dramatist

Crime doesn't pay.
    Proverb

Crises

Don't panic.
    Douglas Adams 1952–2001 English writer, *on the cover of* The Hitch Hiker's Guide to the Galaxy

Comin' in on a wing and a pray'r.
    Harold Adamson 1906–80 American songwriter

Crises

Crisis? What Crisis?
> **Anonymous**, Sun *headline, summarizing James Callaghan on the winter of discontent: 'I don't think other people in the world would share the view* [that] *there is mounting chaos'*

Keep calm and carry on.
> **Anonymous**, *poster designed by the Ministry of Information in 1939 but not used in World War II; re-discovered and popularized in the early 21st century*

You never want a serious crisis to go to waste.
> **Rahm Emanuel** 1959–   American politician, *often quoted as 'Never waste a good crisis'*

The illustrious bishop of Cambrai was of more worth than his chambermaid, and there are few of us that would hesitate to pronounce, if his palace were in flames, and the life of only one of them could be preserved, which of the two ought to be preferred.
> **William Godwin** 1756–1836 English philosopher

For it is your business, when the wall next door catches fire.
> **Horace** 65–8 BC Roman poet

My friends, as I have discovered myself, there are no disasters, only opportunities. And, indeed, opportunities for fresh disasters.
> **Boris Johnson** 1964–   British politician

If you can keep your head when all about you
Are losing theirs and blaming it on you.
> **Rudyard Kipling** 1865–1936 English writer

A trifle consoles us because a trifle upsets us.
> **Blaise Pascal** 1623–62 French scientist and philosopher

We're eyeball to eyeball, and I think the other fellow just blinked.
> **Dean Rusk** 1909–   American politician

I myself have always deprecated…in crisis after crisis, appeals to the Dunkirk spirit as an answer to our problems.
Harold Wilson 1916–95 British statesman

I'm at my best in a messy, middle-of-the-road muddle.
Harold Wilson 1916–95 British statesman

Criticism

A man must serve his time to every trade
Save censure—critics all are ready made.
Lord Byron 1788–1824 English poet

Everything must be like something, so what is this like?
E. M. Forster 1879–1970 English novelist

No theoretician, no writer on art, however interesting he or she might be, could be as interesting as Picasso. A good writer on art may give you an insight to Picasso, but, after all, Picasso was there first.
David Hockney 1937–   British artist

Parodies and caricatures are the most penetrating of criticisms.
Aldous Huxley 1894–1963 English novelist

I don't care anything about reasons, but I know what I like.
Henry James 1843–1916 American novelist

This will never do.
Francis, Lord Jeffrey 1773–1850 Scottish critic, *on Wordsworth's* The Excursion

You *may* abuse a tragedy, though you cannot write one. You may scold a carpenter who has made you a bad table, though you cannot make a table. It is not your trade to make tables.
Samuel Johnson 1709–84 English lexicographer, *on literary criticism*

Criticism

I cry all the way to the bank.

Liberace 1919–87 American showman, *on bad reviews*

People who like this sort of thing will find this the sort of thing they like.

Abraham Lincoln 1809–65 American statesman, *judgement of a book*

One should look long and carefully at oneself before one considers judging others.

Molière 1622–73 French comic dramatist

I am sitting in the smallest room of my house. I have your review before me. In a moment it will be behind me.

Max Reger 1873–1916 German composer, *responding to a savage review*

If you are not criticized, you may not be doing much.

Donald Rumsfeld 1932– American politician

Remember, a statue has never been set up in honour of a critic!

Jean Sibelius 1865–1957 Finnish composer

I never read a book before reviewing it; it prejudices a man so.

Sydney Smith 1771–1845 English essayist

As learned commentators view
In Homer more than Homer knew.

Jonathan Swift 1667–1745 Irish poet and satirist

A critic is a man who knows the way but can't drive the car.

Kenneth Tynan 1927–80 English critic

I maintain that two and two would continue to make four, in spite of the whine of the amateur for three, or the cry of the critic for five.

James McNeill Whistler 1834–1903 American-born painter

Cruelty

Boys throw stones at frogs for fun, but the frogs don't die for 'fun', but in sober earnest.
Bion c.325–c.255 BC Greek philosopher

A robin red breast in a cage
Puts all Heaven in a rage.
William Blake 1757–1827 English poet

Man's inhumanity to man
Makes countless thousands mourn!
Robert Burns 1759–96 Scottish poet

Cruelty, like every other vice, requires no motive outside itself—it only requires opportunity.
George Eliot 1819–80 English novelist

The healthy man does not torture others—generally it is the tortured who turn into torturers.
Carl Gustav Jung 1875–1961 Swiss psychologist

Our language lacks words to express this offence, the demolition of a man.
Primo Levi 1919–87 Italian writer, *of a year spent in Auschwitz*

I must be cruel only to be kind.
William Shakespeare 1564–1616 English dramatist

This was the most unkindest cut of all.
William Shakespeare 1564–1616 English dramatist

All cruel people describe themselves as paragons of frankness.
Tennessee Williams 1911–83 American dramatist

Custom

One can't carry one's father's corpse about everywhere.
  Guillaume Apollinaire 1880–1918 French poet, *on tradition*

Custom reconciles us to everything.
  Edmund Burke 1729–97 Irish-born politician

Tradition means giving votes to the most obscure of all classes, our ancestors. It is the democracy of the dead.
  G. K. Chesterton 1874–1936 English writer

I confess myself to be a great admirer of tradition. The longer you can look back, the farther you can look forward.
  Winston Churchill 1874–1965 British statesman

Actions receive their tincture from the times,
And as they change are virtues made or crimes.
  Daniel Defoe 1660–1731 English novelist

Custom, then, is the great guide of human life.
  David Hume 1711–76 Scottish philosopher

The tradition of all the dead generations weighs like a nightmare on the brain of the living.
  Karl Marx 1818–83 German philosopher

Everyone calls barbarism what is not customary to him.
  Molière 1622–73 French comic dramatist

But to my mind,—though I am native here,
And to the manner born,—it is a custom
More honoured in the breach than the observance.
  William Shakespeare 1564–1616 English dramatist

Laws are sand, customs are rock. Laws can be evaded and punishment escaped, but an openly transgressed custom brings sure punishment.
  Mark Twain 1835–1910 American writer

Cynicism

Kill them all; God will recognize his own.
> **Arnald-Amaury** d. 1225 French abbot, *when asked how the true Catholics could be distinguished from the heretics at the massacre of Béziers*

Nothing matters very much and very few things matter at all.
> **Arthur James Balfour** 1848–1930 British statesman

Never glad confident morning again!
> **Robert Browning** 1812–89 English poet

What makes all doctrines plain and clear?
About two hundred pounds a year.
And that which was proved true before,
Prove false again? Two hundred more.
> **Samuel Butler** 1612–80 English poet

To get practice in being refused.
> **Diogenes** c.400–c.325 BC Greek philosopher, *reply when asked why he was begging for alms from a statue*

Pathos, piety, courage—they exist, but are identical, and so is filth. Everything exists, nothing has value.
> **E. M. Forster** 1879–1970 English novelist

Cynicism is an unpleasant way of saying the truth.
> **Lillian Hellman** 1905–84 American dramatist

Paris is well worth a mass.
> **Henri IV** 1553–1610 French monarch

Cynicism is our shared common language, the Esperanto that actually caught on.
> **Nick Hornby** 1957-   British writer

Dance

SIR HUMPHREY APPLEBY: A cynic is what an idealist calls a realist.

Jonathan Lynn 1943– and **Antony Jay** 1930–2016 English writers, *in* Yes Minister

A man who knows the price of everything and the value of nothing.

Oscar Wilde 1854–1900 Irish dramatist, *definition of a cynic*

 # Dance

A dance is a measured pace, as a verse is a measured speech.

Francis Bacon 1561–1626 English courtier

There may be trouble ahead,
But while there's moonlight and music and love and romance,
Let's face the music and dance.

Irving Berlin 1888–1989 American songwriter

On with the dance! let joy be unconfined;
No sleep till morn, when Youth and Pleasure meet
To chase the glowing Hours with flying feet.

Lord Byron 1788–1824 English poet

This wondrous miracle did Love devise,
For dancing is love's proper exercise.

John Davies 1569–1626 English poet

The truest expression of a people is in its dances and its music. Bodies never lie.

Agnes de Mille 1908–93 American dancer

Dance is the hidden language of the soul.

Martha Graham 1894–1991 American dancer

Come, and trip it as ye go
On the light fantastic toe.

John Milton 1608–74 English poet

[Dancing is] a perpendicular expression of a horizontal desire.
George Bernard Shaw 1856–1950 Irish dramatist

Danger

Risk comes from not knowing what you're doing.
Warren Buffett 1930– American businessman

Dangers by being despised grow great.
Edmund Burke 1729–97 Irish-born politician

Nothing in life is so exhilarating as to be shot at without result.
Winston Churchill 1874–1965 British statesman

When there is no peril in the fight, there is no glory in the triumph.
Pierre Corneille 1606–84 French dramatist

In skating over thin ice, our safety is in our speed.
Ralph Waldo Emerson 1803–82 American writer

Out of this nettle, danger, we pluck this flower, safety.
William Shakespeare 1564–1616 English dramatist

Considering how dangerous everything is nothing is really very frightening.
Gertrude Stein 1874–1946 American writer

Day see also **Night**

This is the day which the Lord hath made: we will rejoice and be glad in it.
Bible

Morning has broken
Like the first morning.
Eleanor Farjeon 1881–1965 English writer

Death

Awake! for Morning in the bowl of night
Has flung the stone that puts the stars to flight.
Edward Fitzgerald 1809–83 English poet

What are days for?
Days are where we live.
Philip Larkin 1922–85 English poet

I have a horror of sunsets, they're so romantic, so operatic.
Marcel Proust 1871–1922 French novelist

Night's candles are burnt out, and jocund day
Stands tiptoe on the misty mountain tops.
William Shakespeare 1564–1616 English dramatist

 # Death see also **Bereavement**

It's not that I'm afraid to die. I just don't want to be there
when it happens.
Woody Allen 1935– American film director

Death is only an horizon, and an horizon is only the limit of
our sight.
Anonymous, *traditional saying, sometimes attributed to William
Penn (1644–1718)*

To die will be an awfully big adventure.
J. M. Barrie 1860–1937 Scottish writer

For dust thou art, and unto dust shalt thou return.
Bible

O death, where is thy sting? O grave, where is thy victory?
Bible

In the midst of life we are in death.
Book of Common Prayer 1662

Forasmuch as it hath pleased Almighty God of his great mercy to take unto himself the soul of our dear brother here departed, we therefore commit his body to the ground; earth to earth, ashes to ashes, dust to dust; in sure and certain hope of the Resurrection to eternal life.

Book of Common Prayer 1662

If I should die, think only this of me:
That there's some corner of a foreign field
That is for ever England.

Rupert Brooke 1887–1915 English poet

However many ways there may be of being alive, it is certain that there are vastly more ways of being dead.

Richard Dawkins 1941– English biologist

Any man's death diminishes me, because I am involved in Mankind; And therefore never send to know for whom the bell tolls; it tolls for thee.

John Donne 1572–1631 English poet

Death be not proud, though some have called thee
Mighty and dreadful, for thou art not so.

John Donne 1572–1631 English poet

The bodies of those that made such a noise and tumult when alive, when dead, lie as quietly among the graves of their neighbours as any others.

Jonathan Edwards 1703–58 American theologian

Death, therefore, the most awful of evils, is nothing to us, seeing that, when we are death is not come, and when death is come, we are not.

Epicurus 341–271 BC Greek philosopher

Death is nothing if one can approach it as such. I was just a tiny night-light, suffocated in its own wax, and on the point of expiring.

E. M. Forster 1879–1970 English novelist

Death

Death is nothing at all; it does not count. I have only slipped away into the next room.

Henry Scott Holland 1847–1918 English theologian

I would rather be tied to the soil as another man's serf, even a poor man's, who hadn't much to live on himself, than be King of all these the dead and destroyed.

Homer fl. 8th century BC Greek poet

Non omnis moriar.
I shall not altogether die.

Horace 65–8 BC Roman poet

Remembering that you are going to die is the best way to avoid the trap of thinking you have something to lose.

Steve Jobs 1955–2011 American computer executive

Depend upon it, Sir, when a man knows he is to be hanged in a fortnight, it concentrates his mind wonderfully.

Samuel Johnson 1709–84 English lexicographer

Now more than ever seems it rich to die,
To cease upon the midnight with no pain.

John Keats 1795–1821 English poet

This parrot is no more! It has ceased to be! It's expired and gone to meet its maker! This is a late parrot! It's a stiff! Bereft of life it rests in peace—if you hadn't nailed it to the perch it would be pushing up the daisies! It's rung down the curtain and joined the choir invisible! THIS IS AN EX–PARROT!

Monty Python's Flying Circus 1969–74 British television programme

And all our calm is in that balm—
Not lost but gone before.

Caroline Norton 1808–77 English poet

Die, my dear Doctor, that's the last thing I shall do!
Lord Palmerston 1784–1865 British statesman

Guns aren't lawful;
Nooses give;
Gas smells awful;
You might as well live.
Dorothy Parker 1893–1967 American critic

We shall die alone.
Blaise Pascal 1623–62 French scientist and philosopher

Abiit ad plures.
He's gone to join the majority [the dead].
Petronius d. AD 65 Roman satirist

Anyone can stop a man's life, but no one his death;
a thousand doors open on to it.
Seneca ('the Younger') c.4 BC–AD 65 Roman philosopher

Nothing in his life
Became him like the leaving it.
William Shakespeare 1564–1616 English dramatist

To die, to sleep;
To sleep: perchance to dream: ay, there's the rub;
For in that sleep of death what dreams may come
When we have shuffled off this mortal coil,
Must give us pause.
William Shakespeare 1564–1616 English dramatist

If there wasn't death, I think you couldn't go on.
Stevie Smith 1902–71 English poet

Death must be distinguished from dying, with which it is
often confused.
Sydney Smith 1771–1845 English essayist

Debt

One death is a tragedy, a million deaths a statistic.
Joseph Stalin 1879–1953 Soviet dictator

For though from out our bourne of time and place
The flood may bear me far,
I hope to see my pilot face to face
When I have crossed the bar.
Alfred, Lord Tennyson 1809–92 English poet

Though lovers be lost love shall not;
And death shall have no dominion.
Dylan Thomas 1914–53 Welsh poet

So it goes.
Kurt Vonnegut 1922–2007 American novelist

I know death hath ten thousand several doors
For men to take their exits.
John Webster c.1580–c.1625 English dramatist

The good die first,
And they whose hearts are dry as summer dust
Burn to the socket.
William Wordsworth 1770–1850 English poet

Nor dread nor hope attend
A dying animal;
A man awaits his end
Dreading and hoping all.
W. B. Yeats 1865–1939 Irish poet

 # Debt

Be not made a beggar by banqueting upon borrowing.
Bible

Rather go to bed supperless than rise in debt.
Benjamin Franklin 1706–90 American statesman and scientist

The human species, according to the best theory I can form of it, is composed of two distinct races, *the men who borrow*, and *the men who lend*.

Charles Lamb 1775–1834 English writer

Should we really let our people starve so we can pay our debts?

Julius Nyerere 1922–99 Tanzanian statesman

You can't put your VISA bill on your American Express card.

P. J. O'Rourke 1947– American writer

A small debt makes a man your debtor; a large one, an enemy.

Seneca ('the Younger') c.4 BC–AD 65 Roman philosopher

Neither a borrower, nor a lender be.

William Shakespeare 1564–1616 English dramatist

Deceit see also **Honesty**, **Lies**

I count false words the foulest plague of all.

Aeschylus c.525–456 BC Greek tragedian

Propaganda is a soft weapon: hold it in your hands too long, and it will move about like a snake, and strike the other way.

Jean Anouilh 1910–87 French dramatist

An open foe may prove a curse,
But a pretended friend is worse.

John Gay 1685–1732 English writer

It was beautiful and simple as all truly great swindles are.

O. Henry 1862–1910 American short-story writer

Deception

Do not be too straight or too soft; straight trees are cut down, but crooked trees remain standing.
Kautilya (Chanakya) fl. *c.*300 BC Hindu statesman

You may fool all the people some of the time; you can even fool some of the people all the time; but you can't fool all of the people all the time.
Abraham Lincoln 1809–65 American statesman

A deception that elevates us is dearer than a host of low truths.
Alexander Pushkin 1799–1837 Russian poet

O what a tangled web we weave,
When first we practise to deceive!
Sir Walter Scott 1771–1832 Scottish novelist

 # Democracy see also **Elections, Politics**

The cure for the ills of Democracy is more Democracy.
John Adams 1735–1826 American statesman

The basis of a democratic state is liberty.
Aristotle 384–322 BC Greek philosopher

Democracy means government by discussion, but it is only effective if you can stop people talking.
Clement Attlee 1883–1967 British statesman

Democracy is the best revenge.
Benazir Bhutto 1953–2007 Pakistani stateswoman

One man shall have one vote.
John Cartwright 1740–1824 English political reformer

Democracy is the worst form of Government except all those other forms that have been tried from time to time.
Winston Churchill 1874–1965 British statesman

As for our majority…one is enough.
Benjamin Disraeli 1804–81 British statesman

So Two cheers for Democracy: one because it admits variety and two because it permits criticism. Two cheers are quite enough: there is no occasion to give three. Only Love the Beloved Republic deserves that.
E. M. Forster 1879–1970 English novelist

All the world over, I will back the masses against the classes.
W. E. Gladstone 1809–98 British statesman

We here highly resolve that the dead shall not have died in vain, that this nation, under God, shall have a new birth of freedom; and that government of the people, by the people, and for the people, shall not perish from the earth.
Abraham Lincoln 1809–65 American statesman

I never could believe that Providence had sent a few men into the world, ready booted and spurred to ride, and millions ready saddled and bridled to be ridden.
Richard Rumbold c.1622–85 English republican conspirator

Democracy substitutes election by the incompetent many for appointment by the corrupt few.
George Bernard Shaw 1856–1950 Irish dramatist

Democracy is not worth a brass farthing if it is being installed by bayonets.
Alexander Solzhenitsyn 1918–2008 Russian novelist

If one must serve, I hold it better to serve a well-bred lion, who is naturally stronger than I am, than two hundred rats of my own breed.
Voltaire 1694–1778 French writer

The world must be made safe for democracy.
Woodrow Wilson 1856–1924 American statesman

Despair see also **Hope**, **Pessimism**

My God, my God, look upon me; why hast thou
forsaken me?
> **Bible**

There is no despair so absolute as that which comes with the
first moments of our first great sorrow, when we have not
yet known what it is to have suffered and be healed, to have
despaired and have recovered hope.
> **George Eliot** 1819–80 English novelist

In a real dark night of the soul it is always three o'clock in
the morning.
> **F. Scott Fitzgerald** 1896–1940 American novelist

Not, I'll not, carrion comfort, Despair, not feast on thee;
Not untwist—slack they may be—these last strands of man
In me or, most weary, cry *I can no more*. I can;
Can something, hope, wish day come, not choose not to be.
> **Gerard Manley Hopkins** 1844–89 English poet

Don't despair, not even over the fact that you don't despair.
> **Franz Kafka** 1883–1924 Czech novelist

Human life begins on the far side of despair.
> **Jean-Paul Sartre** 1905–80 French philosopher

 Determination see also **Persistence**

Ils ne passeront pas.

They shall not pass.
> **Anonymous**, *slogan of the French army at the defence of Verdun,
1916*

Determination

Nil carborundum illegitimi.
Don't let the bastards grind you down.
Anonymous, *cod Latin saying, in circulation during the Second World War, though possibly of earlier origin*

Thought shall be the harder, heart the keener, courage the greater, as our might lessens.
The Battle of Maldon 1000

I can only go one way. I've not got a reverse gear.
Tony Blair 1953– British statesman

Never give in. Never give in, *never, never, never, never*—in nothing, great or small, large or petty—never give in, except to convictions of honour and good sense. Never yield to force: never yield to the apparently overwhelming might of the enemy.
Winston Churchill 1874–1965 British statesman

Say not the struggle naught availeth,
The labour and the wounds are vain,
The enemy faints not, nor faileth,
And as things have been, things remain.
Arthur Hugh Clough 1819–61 English poet

The best way out is always through.
Robert Frost 1874–1963 American poet

I will either find a way, or make one.
Hannibal 247–182 BC Carthaginian general, *on crossing the Alps*

Under the bludgeonings of chance
My head is bloody, but unbowed.
W. E. Henley 1849–1903 English poet

When the going gets tough, the tough get going.
Joseph P. Kennedy 1888–1969 American financier

Determination

With malice toward none; with charity for all; with firmness in the right, as God gives us to see the right, let us strive on to finish the work we are in.
Abraham Lincoln 1809–65 American statesman

Yes we can.
Barack Obama 1961– American statesman

What's the difference between a hockey mom and a pitbull? Lipstick.
Sarah Palin 1964– American politician

Difficulties are just things to overcome after all.
Ernest Shackleton 1874–1922 British explorer

One man that has a mind and knows it can always beat ten men who haven't and don't.
George Bernard Shaw 1856–1950 Irish dramatist

Do not underestimate the determination of a quiet man.
Iain Duncan Smith 1954– British politician

> That which we are, we are;
> One equal temper of heroic hearts,
> Made weak by time and fate, but strong in will
> To strive, to seek, to find, and not to yield.
Alfred, Lord Tennyson 1809–92 English poet

We shall not be diverted from our course. To those waiting with bated breath for that favourite media catch-phrase, the U-turn, I have only this to say. 'You turn if you want to; the lady's not for turning.'
Margaret Thatcher 1925–2013 British stateswoman

Children, if you are tired, keep going; if you are scared, keep going; if you are hungry, keep going; if you want to taste freedom, keep going.
Harriet Tubman c.1820–1913 American abolitionist, *apparently a modern paraphrase of her views*

Diaries

What is more dull than a discreet diary? One might just as well have a discreet soul.

Henry 'Chips' Channon 1897–1958 British politician

To be a good diarist one must have a little snouty, sneaky mind.

Harold Nicolson 1886–1968 English diplomat

One need not write in a diary what one is to remember for ever.

Sylvia Townsend Warner 1893–1978 English writer

I always say, keep a diary and some day it'll keep you.

Mae West 1892–1980 American film actress

I never travel without my diary. One should always have something sensational to read in the train.

Oscar Wilde 1854–1900 Irish dramatist

Diplomacy

To jaw-jaw is always better than to war-war.

Winston Churchill 1874–1965 British statesman

There is only one thing worse than fighting with allies, and that is fighting without them!

Winston Churchill 1874–1965 British statesman

Euphemisms are unpleasant truths wearing diplomatic cologne.

Quentin Crisp 1908–99 English writer

Treaties, you see, are like girls and roses: they last while they last.

Charles de Gaulle 1890–1970 French statesman

Diplomacy

I feel happier now that we have no allies to be polite to and to pamper.

George VI 1895–1952 British monarch

Let us never negotiate out of fear. But let us never fear to negotiate.

John F. Kennedy 1917–63 American statesman

One of the things I learnt when I was negotiating was that until I changed myself I could not change others.

Nelson Mandela 1918–2013 South African statesman

We will extend a hand if you are willing to unclench your fist.

Barack Obama 1961– American statesman

We are prepared to go to the gates of Hell—but no further.

Pius VII 1742–1823 Italian pope, *attempting to reach an agreement with Napoleon*

I'm afraid you've got a bad egg, Mr Jones.
Oh no, my Lord, I assure you! Parts of it are excellent!

Punch 1841–1992 English humorous periodical

Speak softly and carry a big stick; you will go far.

Theodore Roosevelt 1858–1919 American statesman

You can no more make an agreement with those leaders of Colombia than you can nail currant jelly to the wall. And the failure to nail currant jelly to the wall is not due to the nail. It's due to the currant jelly.

Theodore Roosevelt 1858–1919 American statesman

By indirections find directions out.

William Shakespeare 1564–1616 English dramatist

An ambassador is an honest man sent to lie abroad for the good of his country.

Henry Wotton 1568–1639 English diplomat

Discontent see also **Satisfaction**

When you don't have any money, the problem is food.
When you have money, it's sex. When you have both
it's health.
> **J. P. Donleavy** 1926–   Irish-American novelist

We loathe our manna, and we long for quails.
> **John Dryden** 1631–1700 English poet

It is an uneasy lot at best, to be what we call highly taught
and yet not to enjoy: to be present at this great spectacle
of life and never to be liberated from a small hungry
shivering self.
> **George Eliot** 1819–80 English novelist

If I can think of it, it isn't what I want.
> **Randall Jarrell** 1914–65 American poet

> It is a flaw
In happiness, to see beyond our bourn—
It forces us in summer skies to mourn:
It spoils the singing of the nightingale.
> **John Keats** 1795–1821 English poet

It is better to be a human being dissatisfied than a pig
satisfied; better to be Socrates dissatisfied than a fool
satisfied.
> **John Stuart Mill** 1806–73 English philosopher

Whoever is dissatisfied with himself is continually ready for
revenge, and we others will be his victims.
> **Friedrich Nietzsche** 1844–1900 German philosopher

Were there none who were discontented with what they
have, the world would never reach anything better.
> **Florence Nightingale** 1820–1910 English nurse

Discovery

’Tis just like a summer birdcage in a garden; the birds that are without despair to get in, and the birds that are within despair, and are in a consumption, for fear they shall never get out.

John Webster c.1580–c.1625 English dramatist

He spoke with a certain what-is-it in his voice, and I could see that, if not actually disgruntled, he was far from being gruntled.

P. G. Wodehouse 1881–1975 English writer

 Discovery see **Invention**

 Dogs

In the whole history of the world there is but one thing that money cannot buy, to wit: the wag of a dog's tail.

Josh Billings 1818–85 American humorist, *sometimes quoted as 'Money will buy you a pretty good dog, but it won't buy the wag of his tail'*

The great pleasure of a dog is that you may make a fool of yourself with him and not only will he not scold you, but he will make a fool of himself too.

Samuel Butler 1835–1902 English novelist

Near this spot are deposited the remains of one who possessed beauty without vanity, strength without insolence, courage without ferocity, and all the virtues of Man, without his vices.

Lord Byron 1788–1824 English poet, *epitaph on his Newfoundland dog*

To his dog, every man is Napoleon: hence the constant popularity of dogs.

Aldous Huxley 1894–1963 English novelist

Brothers and Sisters, I bid you beware
Of giving your heart to a dog to tear.
> **Rudyard Kipling** 1865–1936 English writer

A door is what a dog is perpetually on the wrong side of.
> **Ogden Nash** 1902–71 American humorist

I am his Highness' dog at Kew;
Pray, tell me sir, whose dog are you?
> **Alexander Pope** 1688–1744 English poet, *engraved on the collar of a dog*

The more one gets to know of men, the more one values dogs.
> **A. Toussenel** 1803–85 French writer, *attributed to Mme Roland in the form 'The more I see of men, the more I like dogs'*

The dog is a gentleman; I hope to go to his heaven, not man's.
> **Mark Twain** 1835–1910 American writer

Doubt see also **Certainty**

Oh! let us never, never doubt
What nobody is sure about!
> **Hilaire Belloc** 1870–1953 British writer

How long halt ye between two opinions?
> **Bible**

I'm a man of no convictions. At least, I think I am.
> **Christopher Hampton** 1946– English dramatist

I am too much of a sceptic to deny the possibility of anything.
> **T. H. Huxley** 1825–95 English biologist

I respect faith but doubt is what gets you an education.
> **Wilson Mizner** 1876–1933 American dramatist

Ten thousand difficulties do not make one doubt.
> **John Henry Newman** 1801–90 English theologian

Drawing

Now, the melancholy god protect thee, and the tailor make thy doublet of changeable taffeta, for thy mind is a very opal.
William Shakespeare 1564–1616 English dramatist

I must have a prodigious quantity of mind; it takes me as much as a week, sometimes, to make it up.
Mark Twain 1835–1910 American writer

Life is doubt,
And faith without doubt is nothing but death.
Miguel de Unamuno 1864–1937 Spanish philosopher

Doubt is not a pleasant condition. But certainty is an absurd one.
Voltaire 1694–1778 French writer

 # Drawing

Not a day without a line.
Apelles Greek painter of the 4th century BC, *proverbial summary of his philosophy*

A picture equals a movement in space.
Emily Carr 1871–1945 Canadian artist

Treat nature in terms of the cylinder, the sphere, the cone, all in perspective.
Paul Cézanne 1839–1906 French painter

I rarely draw what I see—I draw what I feel in my body.
Barbara Hepworth 1903–75 English sculptor

Drawing is the true test of art.
J. A. D. Ingres 1780–1867 French painter

An active line on a walk, moving freely without a goal. A walk for walk's sake.
Paul Klee 1879–1940 German-Swiss painter

Dreams

Have you noticed…there is never any third act in a
nightmare? They bring you to a climax of terror and then
leave you there. They are the work of poor dramatists.
  Max Beerbohm 1872–1956 English critic

The armoured cars of dreams, contrived to let us do
so many a dangerous thing.
  Elizabeth Bishop 1911–79 American poet

All the things one has forgotten scream for help in dreams.
  Elias Canetti 1905–94 Bulgarian-born writer

When we dream that we are dreaming, the moment of
awakening is at hand.
  J. M. Coetzee 1940– South African novelist

The interpretation of dreams is the royal road to a
knowledge of the unconscious activities of the mind.
  Sigmund Freud 1856–1939 Austrian psychoanalyst

The dream of reason produces monsters.
  Goya 1746–1828 Spanish painter

Was it a vision, or a waking dream?
Fled is that music:—do I wake or sleep?
  John Keats 1795–1821 English poet

They who dream by day are cognizant of many things which
escape those who dream only by night.
  Edgar Allan Poe 1809–49 American writer

O God! I could be bounded in a nut-shell, and count myself
a king of infinite space, were it not that I have bad dreams.
  William Shakespeare 1564–1616 English dramatist

The quick Dreams,
The passion-wingèd Ministers of thought.
  Percy Bysshe Shelley 1792–1822 English poet

Drink

One reason why I don't drink is because I wish to know when I am having a good time.
Nancy Astor 1879–1964 British politician

When the wine is in, the wit is out.
Thomas Becon 1512–67 English clergyman

Wine is a mocker, strong drink is raging.
Bible

Freedom and Whisky gang thegither!
Robert Burns 1759–96 Scottish poet

I have taken more out of alcohol than alcohol has taken out of me.
Winston Churchill 1874–1965 British statesman

A man shouldn't fool with booze until he's fifty; then he's a damn fool if he doesn't.
William Faulkner 1897–1962 American novelist

I often wonder what the Vintners buy
One half so precious as the Goods they sell.
Edward Fitzgerald 1809–83 English poet

Drink not the third glass.
George Herbert 1593–1633 English poet

And malt does more than Milton can
To justify God's ways to man.
A. E. Housman 1859–1936 English poet

You're not drunk if you can lie on the floor without holding on.
Dean Martin 1917–95 American actor

Candy
Is dandy
But liquor
Is quicker.
Ogden Nash 1902–71 American humorist

I'm only a beer teetotaller, not a champagne teetotaller.
George Bernard Shaw 1856–1950 Irish dramatist

First the man takes a drink,
Then the drink takes a drink,
Then the drink takes the man!
Edward Rowland Sill 1841–87 American educator, *frequently quoted as a Japanese proverb*

I'm not so think as you drunk I am.
J. C. Squire 1884–1958 English man of letters

Wine is bottled poetry.
Robert Louis Stevenson 1850–94 Scottish novelist

The lips that touch liquor must never touch mine.
George W. Young 1846–1919

Drugs

I'll die young, but it's like kissing God.
Lenny Bruce 1925–66 American comedian, *on his drug addiction*

Junk is the ideal product…the ultimate merchandise. No sales talk necessary. The client will crawl through a sewer and beg to buy.
William S. Burroughs 1914–97 American novelist

I experimented with marijuana a time or two. And I didn't like it, and I didn't inhale.
Bill Clinton 1946– American statesman

The Earth

Thou hast the keys of Paradise, oh just, subtle, and mighty opium!

Thomas De Quincey 1785–1859 English essayist

In this country, don't forget, a habit is no damn private hell. There's no solitary confinement outside of jail. A habit is hell for those you love.

Billie Holiday 1915–59 American singer

Every form of addiction is bad, no matter whether the narcotic be alcohol or morphine or idealism.

Carl Gustav Jung 1875–1961 Swiss psychologist

A drug is neither moral or immoral—it's a chemical compound.

Frank Zappa 1940–93 American rock musician

 # The Earth

The earth is what we all have in common.

Wendell Berry 1934– American poet

The earth is the Lord's, and all that therein is: the compass of the world, and they that dwell therein.

Bible

Topography displays no favourites; North's as near as West. More delicate than the historians' are the map-makers' colours.

Elizabeth Bishop 1911–79 American poet

In every outthrust headland, in every curving beach, in every grain of sand there is a story of the earth.

Rachel Carson 1907–64 American zoologist

How inappropriate to call this planet Earth when it is clearly Ocean.

Arthur C. Clarke 1917–2008 English science fiction writer

Now there is one outstandingly important fact regarding
Spaceship Earth, and that is that no instruction book came
with it.
R. Buckminster Fuller 1895–1983 American designer

In my view, climate change is the most severe problem we
are facing today—more serious even than the threat of
terrorism.
David King 1939- British scientist

To me, it underscores our responsibility to deal more kindly
with one another, and to preserve and cherish the pale blue
dot, the only home we've ever known.
Carl Sagan 1934–96 American astronomer, *of Earth as
photographed by Voyager 1*

Need for a knowledge of geography is greater than the need
of gardens for water after the stars have failed to fulfil their
promise of rain.
Yāqūt d. 1229 Arab geographer

Eating see also **Cookery**, **Food**

Tell me what you eat and I will tell you what you are.
Anthelme Brillat-Savarin 1755–1826 French gourmet

Some hae meat and canna eat,
And some wad eat that want it:
But we hae meat and we can eat,
And sae the Lord be thankit.
Robert Burns 1759–96 Scottish poet

Hunger is the best sauce in the world.
Cervantes 1547–1616 Spanish novelist

It's a very odd thing—
As odd as can be—

Eating

That whatever Miss T eats
Turns into Miss T.
Walter de la Mare 1873–1956 English poet

Gluttony is an emotional escape, a sign something is
eating us.
Peter De Vries 1910–93 American novelist

One can say everything best over a meal.
George Eliot 1819–80 English novelist

ANTHONY HOPKINS: I do wish we could chat longer, but I'm
having an old friend for dinner.
Thomas Harris 1940– and **Ted Tally** 1952– American writer
and American screenwriter, *in the film* The Silence of the
Lambs

I don't eat anything with a face.
Linda McCartney 1941–98 American photographer

Time for a little something.
A. A. Milne 1882–1956 English writer

One should eat to live, and not live to eat.
Molière 1622–73 French comic dramatist

The appetite grows by eating.
François Rabelais c.1494–c.1553 French humanist

Now good digestion wait on appetite,
And health on both!
William Shakespeare 1564–1616 English dramatist

We each day dig our graves with our teeth.
Samuel Smiles 1812–1904 English writer

He sows hurry and reaps indigestion.
Robert Louis Stevenson 1850–94 Scottish novelist

I'll fill hup the chinks wi' cheese.
  R. S. Surtees 1805–64 English novelist

MICHAEL DOUGLAS: Lunch is for wimps.
  Stanley Weiser and **Oliver Stone** 1946– American
  screenwriters, *in the film* Wall Street

One cannot think well, love well, sleep well, if one has not
dined well.
  Virginia Woolf 1882–1941 English novelist

Economics

It's the economy, stupid.
  Anonymous, *slogan of Bill Clinton's first presidential campaign*

There's no such thing as a free lunch.
  Anonymous

There is enough in the world for everyone's need, but not
enough for everyone's greed.
  Frank Buchman 1878–1961 American evangelist

Capitalism is using its money; we socialists throw it away.
  Fidel Castro 1927–2016 Cuban statesman

Inflation is the one form of taxation that can be imposed
without legislation.
  Milton Friedman 1912–2006 American economist

The safest way to double your money is to fold it over and
put it in your pocket.
  Frank McKinney ('Kin') Hubbard 1868–1930 American
  humorist

Gross national product…measures everything, in short,
except that which makes life worthwhile.
  Robert Kennedy 1925–68 American politician

Economics

The green shoots of economic spring are appearing once again.

Norman Lamont 1942– British politician, *often quoted as 'the green shoots of recovery'*

If the policy isn't hurting, it isn't working.

John Major 1943– British statesman, *on controlling inflation*

Government's view of the economy could be summed up in a few short phrases: If it moves, tax it. If it keeps moving, regulate it. And if it stops moving, subsidize it.

Ronald Reagan 1911–2004 American statesman

We have always known that heedless self-interest was bad morals; we know now that it is bad economics.

Franklin D. Roosevelt 1882–1945 American statesman

Wall Street indexes predicted nine out of the last five recessions.

Paul A. Samuelson 1915–2009 American economist

Call a thing immoral or ugly, soul-destroying or a degradation of man, a peril to the peace of the world or to the well-being of future generations: as long as you have not shown it to be 'uneconomic' you have not really questioned its right to exist, grow, and prosper.

E. F. Schumacher 1911–77 German-born economist

It's a recession when your neighbour loses his job; it's a depression when you lose yours.

Harry S. Truman 1884–1972 American statesman

What a country calls its vital economic interests are not the things which enable its citizens to live, but the things which enable it to make war.

Simone Weil 1909–43 French philosopher

MICHAEL DOUGLAS: Greed—for lack of a better word—is good. Greed is right. Greed works.
> **Stanley Weiser** and **Oliver Stone** 1946– American screenwriters American screenwriters, *in the film* Wall Street

It is not that pearls fetch a high price *because* men have dived for them; but on the contrary, men dive for them because they fetch a high price.
> **Richard Whately** 1787–1863 English philosopher

Education see also **Examinations**, **Teaching**

What one knows is, in youth, of little moment; they know enough who know how to learn.
> **Henry Brooks Adams** 1838–1918 American historian

What sculpture is to a block of marble, education is to a human soul.
> **Joseph Addison** 1672–1719 English writer

Give me a child for the first seven years, and you may do what you like with him afterwards.
> **Anonymous**, *attributed as a Jesuit maxim*

The roots of education are bitter, but the fruit is sweet.
> **Aristotle** 384–322 BC Greek philosopher

I said…how, and why, young children, were sooner allured by love, than driven by beating, to attain good learning.
> **Roger Ascham** 1515–68 English scholar

Studies serve for delight, for ornament, and for ability.
> **Francis Bacon** 1561–1626 English courtier

The dread of beatings! Dread of being late!
And, greatest dread of all, the dread of games!
> **John Betjeman** 1906–84 English poet

Education

Ask me my three main priorities for Government, and I tell you: education, education and education.
    Tony Blair 1953– British statesman

That lyf so short, the craft so long to lerne.
    Geoffrey Chaucer c.1343–1400 English poet

In education there should be no class distinction.
    Confucius 551–479 BC Chinese philosopher

C-l-e-a-n, clean, verb active, to make bright, to scour.
W-i-n, win, d-e-r, der, winder, a casement. When the boy knows this out of the book, he goes and does it.
    Charles Dickens 1812–70 English novelist

A University should be a place of light, of liberty, and of learning.
    Benjamin Disraeli 1804–81 British statesman

Study as if you were to live for ever; live as if you were to die tomorrow.
    St Edmund of Abingdon c.1175–1240 English scholar

The value of an education in a liberal arts college is not the learning of many facts but the training of the mind to think something that cannot be learned from textbooks.
    Albert Einstein 1879–1955 German-born theoretical physicist

You send your child to the schoolmaster, but 'tis the schoolboys who educate him.
    Ralph Waldo Emerson 1803–82 American writer

The proper study of mankind is books.
    Aldous Huxley 1894–1963 English novelist

Education is the most powerful weapon which you can use to change the world.
    Nelson Mandela 1918–2013 South African statesman

Effort

If you educate a man you educate one person, but if you educate a woman you educate a family.
Ruby Manikan Indian church leader

My spelling is Wobbly. It's good spelling but it Wobbles, and the letters get in the wrong places.
A. A. Milne 1882–1956 English writer

Education costs money, but then so does ignorance.
Claus Moser 1922–2015 British statistician

Know then thyself, presume not God to scan;
The proper study of mankind is man.
Alexander Pope 1688–1744 English poet

I would I had bestowed that time in the tongues that I have in fencing, dancing, and bear-baiting. O! had I but followed the arts!
William Shakespeare 1564–1616 English dramatist

Education is what survives when what has been learned has been forgotten.
B. F. Skinner 1904–90 American psychologist

What does education often do? It makes a straight-cut ditch of a free, meandering brook.
Henry David Thoreau 1817–62 American writer

The best thing for being sad…is to learn something.
T. H. White 1906–64 English novelist

Effort

We're number two. We try harder.
Anonymous, *advertising slogan for Avis car rentals*

Madam, if a thing is possible, consider it done; the impossible? that will be done.
Charles Alexandre de Calonne 1734–1802 French statesman

Elections

Now, *here*, you see, it takes all the running *you* can do, to keep in the same place. If you want to get somewhere else, you must run at least twice as fast as that!

Lewis Carroll 1832–98 English writer

Oh, how I am tired of the struggle!

Johann Wolfgang von Goethe 1749–1832 German writer

HOMER SIMPSON: Kids, you tried your best, and you failed miserably. The lesson is, never try.

Matt Groening 1954– American humorist

Between us and excellence, the gods have placed the sweat of our brows.

Hesiod fl. 700 BC Greek poet

Mountains will go into labour, and a silly little mouse will be born.

Horace 65–8 BC Roman poet

I had done all that I could; and no man is well pleased to have his all neglected, be it ever so little.

Samuel Johnson 1709–84 English lexicographer

Superhuman effort isn't worth a damn unless it achieves results.

Ernest Shackleton 1874–1922 British explorer

Things won are done; joy's soul lies in the doing.

William Shakespeare 1564–1616 English dramatist

 # Elections see also **Democracy**

Vote early and vote often.

Anonymous, *US election slogan, already current by 1858*

Vote for the man who promises least; he'll be the least disappointing.

Bernard Baruch 1870–1965 American financier

One man shall have one vote.
John Cartwright 1740–1824 English political reformer

Hell, I never vote *for* anybody. I always vote *against*.
W. C. Fields 1880–1946 American humorist

I always voted at my party's call,
And I never thought of thinking for myself at all.
W. S. Gilbert 1836–1911 English writer

To give victory to the right, not bloody bullets, but peaceful ballots only, are necessary.
Abraham Lincoln 1809–65 American statesman, *usually quoted as 'The ballot is stronger than the bullet'*

If voting changed anything, they'd abolish it.
Ken Livingstone 1945– British politician

One of the nuisances of the ballot is that when the oracle has spoken you never know what it means.
Lord Salisbury 1830–1903 British statesman

It's not the voting that's democracy, it's the counting.
Tom Stoppard 1937– British dramatist

Ending

It ain't over till it's over.
Yogi Berra 1925–2015 American baseball player

Better is the end of a thing than the beginning thereof.
Bible

Now this is not the end. It is not even the beginning of the end. But it is, perhaps, the end of the beginning.
Winston Churchill 1874–1965 British statesman, *on the Battle of Egypt*

Enemies

The party's over, it's time to call it a day.
Betty Comden 1917–2006 and **Adolph Green** 1915–2002
American songwriters

This is the way the world ends
Not with a bang but a whimper.
T. S. Eliot 1888–1965 American-born British poet

In my end is my beginning.
Mary, Queen of Scots 1542–87

The opera ain't over 'til the fat lady sings.
Proverb

The rest is silence.
William Shakespeare 1564–1616 English dramatist

This is the beginning of the end.
Charles-Maurice de Talleyrand 1754–1838 French statesman,
*on the announcement of Napoleon's Pyrrhic victory at Borodino,
1812*

They think it's all over—it is now.
Kenneth Wolstenholme 1920–2002 English sports
commentator

 Enemies

He who has a thousand friends has not a friend to spare,
And he who has one enemy will meet him everywhere.
Ali ibn-Abi-Talib *c.*602–661 Arab ruler

Not while I'm alive 'e ain't!
Ernest Bevin 1881–1951 British politician, *reply to the observation
that Nye Bevan was sometimes his own worst enemy*

Love your enemies, do good to them which hate you.
Bible

An injury is much sooner forgotten than an insult.
Lord Chesterfield 1694–1773 English writer

You can calculate the worth of a man by the number of his enemies, and the importance of a work of art by the harm that is spoken of it.
Gustave Flaubert 1821–80 French novelist

Better to have him inside the tent pissing out, than outside pissing in.
Lyndon Baines Johnson 1908–73 American statesman, *of J. Edgar Hoover*

People wish their enemies dead—but I do not; I say give them the gout, give them the stone!
Lady Mary Wortley Montagu 1689–1762 English writer

I have none. I had them all shot.
Ramón María Narváez 1800–68 Spanish statesman, *asked on his deathbed if he forgave his enemies*

The enemies of my enemies are my friends.
Proverb

AL PACINO: Keep your friends close, but your enemies closer.
Mario Puzo 1920–99 and **Francis Ford Coppola** 1939– American novelist and American film director, *in the film* The Godfather: Part II, *often wrongly attributed to Sun Tzu*

There is nothing in the whole world so painful as feeling that one is not liked. It always seems to me that people who hate me must be suffering from some strange form of lunacy.
Sei Shōnagon c.966–c.1013 Japanese diarist

I have always made one prayer to God, a very short one. Here it is, 'My God, make our enemies very ridiculous!'
Voltaire 1694–1778 French writer

England see also **Britain**, **London**

I will not cease from mental fight,
Nor shall my sword sleep in my hand,
Till we have built Jerusalem,
In England's green and pleasant land.
> **William Blake** 1757–1827 English poet

Oh, to be in England
Now that April's there.
> **Robert Browning** 1812–89 English poet

The Thames is liquid history.
> **John Burns** 1858–1943 British politician, *to an American, who
> had compared the Thames disparagingly with the Mississippi*

In England there are sixty different religions, and only one
sauce.
> **Francesco Caracciolo** 1752–99 Neapolitan diplomat

Mad dogs and Englishmen
Go out in the midday sun.
> **Noël Coward** 1899–1973 English dramatist

What should they know of England who only England
know?
> **Rudyard Kipling** 1865–1936 English writer

England is a nation of shopkeepers.
> **Napoleon I** 1769–1821 French emperor

England expects that every man will do his duty.
> **Horatio, Lord Nelson** 1758–1805 British admiral, *at the battle
> of Trafalgar*

There'll always be an England.
> **Ross Parker** 1914–74 and **Hugh Charles** 1907–95 British
> songwriters

Ask any man what nationality he would prefer to be, and ninety-nine out of a hundred will tell you that they would prefer to be Englishmen.

Cecil Rhodes 1853–1902 South African statesman

This royal throne of kings, this sceptred isle,
This earth of majesty, this seat of Mars...
This blessèd plot, this earth, this realm, this England.

William Shakespeare 1564–1616 English dramatist

The froth at top, dregs at bottom, but the middle excellent.

Voltaire 1694–1778 French writer, *comparing the English to their own beer*

You never find an Englishman among the under-dogs—except in England, of course.

Evelyn Waugh 1903–66 English novelist

The English country gentleman galloping after a fox—the unspeakable in full pursuit of the uneatable.

Oscar Wilde 1854–1900 Irish dramatist

We must be free or die, who speak the tongue
That Shakespeare spake; the faith and morals hold
Which Milton held.

William Wordsworth 1770–1850 English poet

The Environment see also **Country**, **Pollution**

Think globally, act locally.

Anonymous, *Friends of the Earth slogan*

Come, friendly bombs, and fall on Slough!
It isn't fit for humans now,
There isn't grass to graze a cow.
Swarm over, Death!

John Betjeman 1906–84 English poet

The Environment

Woe unto them that join house to house, that lay field to field, till there be no place.
  Bible

And was Jerusalem builded here
Among these dark Satanic mills?
  William Blake 1757–1827 English poet

O all ye Green Things upon the Earth, bless ye the Lord.
  Book of Common Prayer 1662

I do not know of any environmental group in any country that does not view its government as an adversary.
  Gro Harlem Brundtland 1939– Norwegian stateswoman

What would the world be, once bereft
Of wet and wildness? Let them be left,
O let them be left, wildness and wet;
Long live the weeds and the wilderness yet.
  Gerard Manley Hopkins 1844–89 English poet

I am I plus my surroundings and if I do not preserve the latter, I do not preserve myself.
  José Ortega y Gasset 1883–1955 Spanish writer

The parks are the lungs of London.
  William Pitt 1708–78 British statesman

Consult the genius of the place in all.
  Alexander Pope 1688–1744 English poet

It's not that easy being green.
  Joe Raposo 1937–89 American songwriter, *sung by the Muppet Kermit the frog*

Small is beautiful.
  E. F. Schumacher 1911–77 German-born economist

Climate change is the greatest market failure the world has ever seen.
  Nicholas Stern 1946– British economist

In wildness is the preservation of the world.
Henry David Thoreau 1817–62 American writer

Envy and Jealousy

Thou shalt not covet thy neighbour's house, thou shalt not covet thy neighbour's wife.
Bible

Jealousy is no more than feeling alone against smiling enemies.
Elizabeth Bowen 1899–1973 Anglo-Irish novelist

The danger chiefly lies in acting well;
No crime's so great as daring to excel.
Charles Churchill 1731–64 English poet

Thou shalt not covet; but tradition
Approves all forms of competition.
Arthur Hugh Clough 1819–61 English poet

Some folks rail against other folks, because other folks have what some folks would be glad of.
Henry Fielding 1707–54 English novelist

Envy can scarcely hold back her tears, when she sees nothing to cry about.
Ovid 43 BC–c.AD 17 Roman poet

To jealousy, nothing is more frightful than laughter.
Françoise Sagan 1935–2004 French novelist

O! beware, my lord, of jealousy;
It is the green-eyed monster which doth mock
The meat it feeds on.
William Shakespeare 1564–1616 English dramatist

Equality see also **Human Rights**

Equality may perhaps be a right, but no power on earth can ever turn it into a fact.

Honoré de Balzac 1799–1850 French novelist

He maketh his sun to rise on the evil and on the good, and sendeth rain on the just and on the unjust.

Bible

A man's a man for a' that.

Robert Burns 1759–96 Scottish poet

When every one is somebodee,
Then no one's anybody.

W. S. Gilbert 1836–1911 English writer

Your levellers wish to level *down* as far as themselves; but they cannot bear levelling *up* to themselves.

Samuel Johnson 1709–84 English lexicographer

I have a dream that one day on the red hills of Georgia the sons of former slaves and the sons of former slave owners will be able to sit down together at the table of brotherhood.

Martin Luther King 1929–68 American civil rights leader

All animals are equal but some animals are more equal than others.

George Orwell 1903–50 English novelist

Hath not a Jew eyes? hath not a Jew hands, organs, dimensions, senses, affections, passions?…If you prick us, do we not bleed? if you tickle us, do we not laugh? if you poison us, do we not die? and if you wrong us, shall we not revenge?

William Shakespeare 1564–1616 English dramatist

Make all men equal today, and God has so created them that they shall all be unequal tomorrow.
Anthony Trollope 1815–82 English novelist

Europe

Whoever speaks of Europe is wrong, [it is] a geographical concept.
Otto von Bismarck 1815–98 German statesman

Fog in Channel—Continent isolated.
Russell Brockbank 1913–79 British cartoonist, *newspaper placard in cartoon*

From Stettin in the Baltic to Trieste in the Adriatic an iron curtain has descended across the Continent.
Winston Churchill 1874–1965 British statesman

Each time we have to choose between Europe and the open sea, we shall always choose the open sea.
Winston Churchill 1874–1965 British statesman

Without Britain Europe would remain only a torso.
Ludwig Erhard 1897–1977 German statesman

It means the end of a thousand years of history.
Hugh Gaitskell 1906–63 British politician, *on a European federation*

If I want to talk to Europe who do I call?
Henry Kissinger 1923– American politician

The policy of European integration is in reality a question of war and peace in the 21st century.
Helmut Kohl 1930– German statesman

Evil

I want the whole of Europe to have one currency; it will make trading much easier.

Napoleon I 1769–1821 French emperor

You're thinking of Europe as Germany and France. I don't. I think that's old Europe. If you look at the entire Nato Europe today, the centre of gravity is shifting to the east.

Donald Rumsfeld 1932– American politician

Better fifty years of Europe than a cycle of Cathay.

Alfred, Lord Tennyson 1809–92 English poet

 # Evil see also **Goodness**

The fearsome, word-and-thought-defying *banality of evil*.

Hannah Arendt 1906–75 American philosopher

I and the public know
What all schoolchildren learn,
Those to whom evil is done
Do evil in return.

W. H. Auden 1907–73 English poet

With love for mankind and hatred of sins.

St Augustine of Hippo AD 354–430 Roman theologian, *often quoted as 'Love the sinner but hate the sin'*

There is no peace, saith the Lord, unto the wicked.

Bible

It is necessary only for the good man to do nothing for evil to triumph.

Edmund Burke 1729–97 Irish-born politician

The face of 'evil' is always the face of total need.

William S. Burroughs 1914–97 American novelist

As soon as men decide that all means are permitted to fight an evil, then their good becomes indistinguishable from the evil that they set out to destroy.
Christopher Dawson 1889–1970 English historian

What we call evil is simply ignorance bumping its head in the dark.
Henry Ford 1863–1947 American car manufacturer

All things truly wicked start from an innocence.
Ernest Hemingway 1899–1961 American novelist

But if he does really think that there is no distinction between virtue and vice, why, Sir, when he leaves our houses, let us count our spoons.
Samuel Johnson 1709–84 English lexicographer

No one ever suddenly became depraved.
Juvenal c.AD 60–c.140 Roman satirist

Farewell remorse! All good to me is lost;
Evil, be thou my good.
John Milton 1608–74 English poet

An orgy looks particularly alluring seen through the mists of righteous indignation.
Malcolm Muggeridge 1903–90 British journalist

By the pricking of my thumbs,
Something wicked this way comes.
William Shakespeare 1564–1616 English dramatist

The line dividing good and evil cuts through the heart of every human being. And who is willing to destroy a piece of his own heart?
Alexander Solzhenitsyn 1918–2008 Russian novelist

Examinations

There are a thousand hacking at the branches of evil to one who is striking at the root.
Henry David Thoreau 1817–62 American writer

 # Examinations

Truth is no more at issue in an examination than thirst at a wine-tasting or fashion at a striptease.
Alan Bennett 1934– English writer

Examinations are formidable even to the best prepared, for the greatest fool may ask more than the wisest man can answer.
Charles Caleb Colton c.1780–1832 English clergyman

Life isn't like coursework, baby. It's one damn essay crisis after another.
Boris Johnson 1964– British politician

I evidently knew more about economics than my examiners.
John Maynard Keynes 1883–1946 English economist, *explaining why he performed badly in the Civil Service examinations*

In examinations those who do not wish to know ask questions of those who cannot tell.
Walter Raleigh 1861–1922 English critic

Do not on any account attempt to write on both sides of the paper at once.
W. C. Sellar 1898–1951 and **R. J. Yeatman** 1898–1968 British writers

Had silicon been a gas, I would have been a major-general by now.
James McNeill Whistler 1834–1903 American-born painter, *having been found 'deficient in chemistry' in a West Point examination*

Exercise see also **Health**

If you walk hard enough, you probably don't need any other God.
>   **Bruce Chatwin** 1940–89 English travel writer

The wise, for cure, on exercise depend;
God never made his work for man to mend.
>   **John Dryden** 1631–1700 English poet

Exercise is the yuppie version of bulimia.
>   **Barbara Ehrenreich** 1941– American sociologist

Exercise is bunk. If you are healthy, you don't need it: if you are sick you shouldn't take it.
>   **Henry Ford** 1863–1947 American car manufacturer

The sovereign invigorator of the body is exercise, and of all the exercises, walking is best.
>   **Thomas Jefferson** 1743–1826 American statesman

A bear, however hard he tries,
Grows tubby without exercise.
>   **A. A. Milne** 1882–1956 English writer

The only exercise I take is walking behind the coffins of friends who took exercise.
>   **Peter O'Toole** 1932–2013 Irish-born British actor

Avoid running at all times.
>   **Leroy ('Satchel') Paige** 1906–82 American baseball player

Those who do not find time for exercise will have to find time for illness.
>   **Proverb**

All you need to run is good shoes.
>   **Paula Radcliffe** 1973– British long-distance runner

Experience

There's no easy way out [of exercise]. If there were, I would have bought it. And believe me, it would be one of my favourite things!

Oprah Winfrey 1954– American talk show hostess

 # Experience

All experience is an arch to build upon.

Henry Brooks Adams 1838–1918 American historian

You may not control all the events that happen to you but you can decide not to be reduced by them.

Maya Angelou 1928–2014 American writer

You should make a point of trying every experience once, excepting incest and folk-dancing.

Anonymous

Experience isn't interesting till it begins to repeat itself—in fact, till it does that, it hardly *is* experience.

Elizabeth Bowen 1899–1973 Anglo-Irish novelist

Everyone knows I'm all in favour of apprenticeships, but let me tell you this is no time for a novice.

Gordon Brown 1951– British statesman

Experience is the best of schoolmasters, only the school fees are heavy.

Thomas Carlyle 1795–1881 Scottish historian

The courtiers who surround him [Louis XVIII] have forgotten nothing and learnt nothing.

Charles Dumouriez 1739–1823 French general

We had the experience but missed the meaning.

T. S. Eliot 1888–1965 American-born British poet

Everything has been said before. But since nobody listens we have to keep going back and beginning all over again.
    André Gide 1869–1951 French novelist

Experience is not what happens to a man; it is what a man does with what happens to him.
    Aldous Huxley 1894–1963 English novelist

HARRISON FORD: It's not the years, honey, it's the mileage.
    George Lucas 1944–   American film director, *in the film* Raiders of the Lost Ark

We took risks, we knew we took them; things have come out against us, and therefore we have no cause for complaint.
    Robert Falcon Scott 1868–1912 English explorer

Education is when you read the fine print; experience is what you get when you don't.
    Pete Seeger 1919–2014 American folk singer

Experience is the name everyone gives to their mistakes.
    Oscar Wilde 1854–1900 Irish dramatist

Facts see also **Knowledge**

In fact the *a priori* reasoning is so entirely satisfactory to me that if the facts won't fit in, why so much the worse for the facts is my feeling.
    Erasmus Darwin 1804–81 English physician, *to his brother Charles, after reading his book,* The Origin of Species

MR GRADGRIND: Now, what I want is, Facts…Facts alone are wanted in life.
    Charles Dickens 1812–70 English novelist

SHERLOCK HOLMES: Data! data! data!…I can't make bricks without clay.
    Arthur Conan Doyle 1859–1930 Scottish-born writer

Failure

What can be asserted without evidence can also be dismissed without evidence.
Christopher Hitchens 1949–2011 English-born American writer

Facts do not cease to exist because they are ignored.
Aldous Huxley 1894–1963 English novelist

When the facts change, I change my mind.
John Maynard Keynes 1883–1946 English economist

Get your facts first, and then you can distort 'em as much as you please.
Mark Twain 1835–1910 American writer

 # Failure see also **Success**

History to the defeated
May say Alas but cannot help or pardon.
W. H. Auden 1907–73 English poet

Ever tried. Ever failed. No matter. Try again. Fail again. Fail better.
Samuel Beckett 1906–89 Irish writer

She knows there's no success like failure
And that failure's no success at all.
Bob Dylan 1941– American singer

Man is not made for defeat. A man can be destroyed but not defeated.
Ernest Hemingway 1899–1961 American novelist

Failure is not an option.
Gene Kranz 1933– American space flight director, *summarized version of announcement to ground crew in Houston as Apollo 13 approached the critical earth-to-moon decision loop*

Vae victis.

Down with the defeated!

Livy 59 BC–AD 17 Roman historian

Show me a good loser and I'll show you a loser.

Vince Lombardi 1913–70 American football coach

There are some defeats more triumphant than victories.

Montaigne 1533–92 French moralist

There is only one step from the sublime to the ridiculous.

Napoleon I 1769–1821 French emperor

We fail!
But screw your courage to the sticking-place,
And we'll not fail.

William Shakespeare 1564–1616 English dramatist

Our business in this world is not to succeed, but to continue to fail, in good spirits.

Robert Louis Stevenson 1850–94 Scottish novelist

Failure is not fatal, but failure to change might be.

John Wooden 1910–2010 American basketball player

Fame

Seven wealthy towns contend for HOMER dead
Through which the living HOMER begged his bread.

Anonymous

There's no such thing as bad publicity except your own obituary.

Brendan Behan 1923–64 Irish dramatist

Let us now praise famous men, and our fathers that begat us.

Bible

Fame

A prophet is not without honour, save in his own country,
and in his own house.
Bible

I awoke one morning and found myself famous.
Lord Byron 1788–1824 English poet

Fame is a fickle food
Upon a shifting plate.
Emily Dickinson 1830–86 American poet

The deed is all, the glory nothing.
Johann Wolfgang von Goethe 1749–1832 German writer

Popularity? It is glory's small change.
Victor Hugo 1802–85 French writer

No path of flowers leads to glory.
Jean de la Fontaine 1621–95 French poet

We're more popular than Jesus now; I don't know which will
go first—rock 'n' roll or Christianity.
John Lennon 1940–80 English pop singer, *of the Beatles*

Fame is the spur that the clear spirit doth raise
(That last infirmity of noble mind)
To scorn delights, and live laborious days.
John Milton 1608–74 English poet

Famous men have the whole earth as their memorial.
Pericles c.495–429 BC Greek statesman

So long as men can breathe, or eyes can see,
So long lives this, and this gives life to thee.
William Shakespeare 1564–1616 English dramatist

You always hide just in the middle of the limelight.
George Bernard Shaw 1856–1950 Irish dramatist, *to
T. E. Lawrence, who had complained of Press attention*

Celebrity is a mask that eats into the face.
John Updike 1932–2009 American writer

In the future everybody will be world famous for fifteen minutes.
Andy Warhol 1927–87 American artist

The Family see also **Children, Parents**

He that hath wife and children hath given hostages to fortune; for they are impediments to great enterprises, either of virtue or mischief.
Francis Bacon 1561–1626 English courtier

Thy wife shall be as the fruitful vine: upon the walls of thine house.
Thy children like the olive-branches: round about thy table.
Bible

As I leave the second most important job I could ever hold, I cherish even more the first—as a husband and father.
Gordon Brown 1951– British statesman, *on resigning as Prime Minister*

We begin our public affections in our families. No cold relation is a zealous citizen.
Edmund Burke 1729–97 Irish-born politician

[It is] time to turn our attention to pressing challenges like…how to make American families more like the Waltons and a little bit less like the Simpsons.
George Bush 1924– American statesman

Believe me, family solidarity is after all the only good thing. I have been deprived of it, so I know.
Marie Curie 1867–1934 Polish-born French physicist

Fashion

One would be in less danger
From the wiles of the stranger
If one's own kin and kith
Were more fun to be with.
  Ogden Nash 1902–71 American humorist

A little more than kin, and less than kind.
  William Shakespeare 1564–1616 English dramatist

If a man's character is to be abused, say what you will, there's nobody like a relation to do the business.
  William Makepeace Thackeray 1811–63 English novelist

All happy families resemble one another, but each unhappy family is unhappy in its own way.
  Leo Tolstoy 1828–1910 Russian novelist

It is no use telling me that there are bad aunts and good aunts. At the core, they are all alike. Sooner or later, out pops the cloven hoof.
  P. G. Wodehouse 1881–1975 English writer

 # Fashion

A little of what you call frippery is very necessary towards looking like the rest of the world.
  Abigail Adams 1744–1818 American letter writer

Fashion often starts off beautiful and becomes ugly, whereas art starts off ugly sometimes and becomes beautiful.
  David Bailey 1938– English photographer

Fashion is made to become unfashionable.
  Coco Chanel 1883–1971 French couturière

One had as good be out of the world, as out of the fashion.
  Colley Cibber 1671–1757 English dramatist

Fate

Haute Couture should be fun, foolish and almost unwearable.
Christian Lacroix 1951– French couturier

I don't design clothes, I design dreams.
Ralph Lauren 1939– American fashion designer

Hip is the sophistication of the wise primitive in a giant jungle.
Norman Mailer 1923–2007 American writer

Fashion is more usually a gentle progression of revisited ideas.
Bruce Oldfield 1950– English fashion designer

Every generation laughs at the old fashions, but follows religiously the new.
Henry David Thoreau 1817–62 American writer

It is charming to totter into vogue.
Horace Walpole 1717–97 English connoisseur

A fashion…is usually a form of ugliness so intolerable that we have to alter it every six months.
Oscar Wilde 1854–1900 Irish dramatist

Fate

Must it be? It must be.
Ludwig van Beethoven 1770–1827 German composer

Canst thou bind the sweet influences of Pleiades, or loose the bands of Orion?
Bible

Fate is not an eagle, it creeps like a rat.
Elizabeth Bowen 1899–1973 Anglo-Irish novelist

Nothing have I found stronger than Necessity.
Euripides c.485–c.406 BC Greek dramatist

Fathers

There once was a man who said, 'Damn!
It is borne in upon me I am
An engine that moves
In predestinate grooves,
I'm not even a bus, I'm a tram.'
Maurice Evan Hare 1886–1967 English limerick writer

What we call fate does not come into us from the outside,
but emerges from us.
Rainer Maria Rilke 1875–1926 German poet

If it be now, 'tis not to come; if it be not to come, it will be
now; if it be not now, yet it will come: the readiness is all.
William Shakespeare 1564–1616 English dramatist

We are merely the stars' tennis-balls, struck and bandied
Which way please them.
John Webster c.1580–c.1625 English dramatist

Every bullet has its billet.
William III 1650–1702 British monarch

 # Fathers

One father is more than a hundred schoolmasters.
George Herbert 1593–1633 English poet

Being a father
Is quite a bother,
But I like it, rather.
Ogden Nash 1902–71 American humorist

I can do one of two things. I can be president of the United
States or I can control Alice. I cannot possibly do both.
Theodore Roosevelt 1858–1919 American statesman, *on his
daughter*

The fundamental defect of fathers, in our competitive society, is that they want their children to be a credit to them.
Bertrand Russell 1872–1970 British philosopher

It doesn't matter who my father was; it matters who I remember he was.
Anne Sexton 1928–74 American poet

It is a wise father that knows his own child.
William Shakespeare 1564–1616 English dramatist

If men do not keep on speaking terms with children, they cease to be men, and become merely machines for eating and for earning money.
John Updike 1932–2009 American writer

Fear

We must travel in the direction of our fear.
John Berryman 1914–72 American poet

No passion so effectually robs the mind of all its powers of acting and reasoning as fear.
Edmund Burke 1729–97 Irish-born politician

If hopes were dupes, fears may be liars.
Arthur Hugh Clough 1819–61 English poet

Be afraid. Be very afraid.
David Cronenberg 1943– Canadian film director

Nothing in life is to be feared, it is only to be understood.
Marie Curie 1867–1934 Polish-born French physicist

I will show you fear in a handful of dust.
T. S. Eliot 1888–1965 American-born British poet

There is no terror in a bang, only in the anticipation of it.
Alfred Hitchcock 1899–1980 British-born film director

Festivals

Fear is, of all passions, that which weakens the judgment most.

Cardinal de Retz 1613–79 French cardinal

The only thing we have to fear is fear itself.

Franklin D. Roosevelt 1882–1945 American statesman

Only the unknown frightens men. But once a man has faced the unknown, that terror becomes the known.

Antoine de Saint-Exupéry 1900–44 French novelist

Present fears
Are less than horrible imaginings.

William Shakespeare 1564–1616 English dramatist

In time we hate that which we often fear.

William Shakespeare 1564–1616 English dramatist

Our deepest fear is not that we are inadequate. Our deepest fear is that we are powerful beyond measure. It is our light, not our darkness, that most frightens us.

Marianne Williamson 1953– American writer

 # Festivals see also **Christmas**

Hogmanay, like all festivals, being but a bank from which we can only draw what we put in.

J. M. Barrie 1860–1937 Scottish writer

Hurrah for the fun!
Is the pudding done?
Hurrah for the pumpkin pie!

Lydia Maria Child 1802–80 American abolitionist, *on Thanksgiving Day*

The true essentials of a feast are only fun and feed.

Oliver Wendell Holmes 1809–94 American physician

The holiest of all holidays are those
Kept by ourselves in silence and apart;
The secret anniversaries of the heart.
   Henry Wadsworth Longfellow 1807–82 American poet

Time has no divisions to mark its passage, there is never
a thunderstorm or blare of trumpets to announce the
beginning of a new month or year. Even when a new
century begins it is only we mortals who ring bells and fire
off pistols.
   Thomas Mann 1875–1955 German novelist

Tonight's December thirty-first,
Something is about to burst…
Hark, it's midnight, children dear.
Duck! Here comes another year!
   Ogden Nash 1902–71 American humorist

Ring out the old, ring in the new,
Ring, happy bells, across the snow:
The year is going, let him go;
Ring out the false, ring in the true.
   Alfred, Lord Tennyson 1809–92 English poet

April 1. This is the day upon which we are reminded of what
we are on the other three hundred and sixty-four.
   Mark Twain 1835–1910 American writer

Fishing

If fishing is a religion, fly fishing is high church.
   Tom Brokaw 1940– American journalist

I love fishing. It's like transcendental meditation with a
punch-line.
   Billy Connolly 1942– Scottish comedian

Flight

Fishing is unquestionably a form of madness but, happily, for the once-bitten there is no cure.
   Lord Home 1903–95 British statesman

All men are equal before fish.
   Herbert Hoover 1874–1964 American statesman

Fly fishing may be a very pleasant amusement; but angling or float fishing I can only compare to a stick and a string, with a worm at one end and a fool at the other.
   Samuel Johnson 1709–84 English lexicographer

It has always been my private conviction that any man who pits his intelligence against a fish and loses has it coming.
   John Steinbeck 1902–68 American novelist

As no man is born an artist, so no man is born an angler.
   Izaak Walton 1593–1683 English writer

 # Flight

Every flyer who ventures across oceans to distant lands is a potential explorer; in his or her breast burns the same fire that urged the adventurers of old to set forth in their sailing-ships for foreign lands.
   Jean Batten 1909–82 New Zealand aviator

Had I been a man I might have explored the Poles, or climbed Mount Everest, but as it was, my spirit found outlet in the air.
   Amy Johnson 1903–41 English aviator

I feel about airplanes the way I feel about diets. It seems to me that they are wonderful things for other people to go on.
   Jean Kerr 1923–2003 American writer

I was astonished at the effect my successful landing in France had on the nations of the world. To me, it was like a match lighting a bonfire.

Charles Lindbergh 1902–74 American aviator

Oh! I have slipped the surly bonds of earth
And danced the skies on laughter-silvered wings;…
And, while with silent lifting mind I've trod
The high, untrespassed sanctity of space,
Put out my hand and touched the face of God.

John Gillespie Magee 1922–41 American airman

I did not fully understand the dread term 'terminal illness' until I saw Heathrow for myself.

Dennis Potter 1935–94 English dramatist

There are only two emotions in a plane: boredom and terror.

Orson Welles 1915–85 American film director

Flowers

Unkempt about those hedges blows
An English unofficial rose.

Rupert Brooke 1887–1915 English poet

Flowers…are a proud assertion that a ray of beauty outvalues all the utilities of the world.

Ralph Waldo Emerson 1803–82 American writer

I sometimes think that never blows so red
The rose as where some buried Caesar bled.

Edward Fitzgerald 1809–83 English poet

People from a planet without flowers would think we must be mad with joy the whole time to have such things about us.

Iris Murdoch 1919–99 English novelist

Food

RICHARD GRIFFITHS: Flowers are essentially tarts; prostitutes for the bees.

> **Bruce Robinson** 1946– English screenwriter, *in the film* Withnail and I

> Daffodils,
> That come before the swallow dares, and take
> The winds of March with beauty.

> **William Shakespeare** 1564–1616 English dramatist

> I wandered lonely as a cloud
> That floats on high o'er vales and hills,
> When all at once I saw a crowd,
> A host, of golden daffodils;
> Beside the lake, beneath the trees,
> Fluttering and dancing in the breeze.

> **William Wordsworth** 1770–1850 English poet

> To me the meanest flower that blows can give
> Thoughts that do often lie too deep for tears.

> **William Wordsworth** 1770–1850 English poet

 # Food see also **Cookery, Eating**

> Shake and shake
> The catsup bottle.
> None will come,
> And then a lot'll.

> **Richard Armour** 1906–89 American poet

I'm President of the United States, and I'm not going to eat any more broccoli!

> **George Bush** 1924– American statesman

Doubtless God could have made a better berry, but doubtless God never did.

> **William Butler** 1535–1618 English physician, *on the strawberry*

Take away that pudding—it has no theme.
Winston Churchill 1874–1965 British statesman

OLIVER TWIST: Please, sir, I want some more.
Charles Dickens 1812–70 English novelist

Cheese, milk's leap toward immortality.
Clifton Fadiman 1904–99 American critic

A cucumber should be well sliced, and dressed with pepper and vinegar, and then thrown out, as good for nothing.
Samuel Johnson 1709–84 English lexicographer

I am a great eater of beef, and I believe that does harm to my wit.
William Shakespeare 1564–1616 English dramatist

There is no love sincerer than the love of food.
George Bernard Shaw 1856–1950 Irish dramatist

A hen's egg is, quite simply, a work of art, a masterpiece of design and construction with, it has to be said, brilliant packaging.
Delia Smith English cook

Serenely full, the epicure would say,
Fate cannot harm me, I have dined to-day.
Sydney Smith 1771–1845 English essayist

Many's the long night I've dreamed of cheese—toasted, mostly.
Robert Louis Stevenson 1850–94 Scottish novelist

Cauliflower is nothing but cabbage with a college education.
Mark Twain 1835–1910 American writer

What moistens the lip and what brightens the eye?
What calls back the past, like the rich pumpkin pie?
John Greenleaf Whittier 1807–92 American poet

Foolishness

The world is full of fools, and he who would not see it should live alone and smash his mirror.
Anonymous

There's a sucker born every minute.
Phineas T. Barnum 1810–91 American showman

For ye suffer fools gladly, seeing ye yourselves are wise.
Bible

Never give a sucker an even break.
W. C. Fields 1880–1946 American humorist

I won't say she was silly, but I think one of us was silly, and it wasn't me.
Elizabeth Gaskell 1810–65 English novelist

Mix a little foolishness with your prudence: it's good to be silly at the right moment.
Horace 65–8 BC Roman poet

A knowledgeable fool is a greater fool than an ignorant fool.
Molière 1622–73 French comic dramatist

Fools rush in where angels fear to tread.
Alexander Pope 1688–1744 English poet

The follies which a man regrets most, in his life, are those which he didn't commit when he had the opportunity.
Helen Rowland 1875–1950 American writer

The ultimate result of shielding men from the effects of folly, is to fill the world with fools.
Herbert Spencer 1820–1903 English philosopher

Let us be thankful for the fools. But for them the rest of us could not succeed.
Mark Twain 1835–1910 American writer

Be wise with speed;
A fool at forty is a fool indeed.
> **Edward Young** 1683–1765 English poet

Football

The great fallacy is that the game is first and last about winning. It is nothing of the kind. The game is about glory, it is about doing things in style and with a flourish, about going out and beating the lot, not waiting for them to die of boredom.
> **Danny Blanchflower** 1926–93 Northern Irish footballer

Football, wherein is nothing but beastly fury, and extreme violence, whereof proceedeth hurt, and consequently rancour and malice do remain with them that be wounded.
> **Thomas Elyot** 1499–1546 English diplomat

Football is an art more central to our culture than anything the Arts Council deigns to recognize.
> **Germaine Greer** 1939– Australian feminist

The natural state of the football fan is bitter disappointment, no matter what the score.
> **Nick Hornby** 1957– British writer

Football is a simple game; 22 men chase a ball for 90 minutes and at the end, the Germans win.
> **Gary Lineker** 1960– English footballer

Oh, he's football crazy, he's football mad
And the football it has robbed him o' the wee bit sense he had.
> **Jimmie McGregor** 1932– Scottish singer

The goal was scored a little bit by the hand of God, another bit by head of Maradona.
> **Diego Maradona** 1960– Argentinian footballer, *on his controversial goal against England in the 1986 World Cup*

Forgiveness

Football? It's the beautiful game.
Pelé 1940– Brazilian footballer

To say that these men paid their shillings to watch twenty-two hirelings kick a ball is merely to say that a violin is wood and catgut, that *Hamlet* is so much paper and ink. For a shilling the Bruddersford United AFC offered you Conflict and Art.
J. B. Priestley 1894–1984 English writer

Some people think football is a matter of life and death…I can assure them it is much more serious than that.
Bill Shankly 1913–81 Scottish footballer

Football and cookery are the two most important subjects in the country.
Delia Smith English cook

 # Forgiveness

Her sins, which are many, are forgiven; for she loved much.
Bible

It is easier to forgive an enemy than to forgive a friend.
William Blake 1757–1827 English poet

I shall be an autocrat: that's my trade. And the good Lord will forgive me: that's his.
Catherine the Great 1729–96 Russian empress

After such knowledge, what forgiveness?
T. S. Eliot 1888–1965 American-born British poet

God may pardon you, but I never can.
Elizabeth I 1533–1603 English monarch

Forgive but never forget.
John F. Kennedy 1917–63 American statesman

Every one says forgiveness is a lovely idea, until they have something to forgive.
C. S. Lewis 1898–1963 English literary scholar

True reconciliation does not consist in merely forgetting the past.
Nelson Mandela 1918–2013 South African statesman

We read that we ought to forgive our enemies; but we do not read that we ought to forgive our friends.
Cosimo de' Medici 1389–1464 Italian statesman

When a deep injury is done to us, we never recover until we forgive.
Alan Paton 1903–88 South African writer

To err is human; to forgive, divine.
Alexander Pope 1688–1744 English poet

Youth, which is forgiven everything, forgives itself nothing: age, which forgives itself everything, is forgiven nothing.
George Bernard Shaw 1856–1950 Irish dramatist

The stupid neither forgive nor forget; the naïve forgive and forget; the wise forgive but do not forget.
Thomas Szasz 1920–2012 Hungarian-born psychiatrist

France

Everything ends this way in France. Weddings, christenings, duels, burials, swindlings, affairs of state—everything is a pretext for a good dinner.
Jean Anouilh 1910–87 French dramatist

France was long a despotism tempered by epigrams.
Thomas Carlyle 1795–1881 Scottish historian

Friendship

How can you govern a country which has 246 varieties of cheese?

Charles de Gaulle 1890–1970 French statesman

France, mother of arts, of warfare, and of laws.

Joachim Du Bellay 1522–60 French poet

Vive la différence, mais vive l'entente cordiale.

Long live the difference, but long live the Entente Cordiale.

Elizabeth II 1926– British monarch

GROUNDSKEEPER WILLIE AS FRENCH TEACHER: Bonjourr, you cheese-eating surrender monkeys.

Matt Groening 1954– American humorist

The French soul is stronger than the French mind, and Voltaire shatters against Joan of Arc.

Victor Hugo 1802–85 French writer

They order, said I, this matter better in France.

Laurence Sterne 1713–68 English novelist

If the French noblesse had been capable of playing cricket with their peasants, their chateaux would never have been burnt.

G. M. Trevelyan 1876–1962 English historian

 # Friendship

Champagne for my real friends, real pain for my sham friends.

Francis Bacon 1909–92 Irish painter

We must take our friends as they are.

James Boswell 1740–95 Scottish lawyer

There is no man so friendless but what he can find a friend sincere enough to tell him disagreeable truths.

Edward Bulwer-Lytton 1803–73 British novelist

Friendship

Should auld acquaintance be forgot
And never brought to mind?
Robert Burns 1759–96 Scottish poet

Friendship is like money, easier made than kept.
Samuel Butler 1835–1902 English novelist

Give me the avowed, erect and manly foe;
Firm I can meet, perhaps return the blow;
But of all plagues, good Heaven, thy wrath can send,
Save me, oh, save me, from the candid friend.
George Canning 1770–1827 British statesman

A woman can become a man's friend only in the following
stages—first an acquaintance, next a mistress, and only then
a friend.
Anton Chekhov 1860–1904 Russian writer

Oh, the comfort—the inexpressible comfort of feeling
safe with a person, having neither to weigh thoughts, nor
measure words, but pouring them all out, just as they are,
chaff and grain together; knowing that a faithful hand will
take and sift them—keep what is worth keeping—and with
the breath of kindness blow the rest away.
Dinah Mulock Craik 1826–87 English novelist

The only reward of virtue is virtue; the only way to have a
friend is to be one.
Ralph Waldo Emerson 1803–82 American writer

Of all the means which wisdom acquires to ensure
happiness throughout the whole of life, by far the most
important is friendship.
Epicurus 341–271 BC Greek philosopher

HUMPHREY BOGART: Louis, I think this is the beginning of a
beautiful friendship.
Julius J. Epstein 1909–2001 and **others** American
screenwriters, *in the film* Casablanca

Friendship

Friends are the sunshine of life.

John Hay 1838–1905 American diplomat

My father always used to say that when you die, if you've got five real friends, you've had a great life.

Lee Iacocca 1924– American businessman

If a man does not make new acquaintance as he advances through life, he will soon find himself left alone. A man, Sir, should keep his friendship in constant repair.

Samuel Johnson 1709–84 English lexicographer

However rare true love may be, true friendship is rarer.

Duc de la Rochefoucauld 1613–80 French moralist

Oh I get by with a little help from my friends,
Mm, I get high with a little help from my friends.

John Lennon 1940–80 and **Paul McCartney** 1942– English pop singers

To like and dislike the same things, that is indeed true friendship.

Sallust 86–35 BC Roman historian

Friendship is constant in all other things
Save in the office and affairs of love.

William Shakespeare 1564–1616 English dramatist

The holy passion of friendship is of so sweet and steady and loyal and enduring a nature that it will last through a whole lifetime, if not asked to lend money.

Mark Twain 1835–1910 American writer

I do not believe that friends are necessarily the people you like best, they are merely the people who got there first.

Peter Ustinov 1921–2004 British actor

The Future

'We are always doing', says he, 'something for Posterity, but I would fain see Posterity do something for us.'
Joseph Addison 1672–1719 English writer

The future ain't what it used to be.
Yogi Berra 1925–2015 American baseball player

Predictions can be very difficult—especially about the future.
Niels Bohr 1885–1962 Danish physicist

You can never plan the future by the past.
Edmund Burke 1729–97 Irish-born politician

I look to the future, because that's where I'm going to spend the rest of my life.
George Burns 1896–1996 American comedian

The empires of the future are the empires of the mind.
Winston Churchill 1874–1965 British statesman

The future belongs to crowds.
Don DeLillo 1936– American novelist

I never think of the future. It comes soon enough.
Albert Einstein 1879–1955 German-born theoretical physicist

You cannot fight against the future. Time is on our side.
W. E. Gladstone 1809–98 British statesman

The best way to predict the future is to invent it.
Alan Kay 1940– American computer scientist

We have trained them [men] to think of the Future as a promised land which favoured heroes attain—not as something which everyone reaches at the rate of sixty minutes an hour, whatever he does, whoever he is.
C. S. Lewis 1898–1963 English literary scholar

Gardens

If you want a picture of the future, imagine a boot stamping on a human face—for ever.
George Orwell 1903–50 English novelist

Lord! we know what we are, but know not what we may be.
William Shakespeare 1564–1616 English dramatist

 # Gardens

I value my garden more for being full of blackbirds than of cherries, and very frankly give them fruit for their songs.
Joseph Addison 1672–1719 English writer

Nothing is more pleasant to the eye than green grass kept finely shorn.
Francis Bacon 1561–1626 English courtier

A garden is a lovesome thing, God wot!
T. E. Brown 1830–97 Manx schoolmaster

What is a weed? A plant whose virtues have not been discovered.
Ralph Waldo Emerson 1803–82 American writer

He that plants trees loves others beside himself.
Thomas Fuller 1654–1734 English physician

The kiss of the sun for pardon,
The song of the birds for mirth,
One is nearer God's Heart in a garden
Than anywhere else on earth.
Dorothy Frances Gurney 1858–1932 English poet

But though an old man, I am but a young gardener.
Thomas Jefferson 1743–1826 American statesman

The Glory of the Garden lies in more than meets the eye.
Rudyard Kipling 1865–1936 English writer

A garden was the primitive prison till man with
Promethean felicity and boldness luckily sinned himself
out of it.
   Charles Lamb 1775–1834 English writer

He who plants a tree
Plants a hope.
   Lucy Larcom 1824–93 American writer

Annihilating all that's made
To a green thought in a green shade.
   Andrew Marvell 1621–78 English poet

Come into the garden, Maud,
I am here at the gate alone.
   Alfred, Lord Tennyson 1809–92 English poet

What a man needs in gardening is a cast iron back, with a
hinge in it.
   Charles Dudley Warner 1829–1900 American writer

The Generation Gap see also **Youth**

The dead might as well try to speak to the living as the old
to the young.
   Willa Cather 1873–1947 American novelist

Come mothers and fathers,
Throughout the land
And don't criticize
What you can't understand.
   Bob Dylan 1941– American singer

Si jeunesse savait; si vieillesse pouvait.
If youth knew; if age could.
   Henri Estienne 1531–98 French printer

Genius

Every generation revolts against its fathers and makes
friends with its grandfathers.
Lewis Mumford 1895–1982 American sociologist

Crabbed age and youth cannot live together:
Youth is full of pleasance, age is full of care.
William Shakespeare 1564–1616 English dramatist

It's all that the young can do for the old, to shock them and
keep them up to date.
George Bernard Shaw 1856–1950 Irish dramatist

Nothing so dates a man as to decry the younger
generation.
Adlai Stevenson 1900–65 American politician

Hope I die before I get old.
Pete Townshend 1945– British rock musician

When I was a boy of 14, my father was so ignorant I could
hardly stand to have the old man around. But when I got
to be 21, I was astonished at how much the old man had
learned in seven years.
Mark Twain 1835–1910 American writer

The old believe everything: the middle-aged suspect
everything: the young know everything.
Oscar Wilde 1854–1900 Irish dramatist

 # Genius

Genius is only a greater aptitude for patience.
Comte de Buffon 1707–88 French naturalist

Everybody has talent at twenty-five. The difficult thing is to
have it at fifty.
Edgar Degas 1834–1917 French artist

Mediocrity knows nothing higher than itself, but talent instantly recognizes genius.
Arthur Conan Doyle 1859–1930 Scottish-born writer

Great wits are sure to madness near allied,
And thin partitions do their bounds divide.
John Dryden 1631–1700 English poet

Genius is one per cent inspiration, ninety-nine per cent perspiration.
Thomas Alva Edison 1847–1931 American inventor

Little minds are interested in the extraordinary; great minds in the commonplace.
Elbert Hubbard 1859–1915 American writer

The true genius is a mind of large general powers, accidentally determined to some particular direction.
Samuel Johnson 1709–84 English lexicographer

Genius does what it must, and Talent does what it can.
Owen Meredith 1831–91 English statesman

Every positive value has its price in negative terms…The genius of Einstein leads to Hiroshima.
Pablo Picasso 1881–1973 Spanish painter

Genius is always allowed some leeway, once the hammer has been pried from its hands and the blood has been cleaned up.
Terry Pratchett 1948–2015 English novelist

It takes a lot of time to be a genius, you have to sit around so much doing nothing, really doing nothing.
Gertrude Stein 1874–1946 American writer

When a true genius appears in the world, you may know him by this sign, that the dunces are all in confederacy against him.
Jonathan Swift 1667–1745 Irish poet and satirist

Gifts

I know of no genius but the genius of hard work.
J. M. W. Turner 1775–1851 English painter

I have nothing to declare except my genius.
Oscar Wilde 1854–1900 Irish dramatist, *at the New York Custom House*

 Gifts see also **Charity**

Surprises are foolish things. The pleasure is not enhanced, and the inconvenience is often considerable.
Jane Austen 1775–1817 English novelist

It is more blessed to give than to receive.
Bible

They gave it me,—for an un-birthday present.
Lewis Carroll 1832–98 English writer

One must be poor to know the luxury of giving.
George Eliot 1819–80 English novelist

Generosity is giving more than you can, and pride is taking less than you need.
Kahlil Gibran 1883–1931 Lebanese-born American writer

A gift though small is welcome.
Homer fl. 8th century BC Greek poet

I know it's not much, but it's the best I can do,
My gift is my song and this one's for you.
Elton John 1947– and **Bernie Taupin** 1950– English pop singer and English songwriter English pop singer and English songwriter

Presents, I often say, endear Absents.
Charles Lamb 1775–1834 English writer

Why is it no one ever sent me yet
One perfect limousine, do you suppose?

Ah no, it's always just my luck to get
One perfect rose.
Dorothy Parker 1893–1967 American critic

SEAN CONNERY: The key to a woman's heart is an
unexpected gift at an unexpected time.
Mike Rich 1959– American screenwriter, *in the film* Finding
Forrester

I am not in the giving vein to-day.
William Shakespeare 1564–1616 English dramatist

God see also **Religion**

The nature of God is a circle of which the centre is
everywhere and the circumference is nowhere.
Anonymous

There's probably no God. Now stop worrying and enjoy
your life.
Anonymous, *advertisement on London buses, supported by
English evolutionary biologist Richard Dawkins (1941–)*

In the beginning was the Word, and the Word was with
God, and the Word was God.
Bible

He that loveth not knoweth not God; for God is love.
Bible

When men stop believing in God they don't believe in
nothing; they believe in anything.
G. K. Chesterton 1874–1936 English writer

God moves in a mysterious way
His wonders to perform.
William Cowper 1731–1800 English poet

God

God is subtle but he is not malicious.
Albert Einstein 1879–1955 German-born theoretical physicist

Operationally, God is beginning to resemble not a ruler but the last fading smile of a cosmic Cheshire cat.
Julian Huxley 1887–1975 English biologist

An honest God is the noblest work of man.
Robert G. Ingersoll 1833–99 American agnostic

Many roads lead to God. I have chosen that of music and dance.
Jalal ad-Din ar-Rumi 1207–73 Persian poet

God is the breath of all breath.
Kabir c.1398–c.1448 North Indian poet and mystic

God seems to have left the receiver off the hook, and time is running out.
Arthur Koestler 1905–83 Hungarian-born writer

Praise belongs to God, the Lord of all Being,
the All-merciful, the All-compassionate.
The Koran

Though the mills of God grind slowly, yet they grind
  exceeding small;
Though with patience He stands waiting, with exactness
  grinds He all.
Henry Wadsworth Longfellow 1807–82 American poet

Whatever your heart clings to and confides in, that is really your God.
Martin Luther 1483–1546 German theologian

If the triangles were to make a God they would give him three sides.
Montesquieu 1689–1755 French political philosopher

The Buddha, the Godhead, resides quite as comfortably in the circuits of a digital computer or the gears of a cycle transmission as he does at the top of a mountain or in the petals of a flower.
> **Robert M. Pirsig** 1928–2017 American writer

Hear, O Israel: the Lord our God, the Lord is One.
> **The Siddur**

O Lord, to what a state dost Thou bring those who love Thee!
> **St Teresa of Ávila** 1512–82 Spanish mystic

For man proposes, but God disposes.
> **Thomas à Kempis** c.1380–1471 German writer

If God did not exist, it would be necessary to invent him.
> **Voltaire** 1694–1778 French writer

Our God, our help in ages past
Our hope for years to come,
Our shelter from the stormy blast,
And our eternal home.
> **Isaac Watts** 1674–1748 English hymn-writer

Golf

If you watch a game, it's fun. If you play it, it's recreation. If you work at it, it's golf.
> **Bob Hope** 1903–2003 American comedian

Golf is so popular simply because it is the best game in the world at which to be bad.
> **A. A. Milne** 1882–1956 English writer

Golf is a good walk spoiled.
> **Mark Twain** 1835–1910 American writer

Good Looks

The least thing upset him on the links. He missed short putts because of the uproar of the butterflies in the adjoining meadows.
P. G. Wodehouse 1881–1975 English writer

Golf…is the infallible test. The man who can go into a patch of rough alone, with the knowledge that only God is watching him, and play his ball where it lies, is the man who will serve you faithfully and well.
P. G. Wodehouse 1881–1975 English writer

 # Good Looks

A pretty girl is like a melody
That haunts you night and day.
Irving Berlin 1888–1989 American songwriter

And she was fayr as is the rose in May.
Geoffrey Chaucer c.1343–1400 English poet

When a woman isn't beautiful, people always say, 'You have lovely eyes, you have lovely hair.'
Anton Chekhov 1860–1904 Russian writer

Beauty is the lover's gift.
William Congreve 1670–1729 English dramatist

Is it too much to ask that women be spared the daily struggle for superhuman beauty in order to offer it to the caresses of a subhumanly ugly mate?
Germaine Greer 1939– Australian feminist

I'm tired of all this nonsense about beauty being only skin-deep. That's deep enough. What do you want—an adorable pancreas?
Jean Kerr 1923–2003 American writer

The Lord prefers common-looking people. That is why he makes so many of them.
Abraham Lincoln 1809–65 American statesman

A beautiful face is a mute recommendation.
Publilius Syrus fl. 1st century BC Roman writer

Shall I compare thee to a summer's day?
Thou art more lovely and more temperate.
William Shakespeare 1564–1616 English dramatist

Goodness see also **Evil**

Every art and every investigation, and likewise every practical pursuit or undertaking, seems to aim at some good: hence it has been well said that the Good is That at which all things aim.
Aristotle 384–322 BC Greek philosopher

He who would do good to another, must do it in minute particulars.
William Blake 1757–1827 English poet

No one can be good for long if goodness is not in demand.
Bertolt Brecht 1898–1956 German dramatist

Integrity has no need of rules.
Albert Camus 1913–60 French writer

No people do so much harm as those who go about doing good.
Mandell Creighton 1843–1901 English prelate

What after all
Is a halo? It's only one more thing to keep clean.
Christopher Fry 1907–2005 English dramatist

I expect to pass through this world but once; any good thing therefore that I can do, or any kindness that I can show to

Goodness

any fellow-creature, let me do it now; let me not defer or neglect it, for I shall not pass this way again.
Stephen Grellet 1773–1855 French missionary

Be good, sweet maid, and let who will be clever.
Charles Kingsley 1819–75 English writer

Good and evil shall not be held equal. Turn away evil with that which is better; and behold the man between whom and thyself there was enmity, shall become, as it were, thy warmest friend.
The Koran

A man who wants to act virtuously in every way necessarily comes to grief among so many who are not virtuous.
Niccolò Machiavelli 1469–1527 Italian political philosopher

Virtue she finds too painful an endeavour,
Content to dwell in decencies for ever.
Alexander Pope 1688–1744 English poet

Dost thou think, because thou art virtuous, there shall be no more cakes and ale?
William Shakespeare 1564–1616 English dramatist

How far that little candle throws his beams!
So shines a good deed in a naughty world.
William Shakespeare 1564–1616 English dramatist

Our goodness derives not from our capacity to think but to love.
St Teresa of Ávila 1512–82 Spanish mystic

Would that we had spent one whole day well in this world!
Thomas à Kempis c.1380–1471 German writer

Virtue knows to a farthing what it has lost by not having been vice.
Horace Walpole 1717–97 English connoisseur

'Goodness, what beautiful diamonds!'
'Goodness had nothing to do with it.'
Mae West 1892–1980 American film actress

That best portion of a good man's life,
His little, nameless, unremembered, acts
Of kindness and of love.
William Wordsworth 1770–1850 English poet

Gossip

There is so much good in the worst of us,
And so much bad in the best of us,
That it hardly becomes any of us
To talk about the rest of us.
Anonymous

Careless talk costs lives.
Anonymous, *Second World War security slogan*

Every man is surrounded by a neighbourhood of voluntary
spies.
Jane Austen 1775–1817 English novelist

They come together like the Coroner's Inquest, to sit upon
the murdered reputations of the week.
William Congreve 1670–1729 English dramatist

Gossip is a sort of smoke that comes from the dirty tobacco-
pipes of those who diffuse it: it proves nothing but the bad
taste of the smoker.
George Eliot 1819–80 English novelist

Love and scandal are the best sweeteners of tea.
Henry Fielding 1707–54 English novelist

Like all gossip—it's merely one of those half-alive things
that try to crowd out real life.
E. M. Forster 1879–1970 English novelist

Government

No one gossips about other people's secret virtues.
Bertrand Russell 1872–1970 British philosopher

It takes your enemy and your friend, working together, to hurt you to the heart: the one to slander you and the other to get the news to you.
Mark Twain 1835–1910 American writer

There is only one thing in the world worse than being talked about, and that is not being talked about.
Oscar Wilde 1854–1900 Irish dramatist

 # Government see also **Politics**

Let them hate, so long as they fear.
Accius 170–c.86 BC Roman poet

The happiness of society is the end of government.
John Adams 1735–1826 American statesman

Dullness in matters of government is a good sign, and not a bad one.
Walter Bagehot 1826–77 English economist

The object of government in peace and in war is not the glory of rulers or of races, but the happiness of the common man.
William Henry Beveridge 1879–1963 British economist

England is the mother of Parliaments.
John Bright 1811–89 English politician

Dear Chief Secretary, I'm afraid there is no money.
Liam Byrne 1970– British politician, *letter left for his successor as Chief Secretary to the Treasury*

The poor have sometimes objected to being governed badly; the rich have always objected to being governed at all.
G. K. Chesterton 1874–1936 English writer

It is a 'beautiful maxim' that it is necessary to save five *sous* on unessential things, and to pour out millions when it is a question of your glory.

Jean-Baptiste Colbert 1619–83 French statesman

No Government can be long secure without a formidable Opposition.

Benjamin Disraeli 1804–81 British statesman

Though God hath raised me high, yet this I count the glory of my crown: that I have reigned with your loves.

Elizabeth I 1533–1603 English monarch

If the Government is big enough to give you everything you want, it is big enough to take away everything you have.

Gerald Ford 1909–2006 American statesman

The state is like the human body. Not all of its functions are dignified.

Anatole France 1844–1924 French man of letters

My people and I have come to an agreement which satisfies us both. They are to say what they please, and I am to do what I please.

Frederick the Great 1712–86 Prussian monarch

Your business is not to govern the country but it is, if you think fit, to call to account those who do govern it.

W. E. Gladstone 1809–98 British statesman, *to the House of Commons*

Many journalists have fallen for the conspiracy theory of government. I do assure you that they would produce more accurate work if they adhered to the cock-up theory.

Bernard Ingham 1932– British journalist

The important thing for Government is not to do things which individuals are doing already, and to do them a little

Greatness

better or a little worse; but to do those things which at present are not done at all.

John Maynard Keynes 1883–1946 English economist

To govern is to choose.

Duc de Lévis 1764–1830 French soldier

It is much safer for a prince to be feared than loved, if he is to fail in one of the two.

Niccolò Machiavelli 1469–1527 Italian political philosopher

If men were angels, no government would be necessary.

James Madison 1751–1836 American statesman

BIG BROTHER IS WATCHING YOU.

George Orwell 1903–50 English novelist

The best government is that which governs least.

John L. O'Sullivan 1813–95 American journalist

For forms of government let fools contest;
Whate'er is best administered is best.

Alexander Pope 1688–1744 English poet

Wherever you have an efficient government you have a dictatorship.

Harry S. Truman 1884–1972 American statesman

Governments need both shepherds and butchers.

Voltaire 1694–1778 French writer

 # Greatness

The beauty of Israel is slain upon thy high places: how are the mighty fallen!

Bible

JOHN CUSACK: I'm looking for a dare-to-be-great situation.

Cameron Crowe 1957– American film director, *in the film* Say Anything

To be great is to be misunderstood.
Ralph Waldo Emerson 1803–82 American writer

A man does not attain the status of Galileo merely because he is persecuted; he must also be right.
Stephen Jay Gould 1941–2002 American palaeontologist

The glory of great men should always be measured against the means they used to acquire it.
Duc de la Rochefoucauld 1613–80 French moralist

If any man seeks for greatness, let him forget greatness, and ask for truth, and he will find both.
Horace Mann 1796–1859 American educationist

The first test of a truly great man is his humility.
John Ruskin 1819–1900 English critic

But be not afraid of greatness: some men are born great, some achieve greatness, and some have greatness thrust upon them.
William Shakespeare 1564–1616 English dramatist

Habit

The less of routine, the more of life.
Amos Bronson Alcott 1799–1888 American reformer

Routine, in an intelligent man, is a sign of ambition.
W. H. Auden 1907–73 English poet

Habit is a great deadener.
Samuel Beckett 1906–89 Irish writer

Habit with him was all the test of truth,
'It must be right: I've done it from my youth.'
George Crabbe 1754–1832 English poet

Happiness

Habit and routine have an unbelievable power to waste and destroy.

Henri de Lubac 1896–1991 French theologian

Sow an act, and you reap a habit. Sow a habit and you reap a character. Sow a character, and you reap a destiny.

Charles Reade 1814–84 English writer

Good habits: they are never good, because they are habits.

Jean-Paul Sartre 1905–80 French philosopher

Happiness

Mirth is like a flash of lightning that breaks through a gloom of clouds, and glitters for a moment: cheerfulness keeps up a kind of day-light in the mind.

Joseph Addison 1672–1719 English writer

A large income is the best recipe for happiness I ever heard of. It certainly may secure all the myrtle and turkey part of it.

Jane Austen 1775–1817 English novelist

There may be Peace without Joy, and Joy without Peace, but the two combined make Happiness.

John Buchan 1875–1940 Scottish novelist

Happiness is…finding two olives in your martini when you're hungry.

Johnny Carson 1925–2005 American comedian

Happiness is a mystery like religion, and should never be rationalized.

G. K. Chesterton 1874–1936 English writer

If you want others to be happy, practise compassion. If you want to be happy, practise compassion.

Dalai Lama 1935– Tibetan monk

Happiness

Happiness resides not in possessions and not in gold,
the feeling of happiness dwells in the soul.
> **Democritus** c.460–c.370 BC Greek philosopher

To be stupid, and selfish, and to have good health are the
three requirements for happiness, though if stupidity is
lacking, the others are useless.
> **Gustave Flaubert** 1821–80 French novelist

Happiness makes up in height for what it lacks in length.
> **Robert Frost** 1874–1963 American poet

Point me out the happy man and I will point you out
either egotism, selfishness, evil—or else an absolute
ignorance.
> **Graham Greene** 1904–91 English novelist

Happiness is a how, not a what; a talent, not an object.
> **Hermann Hesse** 1877–1962 German writer

I can sympathize with people's pains, but not with their
pleasures. There is something curiously boring about
somebody else's happiness.
> **Aldous Huxley** 1894–1963 English novelist

Happiness is not an ideal of reason but of imagination.
> **Immanuel Kant** 1724–1804 German philosopher

A man enjoys the happiness he feels, a woman the
happiness she gives.
> **Pierre Choderlos de Laclos** 1741–1803 French soldier

Happiness writes white.
> **Philip Larkin** 1922–85 English poet

Happiness is a warm gun.
> **John Lennon** 1940–80 English pop singer

Happiness

Ask yourself whether you are happy, and you cease to be so.

John Stuart Mill 1806–73 English philosopher

Not to admire, is all the art I know,
To make men happy, and to keep them so.

Alexander Pope 1688–1744 English poet

To be without some of the things you want is an indispensable part of happiness.

Bertrand Russell 1872–1970 British philosopher

Freude, schöner Götterfunken,
Tochter aus Elysium.

Joy, beautiful radiance of the gods, daughter of Elysium.

Friedrich von Schiller 1759–1805 German poet

But a lifetime of happiness! No man alive could bear it: it would be hell on earth.

George Bernard Shaw 1856–1950 Irish dramatist

Call no man happy before he dies, he is at best but fortunate.

Solon c.640–after 556 BC Greek statesman

It is not how much we have, but how much we enjoy, that makes happiness.

C. H. Spurgeon 1834–92 English preacher

There's only one way of being comfortable, and that is to stop running round after happiness. If you make up your mind not to be happy there's no reason why you shouldn't have a fairly good time.

Edith Wharton 1862–1937 American novelist, *often quoted as 'If only we'd stop trying to be happy we could have a pretty good time'*

Hatred

Better is a dinner of herbs where love is, than a stalled ox and hatred therewith.
Bible

I do not love thee, Dr Fell.
The reason why I cannot tell;
But this I know, and know full well,
I do not love thee, Dr Fell.
Thomas Brown 1663–1704 English satirist

Now hatred is by far the longest pleasure;
Men love in haste, but they detest at leisure.
Lord Byron 1788–1824 English poet

Love, friendship, respect do not unite people as much as common hatred for something.
Anton Chekhov 1860–1904 Russian writer

I never hated a man enough to give him diamonds back.
Zsa Zsa Gabor 1919–2016 Hungarian-born film actress

We can scarcely hate any one that we know.
William Hazlitt 1778–1830 English essayist

If you hate a person, you hate something in him that is part of yourself. What isn't part of ourselves doesn't disturb us.
Hermann Hesse 1877–1962 German writer

Returning hate for hate multiplies hate, adding deeper darkness to a night already devoid of stars. Darkness cannot drive out darkness; only light can do that. Hate cannot drive out hate; only love can do that.
Martin Luther King 1929–68 American civil rights leader

No one is born hating another person because of the colour of his skin, or his background, or his religion. People must learn to hate, and if they can learn to hate, they can be taught to love, for love comes more naturally to the human heart than its opposite.

Nelson Mandela 1918–2013 South African statesman

Always remember, others may hate you. Those who hate you don't win unless you hate them. And then you destroy yourself.

Richard Nixon 1913–94 American statesman

For hate is not conquered by hate: hate is conquered by love. This is a law eternal.

Pali Tripitaka c. 2nd century BC Buddhist sacred texts

Health see also **Exercise, Sickness**

The first law of dietetics seems to be: if it tastes good, it's bad for you.

Isaac Asimov 1920–92 Russian-born science fiction writer

The first wealth is health.

Ralph Waldo Emerson 1803–82 American writer

Health is worth more than learning.

Thomas Jefferson 1743–1826 American statesman

Mens sana in corpore sano.

A sound mind in a sound body.

Juvenal c.AD 60–c.140 Roman satirist

Life's not just being alive, but being well.

Martial c.AD 40–c.104 Roman epigrammatist

The best doctors are Dr Diet, Dr Quiet, and Dr Merryman.

Proverb

Choose rather to be strong in soul than strong of body.

Pythagoras 580–500 BC Greek philosopher

Look to your health; and if you have it, praise God, and value it next to a good conscience; for health is the second blessing that we mortals are capable of; a blessing that money cannot buy.
Izaak Walton 1593–1683 English writer

The Heart

The desires of the heart are as crooked as corkscrews
Not to be born is the best for man.
W. H. Auden 1907–73 English poet

There is a road from the eye to the heart that does not go through the intellect.
G. K. Chesterton 1874–1936 English writer

The human heart likes a little disorder in its geometry.
Louis de Bernières 1954–   British novelist

A man who has not passed through the inferno of his passions has never overcome them.
Carl Gustav Jung 1875–1961 Swiss psychologist

Calm of mind, all passion spent.
John Milton 1608–74 English poet

The heart is an organ of fire.
Michael Ondaatje 1943–   Canadian writer

The heart has its reasons which reason knows nothing of.
Blaise Pascal 1623–62 French scientist and philosopher

Unlearn'd, he knew no schoolman's subtle art,
No language, but the language of the heart.
Alexander Pope 1688–1744 English poet

A man whose blood
Is very snow-broth; one who never feels
The wanton stings and motions of the sense.
William Shakespeare 1564–1616 English dramatist

Heaven

The heart of another is a dark forest.
Ivan Turgenev 1818–83 Russian novelist

Now that my ladder's gone
I must lie down where all ladders start
In the foul rag and bone shop of the heart.
W. B. Yeats 1865–1939 Irish poet

 # Heaven

And I saw a new heaven and a new earth: for the first heaven and the first earth were passed away; and there was no more sea.
Bible

The true paradises are the paradises that we have lost.
Marcel Proust 1871–1922 French novelist

HENRY LUTTRELL: My idea of heaven is, eating *pâté de foie gras* to the sound of trumpets.
Sydney Smith 1771–1845 English essayist

I will spend my heaven doing good on earth.
St Teresa of Lisieux 1873–97 French nun

Heaven for climate, and hell for society.
Mark Twain 1835–1910 American writer

 # Hell

Hell, madam, is to love no more.
Georges Bernanos 1888–1948 French writer

Abandon all hope, you who enter!
Dante Alighieri 1265–1321 Italian poet, *inscription at the entrance to Hell*

What is hell?
Hell is oneself,
Hell is alone, the other figures in it
Merely projections.
T. S. Eliot 1888–1965 American-born British poet

Hell is other people.
Jean-Paul Sartre 1905–80 French philosopher

A perpetual holiday is a good working definition of hell.
George Bernard Shaw 1856–1950 Irish dramatist

Hell is a city much like London.
Percy Bysshe Shelley 1792–1822 English poet

Heroes

We can be heroes
Just for one day.
David Bowie 1947–2016 English rock musician

ANDREA: Unhappy the land that has no heroes!…
GALILEO: No. Unhappy the land that needs heroes.
Bertolt Brecht 1898–1956 German dramatist

No man is a hero to his valet.
Mme Cornuel 1605–94 French society hostess

Every hero becomes a bore at last.
Ralph Waldo Emerson 1803–82 American writer

Ultimately a hero is a man who would argue with the Gods,
and so awakens devils to contest his vision.
Norman Mailer 1923–2007 American writer

Heroing is one of the shortest-lived professions there is.
Will Rogers 1879–1935 American actor

A hero is the one who does what he can. The others don't.
Romain Rolland 1866–1944 French writer

In this world I would rather live two days like a tiger, than two hundred years like a sheep.
Tipu Sultan c.1750-99

 # History

If history records good things of good men, the thoughtful hearer is encouraged to imitate what is good.
The Venerable Bede AD 673-735 English historian

History repeats itself; historians repeat one another.
Rupert Brooke 1887-1915 English poet

History is the essence of innumerable biographies.
Thomas Carlyle 1795-1881 Scottish historian

To be ignorant of what occurred before you were born is to remain forever a child.
Cicero 106-43 BC Roman statesman

History is philosophy from examples.
Dionysius of Halicarnassus fl. 30-7 BC Greek historian

History is more or less bunk.
Henry Ford 1863-1947 American car manufacturer

History is past politics, and politics is present history.
E. A. Freeman 1823-92 English historian

History…is, indeed, little more than the register of the crimes, follies, and misfortunes of mankind.
Edward Gibbon 1737-94 English historian

War makes rattling good history; but Peace is poor reading.
Thomas Hardy 1840-1928 English novelist

Hegel says somewhere that all great events and personalities in world history reappear in one fashion or another. He forgot to add: the first time as tragedy, the second as farce.
Karl Marx 1818-83 German philosopher

Happy the people whose annals are blank in history-books!
Montesquieu 1689–1755 French political philosopher

History is not what you thought. *It is what you can remember.*
W. C. Sellar 1898–1951 and **R. J. Yeatman** 1898–1968 British writers

Human history becomes more and more a race between education and catastrophe.
H. G. Wells 1866–1946 English novelist

Home see also **Houses, Housework**

Home is home, though it be never so homely.
John Clarke d. 1658 English schoolmaster

'Home is the place where, when you have to go there,
They have to take you in.'
'I should have called it
Something you somehow haven't to deserve.'
Robert Frost 1874–1963 American poet

What's the good of a home if you are never in it?
George Grossmith 1847–1912 and **Weedon Grossmith** 1854–1919 English writers

One never reaches home. But wherever friendly paths intersect the whole world looks like home for a time.
Hermann Hesse 1877–1962 German writer

Any old place I can hang my hat is home sweet home to me.
William Jerome 1865–1932 American songwriter

The accent of one's birthplace lingers in the mind and in the heart as it does in one's speech.
Duc de la Rochefoucauld 1613–80 French moralist

Honesty

E.T. phone home.
> **Melissa Mathison** 1950– American screenwriter, *in the film* E.T.

Mid pleasures and palaces though we may roam,
Be it ever so humble, there's no place like home.
> **J. H. Payne** 1791–1852 American actor

Home is where you come to when you have nothing better to do.
> **Margaret Thatcher** 1925–2013 British stateswoman

 # Honesty see also **Deceit**

Honesty is praised and left to shiver.
> **Juvenal** c.AD 60–c.140 Roman satirist

honesty is a good
thing but
it is not profitable to
its possessor
unless it is
kept under control.
> **Don Marquis** 1878–1937 American poet and journalist

An honest man's the noblest work of God.
> **Alexander Pope** 1688–1744 English poet

Speak what we feel, not what we ought to say.
> **William Shakespeare** 1564–1616 English dramatist

It is dangerous to be sincere unless you are also stupid.
> **George Bernard Shaw** 1856–1950 Irish dramatist

I am afraid we must make the world honest before we can honestly say to our children that honesty is the best policy.
> **George Bernard Shaw** 1856–1950 Irish dramatist

Honour

The louder he talked of his honour, the faster we counted our spoons.
Ralph Waldo Emerson 1803–82 American writer

GROUCHO MARX: Remember, you're fighting for this woman's honour…which is probably more than she ever did.
Bert Kalmar 1884–1947 and **others** American screenwriters, *in the film* Duck Soup

I could not love thee, Dear, so much,
Loved I not honour more.
Richard Lovelace 1618–58 English poet

But he that filches from me my good name
Robs me of that which not enriches him,
And makes me poor indeed.
William Shakespeare 1564–1616 English dramatist

O! I have lost my reputation. I have lost the immortal part of myself, and what remains is bestial.
William Shakespeare 1564–1616 English dramatist

His honour rooted in dishonour stood,
And faith unfaithful kept him falsely true.
Alfred, Lord Tennyson 1809–92 English poet

Honours

The rank is but the guinea's stamp,
The man's the gowd for a' that!
Robert Burns 1759–96 Scottish poet

A medal glitters, but it also casts a shadow.
Winston Churchill 1874–1965 British statesman, *on the envy caused by the award of honours*

Hope

What I like about the Order of the Garter is that there is no damned merit about it.
Lord Melbourne 1779–1848 British statesman

When I want a peerage, I shall buy it like an honest man.
Lord Northcliffe 1865–1922 British newspaper proprietor

There is no stronger craving in the world than that of the rich for titles, except perhaps that of the titled for riches.
Hesketh Pearson 1887–1964 English biographer

Titles distinguish the mediocre, embarrass the superior, and are disgraced by the inferior.
George Bernard Shaw 1856–1950 Irish dramatist

What harm have I ever done to the Labour Party?
R. H. Tawney 1880–1962 British economic historian, *on declining the offer of a peerage*

Kind hearts are more than coronets,
And simple faith than Norman blood.
Alfred, Lord Tennyson 1809–92 English poet

 # Hope see also **Despair**, **Optimism**

Hope is a good breakfast, but it is a bad supper.
Francis Bacon 1561–1626 English courtier

Hope deferred maketh the heart sick: but when the desire cometh, it is a tree of life.
Bible

He that lives upon hope will die fasting.
Benjamin Franklin 1706–90 American statesman and scientist

Walk on, walk on, with hope in your heart,
And you'll never walk alone.
Oscar Hammerstein II 1895–1960 American songwriter

Hope is definitely not the same thing as optimism. It is not the conviction that something will turn out well, but the certainty that something makes sense, regardless of how it turns out.

Václav Havel 1936–2011 Czech statesman

He that lives in hope danceth without music.

George Herbert 1593–1633 English poet

Nil desperandum.

Never despair.

Horace 65–8 BC Roman poet

Plenty of hope—for God—an abundance of hope—only not for us.

Franz Kafka 1883–1924 Czech novelist, *often quoted as 'There is hope but not for us'*

Hope is like a road in the country; there was never a road, but when many people walk on it, the road comes into existence.

Lu Xun 1881–1936 Chinese writer

After all, tomorrow is another day.

Margaret Mitchell 1900–49 American novelist

Hope springs eternal in the human breast:
Man never Is, but always To be blest.

Alexander Pope 1688–1744 English poet

Hospitality

It was a delightful visit;– perfect, in being much too short.

Jane Austen 1775–1817 English novelist

Be not forgetful to entertain strangers: for thereby some have entertained angels unawares.

Bible

Houses

Come in the evening, or come in the morning,
Come when you're looked for, or come without warning.
Thomas Davis 1814–45 Irish poet

Hospitality consists in a little fire, a little food, and an immense quiet.
Ralph Waldo Emerson 1803–82 American writer

A host is like a general: misfortunes often reveal his genius.
Horace 65–8 BC Roman poet

Some people can stay longer in an hour than others can in a week.
William Dean Howells 1837–1920 American writer

For I, who hold sage Homer's rule the best,
Welcome the coming, speed the going guest.
Alexander Pope 1688–1744 English poet

       Unbidden guests
Are often welcomest when they are gone.
William Shakespeare 1564–1616 English dramatist

This door will open at a touch to welcome every friend.
Henry Van Dyke 1852–1933 American minister

 # Houses see also **Home**

Houses are built to live in and not to look on; therefore let use be preferred before uniformity, except where both may be had.
Francis Bacon 1561–1626 English courtier

For a man's house is his castle, *et domus sua cuique est tutissimum refugium* [and each man's home is his safest refuge].
Edward Coke 1552–1634 English jurist

It takes a heap o' livin' in a house t' make it home.
Edgar A. Guest 1881–1959 American writer

A house is a machine for living in.
Le Corbusier 1887–1965 French architect

Have nothing in your houses that you do not know to be useful, or believe to be beautiful.
William Morris 1834–96 English artist

Does anybody mind if I don't live in a house that is quaint?
Because, for one thing, quaint houses are generally houses
  where plumbing ain't.
Ogden Nash 1902–71 American humorist

A comfortable house is a great source of happiness. It ranks immediately after health and a good conscience.
Sydney Smith 1771–1845 English essayist

But every house where Love abides
And Friendship is a guest,
Is surely home, and home, sweet home,
For there the heart can rest.
Henry Van Dyke 1852–1933 American minister

Housework see also **Home**

Conran's Law of Housework—it expands to fill the time available plus half an hour.
Shirley Conran 1932– English writer

There was no need to do any housework at all. After the first four years the dirt doesn't get any worse.
Quentin Crisp 1908–99 English writer

Cleaning your house while your kids are still growing is like shovelling the walk before it stops snowing.
Phyllis Diller 1917–2012 American actress

Housework

'I hate discussions of feminism that end up with who does the dishes,' she said. So do I. But at the end, there are always the damned dishes.

Marilyn French 1929–2009 American writer

Dirt is only matter out of place.

John Chipman Gray 1839–1915 American lawyer

At the worst, a house unkempt cannot be so distressing as a life unlived.

Rose Macaulay 1881–1958 English novelist

The dust comes secretly day after day,
Lies on my ledge and dulls my shining things.
But O this dust that I shall drive away
Is flowers and Kings,
Is Solomon's temple, poets, Nineveh.

Viola Meynell 1886–1956 English writer

There is scarcely any less bother in the running of a family than in that of an entire state. And domestic business is no less importunate for being less important.

Montaigne 1533–92 French moralist

God walks among the pots and pans.

St Teresa of Ávila 1512–82 Spanish mystic

MR PRITCHARD: I must dust the blinds and then I must raise them.
MRS OGMORE-PRITCHARD: And before you let the sun in, mind it wipes its shoes.

Dylan Thomas 1914–53 Welsh poet

Hatred of domestic work is a natural and admirable result of civilization.

Rebecca West 1892–1983 English writer

The Human Race

We are born of risen apes, not fallen angels, and the apes were armed killers beside.

Robert Ardrey 1908–80 American dramatist

There's a man all over for you, blaming on his boots the faults of his feet.

Samuel Beckett 1906–89 Irish writer

We carry within us the wonders we seek without us: there is all Africa and her prodigies in us.

Sir Thomas Browne 1605–82 English writer

By nature men are alike. Through practice they have become far apart.

Confucius 551–479 BC Chinese philosopher

What is man, when you come to think upon him, but a minutely set, ingenious machine for turning, with infinite artfulness, the red wine of Shiraz into urine?

Isak Dinesen 1885–1962 Danish writer

Is man an ape or an angel? Now I am on the side of the angels.

Benjamin Disraeli 1804–81 British statesman

Man is a tool-making animal.

Benjamin Franklin 1706–90 American statesman and scientist

Man is the only animal that laughs and weeps; for he is the only animal that is struck with the difference between what things are and what they ought to be.

William Hazlitt 1778–1830 English essayist

The life of man is of no greater importance to the universe than that of an oyster.

David Hume 1711–76 Scottish philosopher

The Human Race

Out of the crooked timber of humanity no straight thing
can ever be made.
    Immanuel Kant 1724–1804 German philosopher

In the final analysis, our most basic common link is that
we all inhabit this small planet. We all breathe the same air.
We all cherish our children's future. And we are all mortal.
    John F. Kennedy 1917–63 American statesman

O mankind, We have created you
male and female, and appointed you
races and tribes, that you may know
one another.
    The Koran

To say, for example, that a man is made up of certain
chemical elements is a satisfactory description only for
those who intend to use him as a fertilizer.
    H. J. Muller 1890–1967 American geneticist

I teach you the superman. Man is something to be
surpassed.
    Friedrich Nietzsche 1844–1900 German philosopher

Man is only a reed, the weakest thing in nature; but he is a
thinking reed.
    Blaise Pascal 1623–62 French scientist and philosopher

Man is the measure of all things.
    Protagoras b. c.485 BC Greek sophist

The children of Adam are limbs to each other, having been
created of one essence.
    Sadi c.1213–c.91 Persian poet

How beauteous mankind is! O brave new world,
That has such people in't.
    William Shakespeare 1564–1616 English dramatist

What a piece of work is a man! How noble in reason! how infinite in faculty! in form, in moving, how express and admirable! in action how like an angel! in apprehension how like a god! the beauty of the world! the paragon of animals!

William Shakespeare 1564–1616 English dramatist

Man is the Only Animal that Blushes. Or needs to.

Mark Twain 1835–1910 American writer

We're all of us guinea pigs in the laboratory of God. Humanity is just a work in progress.

Tennessee Williams 1911–83 American dramatist

Human Rights

We hold these truths to be self-evident, that all men are created equal, that they are endowed by their Creator with certain unalienable rights, that among these are life, liberty and the pursuit of happiness.

American Declaration of Independence 1776

Liberté! Égalité! Fraternité!
Freedom! Equality! Brotherhood!

Anonymous, *motto of the French Revolution*

Men, their rights, and nothing more; women, their rights, and nothing less.

Susan Brownell Anthony 1820–1906 American feminist

Natural rights is simple nonsense: natural and imprescriptible rights, rhetorical nonsense—nonsense upon stilts.

Jeremy Bentham 1748–1832 English philosopher

No man can put a chain about the ankle of his fellow man without at last finding the other end fastened about his own neck.

Frederick Douglass c.1818–95 American former slave

Humour

The rights of man come not from the generosity of the state, but from the hand of God.
John F. Kennedy 1917–63 American statesman

To no man will we sell, or deny, or delay, right or justice.
Magna Carta 1215

The poorest he that is in England hath a life to live as the greatest he.
Thomas Rainborowe d. 1648 English soldier

We look forward to a world founded upon four essential human freedoms. The first is freedom of speech and expression—everywhere in the world. The second is freedom of every person to worship God in his own way—everywhere in the world. The third is freedom from want… The fourth is freedom from fear.
Franklin D. Roosevelt 1882–1945 American statesman

That little man…he says women can't have as much rights as men, cause Christ wasn't a woman. Where did your Christ come from? From God and a woman. Man had nothing to do with Him.
Sojourner Truth c.1797–1883 American evangelist

All human beings are born free and equal in dignity and rights.
Universal Declaration of Human Rights 1948

 # Humour see also **Wit**

Among those whom I like or admire, I can find no common denominator, but among those whom I love, I can: all of them make me laugh.
W. H. Auden 1907–73 English poet

For what do we live, but to make sport for our neighbours, and laugh at them in our turn?
Jane Austen 1775–1817 English novelist

I make myself laugh at everything, for fear of having to weep at it.
Pierre-Augustin Caron de Beaumarchais 1732–99 French dramatist

Comedy is tragedy plus time.
Carol Burnett 1936– American comedienne

Of all days, the one most surely wasted is the one on which one has not laughed.
Nicolas-Sébastien Chamfort 1741–94 French writer

A difference of taste in jokes is a great strain on the affections.
George Eliot 1819–80 English novelist

The funniest thing about comedy is that you never know why people laugh. I know *what* makes them laugh but trying to get your hands on the *why* of it is like trying to pick an eel out of a tub of water.
W. C. Fields 1880–1946 American humorist

What do you mean, funny? Funny-peculiar or funny ha-ha?
Ian Hay 1876–1952 Scottish writer

[A pun] is a pistol let off at the ear; not a feather to tickle the intellect.
Charles Lamb 1775–1834 English writer

Every joke is a tiny revolution.
George Orwell 1903–50 English novelist

Laughter is pleasant, but the exertion is too much for me.
Thomas Love Peacock 1785–1866 English writer

Hypocrisy

Everything is funny as long as it is happening to Somebody Else.
Will Rogers 1879–1935 American actor

Humour is emotional chaos remembered in tranquillity.
James Thurber 1894–1961 American humorist

Against the assault of laughter nothing can stand.
Mark Twain 1835–1910 American writer

We are not amused.
Queen Victoria 1819–1901 British monarch

It's hard to be funny when you have to be clean.
Mae West 1892–1980 American film actress

 # Hypocrisy

Ye are like unto whited sepulchres, which indeed appear beautiful outward, but are within full of dead men's bones, and of all uncleanness.
Bible

Compound for sins, they are inclined to,
By damning those they have no mind to.
Samuel Butler 1612–80 English poet

The smylere with the knyf under the cloke.
Geoffrey Chaucer c.1343–1400 English poet

Keep up appearances; there lies the test;
The world will give thee credit for the rest.
Outward be fair, however foul within;
Sin if thou wilt, but then in secret sin.
Charles Churchill 1731–64 English poet

Hypocrisy is a tribute which vice pays to virtue.
Duc de la Rochefoucauld 1613–80 French moralist

Hypocrisy, the only evil that walks
Invisible, except to God alone.
    John Milton 1608–74 English poet

       I want that glib and oily art
To speak and purpose not.
    William Shakespeare 1564–1616 English dramatist

All Reformers, however strict their social conscience, live in
houses just as big as they can pay for.
    Logan Pearsall Smith 1865–1946 American writer

I sit on a man's back, choking him and making him carry
me, and yet assure myself and others that I am very sorry
for him and wish to ease his lot by all possible means—
except by getting off his back.
    Leo Tolstoy 1828–1910 Russian novelist

Idealism

A cause may be inconvenient, but it's magnificent. It's like
champagne or high heels, and one must be prepared to
suffer for it.
    Arnold Bennett 1867–1931 English novelist

Where there is no vision, the people perish.
    Bible

Oh, the vision thing.
    George Bush 1924– American statesman, *responding to the
suggestion that he turn his attention from short-term campaign
objectives and look to the longer term*

There's only one corner of the universe you can be certain of
improving, and that's your own self.
    Aldous Huxley 1894–1963 English novelist

Ideas

Each time a man stands up for an ideal…he sends forth
a tiny ripple of hope, and…those ripples build a current
which can sweep down the mightiest walls of oppression
and resistance.

Robert Kennedy 1925-68 American politician

If a man hasn't discovered something he will die for, he isn't
fit to live.

Martin Luther King 1929-68 American civil rights leader

The first thing a man will do for his ideals is lie.

J. A. Schumpeter 1883-1950 American economist

We are all in the gutter, but some of us are looking at the
stars.

Oscar Wilde 1854-1900 Irish dramatist

I have spread my dreams under your feet;
Tread softly because you tread on my dreams.

W. B. Yeats 1865-1939 Irish poet

 # Ideas see also **Thinking**

There is one thing stronger than all the armies in the world;
and that is an idea whose time has come.

Anonymous

Probable impossibilities are to be preferred to improbable
possibilities.

Aristotle 384-322 BC Greek philosopher

It isn't that they can't see the solution. It is that they can't see
the problem.

G. K. Chesterton 1874-1936 English writer

The value of an idea lies in the using of it.

Thomas Alva Edison 1847-1931 American inventor

I think that only daring speculation can lead us further and not accumulation of facts.

Albert Einstein 1879–1955 German-born theoretical physicist

Every now and then a man's mind is stretched by a new idea or sensation, and never shrinks back to its former dimensions.

Oliver Wendell Holmes 1809–94 American physician

A stand can be made against invasion by an army; no stand can be made against invasion by an idea.

Victor Hugo 1802–85 French writer

He who receives an idea from me, receives instruction himself without lessening mine; as he who lights his taper at mine, receives light without darkening me.

Thomas Jefferson 1743–1826 American statesman

MICHAEL CAINE: Hang on a minute lads, I've got a great idea.

Troy Kennedy-Martin 1932–2009 British screenwriter, *in the film* The Italian Job

When you are a Bear of Very Little Brain, and you Think of Things, you find sometimes that a Thing which seemed very Thingish inside you is quite different when it gets out into the open and has other people looking at it.

A. A. Milne 1882–1956 English writer

You see things; and you say 'Why?' But I dream things that never were; and I say 'Why not?'

George Bernard Shaw 1856–1950 Irish dramatist

Ideas won't keep. Something must be done about them.

Alfred North Whitehead 1861–1947 English philosopher

Idleness

A man who has nothing to do with his own time has no conscience in his intrusion on that of others.
Jane Austen 1775–1817 English novelist

Go to the ant thou sluggard; consider her ways, and be wise.
Bible

The foul sluggard's comfort: 'It will last my time.'
Thomas Carlyle 1795–1881 Scottish historian

Idleness is only the refuge of weak minds.
Lord Chesterfield 1694–1773 English writer

It is better to wear out than to rust out.
Richard Cumberland 1631–1718 English divine

It is impossible to enjoy idling thoroughly unless one has plenty of work to do.
Jerome K. Jerome 1859–1927 English writer

I was raised to feel that doing nothing was a sin. I had to learn to do nothing.
Jenny Joseph 1932– English poet

Far from idleness being the root of evil, rather it is the true good.
Sören Kierkegaard 1813–55 Danish philosopher

Inactivity is death.
Benito Mussolini 1883–1945 Italian dictator

The time you enjoy wasting is not wasted time.
Laurence Peter 1919–90 Canadian writer, *commenting on a remark by Bertrand Russell*

For Satan finds some mischief still
For idle hands to do.
Isaac Watts 1674–1748 English hymn-writer

Procrastination is the thief of time.
Edward Young 1683–1765 English poet

Ignorance ✳

Ignorance is not innocence but sin.
Robert Browning 1812–89 English poet

Ignorance more frequently begets confidence than does knowledge: it is those who know little, and not those who know much, who so positively assert that this or that problem will never be solved by science.
Charles Darwin 1809–82 English naturalist

To be conscious that you are ignorant is a great step to knowledge.
Benjamin Disraeli 1804–81 British statesman

Whatever Nature has in store for mankind, unpleasant as it may be, men must accept, for ignorance is never better than knowledge.
Enrico Fermi 1901–54 Italian-born American physicist

> Where ignorance is bliss,
'Tis folly to be wise.
Thomas Gray 1716–71 English poet

Ignorance, madam, pure ignorance.
Samuel Johnson 1709–84 English lexicographer, *on being asked why he had defined* pastern *as the 'knee' of a horse*

You know everybody is ignorant, only on different subjects.
Will Rogers 1879–1935 American actor

Learn to say, 'I don't know'. If used when appropriate, it will be often.
Donald Rumsfeld 1932– American politician

Imagination

If one does not know to which port one is sailing, no wind is favourable.

Seneca ('the Younger') c.4 BC–AD 65 Roman philosopher

As any fule kno.

Geoffrey Willans 1911–58 and **Ronald Searle** 1920–2011
English writers

 # Imagination

Imagination is the highest kite that can fly.

Lauren Bacall 1924–2014 American actress

All fantasy should have a solid base in reality.

Max Beerbohm 1872–1956 English critic

To see a world in a grain of sand
And a heaven in a wild flower
Hold infinity in the palm of your hand
And eternity in an hour.

William Blake 1757–1827 English poet

Go, and catch a falling star,
Get with child a mandrake root,
Tell me, where all past years are,
Or who cleft the Devil's foot.
Teach me to hear mermaids singing.

John Donne 1572–1631 English poet

Where there is no imagination there is no horror.

Arthur Conan Doyle 1859–1930 Scottish-born writer

Imagination is more important than knowledge. Knowledge is limited. Imagination encircles the world.

Albert Einstein 1879–1955 German-born theoretical physicist

Were it not for imagination, Sir, a man would be as happy in the arms of a chambermaid as of a Duchess.

Samuel Johnson 1709–84 English lexicographer

Heard melodies are sweet, but those unheard
Are sweeter.
John Keats 1795–1821 English poet

Imagine there's no heaven
It's easy if you try.
John Lennon 1940–80 English pop singer

His imagination resembled the wings of an ostrich.
It enabled him to run, though not to soar.
Lord Macaulay 1800–59 English historian

Fantasy is like an exercise bicycle for the mind.
Terry Pratchett 1948–2015 English novelist

The lunatic, the lover, and the poet,
Are of imagination all compact.
William Shakespeare 1564–1616 English dramatist

Must then a Christ perish in torment in every age to save
those that have no imagination?
George Bernard Shaw 1856–1950 Irish dramatist

Whither is fled the visionary gleam?
Where is it now, the glory and the dream?
William Wordsworth 1770–1850 English poet

India

Nothing in India is identifiable, the mere asking of a
question causes it to disappear or to merge in something
else.
E. M. Forster 1879–1970 English novelist

The brightest jewel that now remained in his Majesty's
crown.
Charles James Fox 1749–1806 English politician, *on India*

Indifference

If there is a paradise on earth, it is this, it is this, it is this.

Amir Khusrau 1253–1325 Persian poet, *inscribed on the wall of the Diwan-i-Khas [the hall of special audience] in the Red Fort at Delhi*

India will go on.

R. K. Narayan 1906–2001 Indian novelist

At the stroke of the midnight hour, while the world sleeps, India will awake to life and freedom. A moment comes, which comes but rarely in history, when we step out from the old to the new, when an age ends, and when the soul of a nation, long suppressed, finds utterance.

Jawaharlal Nehru 1889–1964 Indian statesman

If there is one place on the face of the earth where all the dreams of living men have found a home from the very earliest days when man began the dream of existence, it is India.

Romain Rolland 1866–1944 French writer

Nothing has been left undone, either by man or Nature, to make India the most extraordinary country that the sun visits on his rounds.

Mark Twain 1835–1910 American writer

 # Indifference

All colours will agree in the dark.

Francis Bacon 1561–1626 English courtier

Because thou art lukewarm, and neither cold nor hot, I will spew thee out of my mouth.

Bible

Catholics and Communists have committed great crimes, but at least they have not stood aside, like an established society, and been indifferent. I would rather have blood on my hands than water like Pilate.

Graham Greene 1904–91 English novelist

Let them eat cake.

Marie-Antoinette 1755–93 French queen, *on being told that her people had no bread; the saying is of older origin*

I wish I could care what you do or where you go but I can't…My dear, I don't give a damn.

Margaret Mitchell 1900–49 American novelist, *'Frankly, my dear, I don't give a damn!' in Sidney Howard's screenplay for* Gone With the Wind

Vacant heart and hand, and eye,—
Easy live and quiet die.

Sir Walter Scott 1771–1832 Scottish novelist

It is the disease of not listening, the malady of not marking, that I am troubled withal.

William Shakespeare 1564–1616 English dramatist

The worst sin towards our fellow creatures is not to hate them, but to be indifferent to them: that's the essence of inhumanity.

George Bernard Shaw 1856–1950 Irish dramatist

I was much further out than you thought
And not waving but drowning.

Stevie Smith 1902–71 English poet

The opposite of love is not hate, it's indifference. The opposite of art is not ugliness, it's indifference. The opposite of faith is not heresy, it's indifference. And the opposite of life is not death, it's indifference.

Elie Wiesel 1928–2016 Romanian-born American writer

Individuality

Cast a cold eye
On life, on death.
Horseman pass by!
W. B. Yeats 1865–1939 Irish poet

 # Individuality

A dead thing can go with the stream, but only a living thing can go against it.
G. K. Chesterton 1874–1936 English writer

It is easier to live through someone else than to become complete yourself.
Betty Friedan 1921–2006 American feminist

In friendship or in love, the two side by side raise hands together to find what one cannot reach alone.
Kahlil Gibran 1883–1931 Lebanese-born American writer

I'm not alone, I'm free. I no longer have to be a credit, I don't have to be a symbol to anybody, I don't have to be a first to anybody. I don't have to be an imitation of a white woman that Hollywood sort of hoped I'd become. I'm me, and I'm like nobody else.
Lena Mary Calhoun Horne 1917–2010 American singer and actor

That so few now dare to be eccentric marks the chief danger of the time.
John Stuart Mill 1806–73 English philosopher

I am not an eccentric. It's just that I am more alive than most people. I am an unpopular electric eel in a pool of catfish.
Edith Sitwell 1887–1964 English poet

Most people are other people. Their thoughts are someone else's opinions, their lives a mimicry, their passions a quotation.

Oscar Wilde 1854–1900 Irish dramatist

Insight ✳

[See] things not as they are, but as they might be.

Felix Adler 1851–1933 American philosopher

If the doors of perception were cleansed everything would appear to man as it is, infinite.

William Blake 1757–1827 English poet

One sees great things from the valley; only small things from the peak.

G. K. Chesterton 1874–1936 English writer

If we had a keen vision and feeling of all ordinary human life, it would be like hearing the grass grow and the squirrel's heart beat, and we should die of that roar which lies on the other side of silence.

George Eliot 1819–80 English novelist

The crown of life is neither happiness nor annihilation; it is understanding.

Winifred Holtby 1898–1935 British novelist

Come to the edge.
We might fall.
Come to the edge.
It's too high!
COME TO THE EDGE!
And they came
and he pushed
and they flew…

Christopher Logue 1926–2011 English poet

Intelligence

To understand just one life, you have to swallow the world.
Salman Rushdie 1947– Indian-born British novelist

It is only with the heart that one can see rightly; what is
essential is invisible to the eye.
Antoine de Saint-Exupéry 1900–44 French novelist

Every man takes the limits of his own field of vision for the
limits of the world.
Arthur Schopenhauer 1788–1860 German philosopher

Tout comprendre rend très indulgent.

To be totally understanding makes one very indulgent.
Mme de Staël 1766–1817 French writer

Everything I have written seems like straw by comparison
with what I have seen and what has been revealed to me.
St Thomas Aquinas c.1225–74 Italian theologian, *following a
mystical experience, after which he did no more teaching or writing*

 # Intelligence

To the man-in-the-street, who, I'm sorry to say,
Is a keen observer of life,
The word 'Intellectual' suggests straight away
A man who's untrue to his wife.
W. H. Auden 1907–73 English poet

A man is not necessarily intelligent because he has plenty
of ideas, any more than he is a good general because he has
plenty of soldiers.
Nicolas-Sébastien Chamfort 1741–94 French writer

'Excellent,' I cried. 'Elementary,' said he.
Arthur Conan Doyle 1859–1930 Scottish-born writer,
commonly quoted as 'Elementary, my dear Watson'

As a human being, one has been endowed with just enough intelligence to be able to see clearly how utterly inadequate that intelligence is when confronted with what exists.

Albert Einstein 1879–1955 German-born theoretical physicist

The test of a first-rate intelligence is the ability to hold two opposed ideas in the mind at the same time, and still retain the ability to function.

F. Scott Fitzgerald 1896–1940 American novelist

So dumb he can't fart and chew gum at the same time.

Lyndon Baines Johnson 1908–73 American statesman, *of Gerald Ford*

Sir, I have found you an argument; but I am not obliged to find you an understanding.

Samuel Johnson 1709–84 English lexicographer

I think, therefore I am is the statement of an intellectual who underrates toothaches.

Milan Kundera 1929– Czech novelist

No one in this world, so far as I know—and I have searched the records for years, and employed agents to help me—has ever lost money by underestimating the intelligence of the great masses of the plain people.

H. L. Mencken 1880–1956 American journalist

You beat your pate, and fancy wit will come:
Knock as you please, there's nobody at home.

Alexander Pope 1688–1744 English poet

With stupidity the gods themselves struggle in vain.

Friedrich von Schiller 1759–1805 German poet

Rule no. 11: Be nice to nerds. Chances are you'll end up working for one.

Charles J. Sykes 1954– American writer, *often wrongly attributed to the American computer entrepreneur Bill Gates*

Invention and Discovery

When man wanted to make a machine that would walk he created the wheel, which does not resemble a leg.
Guillaume Apollinaire 1880–1918 French poet

Eureka!
I've got it!
Archimedes c.287–212 BC Greek mathematician

Printing, gunpowder, and the mariner's needle [compass]… these three have changed the whole face and state of things throughout the world.
Francis Bacon 1561–1626 English courtier

Through the unknown, we'll find the new.
Charles Baudelaire 1821–67 French poet

The discovery of a new dish does more for human happiness than the discovery of a star.
Anthelme Brillat-Savarin 1755–1826 French gourmet

LORD CARNARVON: Can you see anything?
CARTER: Yes, wonderful things.
Howard Carter 1874–1939 English archaeologist, *on first looking into the tomb of Tutankhamun*

Why sir, there is every possibility that you will soon be able to tax it!
Michael Faraday 1791–1867 English scientist, *to Gladstone, when asked about the usefulness of electricity*

What is the use of a new-born child?
Benjamin Franklin 1706–90 American statesman and scientist, *when asked what was the use of a new invention*

Invention and Discovery

SALVIATI: Now you see how easy it is to understand.
SAGREDO: So are all truths, once they are discovered.
Galileo Galilei 1564–1642 Italian astronomer, *often quoted as 'All truths are easy to understand, once they are discovered; the point is, to discover them'*

Then felt I like some watcher of the skies
When a new planet swims into his ken.
John Keats 1795–1821 English poet

Praise without end the go-ahead zeal
of whoever it was invented the wheel;
but never a word for the poor soul's sake
that thought ahead, and invented the brake.
Howard Nemerov 1920–91 American writer

I don't know what I may seem to the world, but as to myself,
I seem to have been only like a boy playing on the sea-shore
and diverting myself in now and then finding a smoother
pebble or a prettier shell than ordinary, whilst the great
ocean of truth lay all undiscovered before me.
Isaac Newton 1642–1727 English mathematician

I remembered the line from the Hindu scripture, the *Bhagavad Gita*…'I am become death, the destroyer of worlds.'
J. Robert Oppenheimer 1904–67 American physicist, *on the explosion of the first atomic bomb near Alamogordo, New Mexico*

If you wish to make an apple pie from scratch, you must
first invent the universe.
Carl Sagan 1934–96 American astronomer

Discovery consists of seeing what everybody has seen and
thinking what nobody has thought.
Albert von Szent-Györgyi 1893–1986 Hungarian-born biochemist

Name the greatest of all the inventors. Accident.
Mark Twain 1835–1910 American writer

Ireland

For the great Gaels of Ireland
Are the men that God made mad,
For all their wars are merry,
And all their songs are sad.
    G. K. Chesterton 1874–1936 English writer

Ulster will fight; Ulster will be right.
    Lord Randolph Churchill 1849–94 British politician

        The famous
Northern reticence, the tight gag of place
And times.
    Seamus Heaney 1939–2013 Irish poet

Ireland is the old sow that eats her farrow.
    James Joyce 1882–1941 Irish novelist

Ireland is a small but insuppressible island half an hour
nearer the sunset than Great Britain.
    Thomas Kettle 1880–1916 Irish economist

In Ireland the inevitable never happens and the unexpected
constantly occurs.
    John Pentland Mahaffy 1839–1919 Irish writer

Spenser's Ireland
has not altered;—
a place as kind as it is green,
the greenest place I've never seen.
    Marianne Moore 1887–1972 American poet

To be Irish is to know that in the end the world will break
your heart.
    Daniel P. Moynihan 1927–2003 American politician

Romantic Ireland's dead and gone,
It's with O'Leary in the grave.
W. B. Yeats 1865–1939 Irish poet

Jealousy see Envy

Journalism see also News

The Times has made many ministries.
Walter Bagehot 1826–77 English economist

I read the newspapers avidly. It is my one form of
continuous fiction.
Aneurin Bevan 1897–1960 British politician

When seagulls follow a trawler, it is because they think
sardines will be thrown into the sea.
Eric Cantona 1966–   French footballer, *at a press conference*

When the legend becomes fact, print the legend.
Willis Goldbeck and **James Warner Bellah** American
screenwriters, *in the film* The Man Who Shot Liberty Valance

You furnish the pictures and I'll furnish the war.
William Randolph Hearst 1863–1951 American newspaper
publisher, *message to the artist Frederic Remington in Havana,
Cuba, during the Spanish-American War of 1898*

Power without responsibility: the prerogative of the harlot
throughout the ages.
Rudyard Kipling 1865–1936 English writer, *summing up Lord
Beaverbrook's political standpoint* vis-à-vis *the* Daily Express

A good newspaper, I suppose, is a nation talking to itself.
Arthur Miller 1915–2005 American dramatist

Journalism

All the news that's fit to print.
Adolph S. Ochs 1858–1935 American publisher, *motto of the New York Times*

A cynical, mercenary, demagogic, corrupt press will produce in time a people as base as itself.
Joseph Pulitzer 1847–1911 Hungarian-born American editor

The men with the muck-rakes are often indispensable to the well-being of society; but only if they know when to stop raking the muck.
Theodore Roosevelt 1858–1919 American statesman

Comment is free, but facts are sacred.
C. P. Scott 1846–1932 British journalist

Ever noticed that no matter what happens in one day, it exactly fits in the newspaper?
Jerry Seinfeld 1954– American comedian

Comment is free but facts are on expenses.
Tom Stoppard 1937– British dramatist

We must try to find ways to starve the terrorist and the hijacker of the oxygen of publicity on which they depend.
Margaret Thatcher 1925–2013 British stateswoman

The report of my death was an exaggeration.
Mark Twain 1835–1910 American writer, *usually quoted as 'Reports of my death have been greatly exaggerated'*

Journalism—an ability to meet the challenge of filling the space.
Rebecca West 1892–1983 English writer

Rock journalism is people who can't write interviewing people who can't talk for people who can't read.
Frank Zappa 1940–93 American rock musician

Justice see also **Law**

Jedem das Seine.
To each his own.
> **Anonymous**, *inscription on the gate of Buchenwald concentration camp; often quoted as 'Everyone gets what he deserves'*

Audi partem alteram.
Hear the other side.
> **St Augustine of Hippo** AD 354–430 Roman theologian

Publicity is the very soul of justice. It is the keenest spur to exertion, and the surest of all guards against improbity.
> **Jeremy Bentham** 1748–1832 English philosopher

Life for life,
Eye for eye, tooth for tooth.
> **Bible**

It is better that ten guilty persons escape than one innocent suffer.
> **William Blackstone** 1723–80 English jurist

When I hear of an 'equity' in a case like this, I am reminded of a blind man in a dark room—looking for a black hat—which isn't there.
> **Lord Bowen** 1835–94 English judge

No! No! Sentence first—verdict afterwards.
> **Lewis Carroll** 1832–98 English writer

Justice is truth in action.
> **Benjamin Disraeli** 1804–81 British statesman

All sensible people are selfish, and nature is tugging at every contract to make the terms of it fair.
> **Ralph Waldo Emerson** 1803–82 American writer

Justice

Fiat justitia et pereat mundus.
Let justice be done, though the world perish.
Ferdinand I 1503–64 Holy Roman emperor

Justice should not only be done, but should manifestly and undoubtedly be seen to be done.
Lord Hewart 1870–1943 British lawyer

Injustice anywhere is a threat to justice everywhere.
Martin Luther King 1929–68 American civil rights leader

I have always found that mercy bears richer fruits than strict justice.
Abraham Lincoln 1809–65 American statesman

In England, justice is open to all—like the Ritz Hotel.
James Mathew 1830–1908 Irish judge

Here [Paris] they hang a man first, and try him afterwards.
Molière 1622–73 French comic dramatist

The quality of mercy is not strained,
It droppeth as the gentle rain from heaven
Upon the place beneath: it is twice blessed;
It blesseth him that gives and him that takes.
William Shakespeare 1564–1616 English dramatist

Thrice is he armed that hath his quarrel just.
William Shakespeare 1564–1616 English dramatist

Two wrongs don't make a right, but they make a good excuse.
Thomas Szasz 1920–2012 Hungarian-born psychiatrist

It is justice, not charity, that is wanting in the world.
Mary Wollstonecraft 1759–97 English feminist

Kissing

A kiss is a lovely trick designed by nature to stop speech
when words become superfluous.
> **Ingrid Bergman** 1915–82 Swedish actress

It's like kissing Hitler.
> **Tony Curtis** 1925–2010 American actor, *when asked what it was
> like to kiss Marilyn Monroe*

A fine romance with no kisses.
A fine romance, my friend, this is.
> **Dorothy Fields** 1905–74 American songwriter

To let a fool kiss you is stupid,
To let a kiss fool you is worse.
> **E. Y. ('Yip') Harburg** 1898–1981 American songwriter

Where do the noses go? I always wondered where the noses
would go.
> **Ernest Hemingway** 1899–1961 American novelist

You must remember this, a kiss is still a kiss,
A sigh is just a sigh;
The fundamental things apply,
As time goes by.
> **Herman Hupfeld** 1894–1951 American songwriter

A kiss can be a comma, a question mark or an exclamation
point. That's basic spelling that every woman ought to know.
> **Mistinguett** 1875–1956 French actress

O Love, O fire! once he drew
With one long kiss my whole soul through
My lips, as sunlight drinketh dew.
> **Alfred, Lord Tennyson** 1809–92 English poet

Knowledge

 # Knowledge see also **Facts**, **Wisdom**

Everyman, I will go with thee, and be thy guide,
In thy most need to go by thy side.
> **Anonymous**, Everyman (c.*1509–19*) *spoken by Knowledge*

The fox knows many things—the hedgehog one *big* one.
> **Archilochus** Greek poet of the 7th century BC

All men by nature desire knowledge.
> **Aristotle** 384–322 BC Greek philosopher

For also knowledge itself is power.
> **Francis Bacon** 1561–1626 English courtier

For now we see through a glass, darkly; but then face to
face: now I know in part; but then shall I know even as also
I am known.
> **Bible**

It is better to know nothing than to know what ain't so.
> **Josh Billings** 1818–85 American humorist

The place to observe nature is where you are: the walk to
take to-day is the walk you took yesterday. You will not find
just the same things.
> **John Burroughs** 1837–1921 American naturalist, *often quoted as
'To learn something new, take the path that you took yesterday'*

An expert is one who knows more and more about less and
less.
> **Nicholas Murray Butler** 1862–1947 American philosopher

Knowledge may give weight, but accomplishments give
lustre, and many more people see than weigh.
> **Lord Chesterfield** 1694–1773 English writer

Knowledge

There is no such thing on earth as an uninteresting subject;
the only thing that can exist is an uninterested person.
G. K. Chesterton 1874–1936 English writer

Where is the wisdom we have lost in knowledge?
Where is the knowledge we have lost in information?
T. S. Eliot 1888–1965 American-born British poet

Knowledge is of two kinds. We know a subject ourselves,
or we know where we can find information upon it.
Samuel Johnson 1709–84 English lexicographer

All wish to possess knowledge, but no one is willing to pay
the price.
Juvenal c.AD 60–c.140 Roman satirist

Dare to know! Have the courage to use your own reason!
This is the motto of the Enlightenment.
Immanuel Kant 1724–1804 German philosopher

The motto of all the mongoose family is, 'Run and find out.'
Rudyard Kipling 1865–1936 English writer

We have learned the answers, all the answers:
It is the question that we do not know.
Archibald MacLeish 1892–1982 American poet

Que sais-je?
What do I know?
Montaigne 1533–92 French moralist

Satisfaction of one's curiosity is one of the greatest sources
of happiness in life.
Linus Pauling 1901– 94 American chemist

A little learning is a dangerous thing;
Drink deep, or taste not the Pierian spring.
Alexander Pope 1688–1744 English poet

Knowledge

Knowledge without conscience is but the ruin of the soul.
François Rabelais c.1494–c.1553 French humanist

There are known knowns; there are things we know we know. We also know there are known unknowns; that is to say we know there are some things we do not know. But there are also unknown unknowns—the ones we don't know we don't know.
Donald Rumsfeld 1932– American politician

The larger the island of knowledge, the longer the shoreline of wonder.
Ralph W. Sockman 1889–1970 American clergyman

I know nothing except the fact of my ignorance.
Socrates 469–399 BC Greek philosopher

Everybody gets so much information all day long that they lose their common sense.
Gertrude Stein 1874–1946 American writer

Knowledge is good. It does not have to look good or sound good or even do good. It is good just by being knowledge. And the only thing that makes it knowledge is that it is true. You can't have too much of it and there is no little too little to be worth having.
Tom Stoppard 1937– British dramatist

UMA THURMAN: That was a little bit more information than I needed to know.
Quentin Tarantino 1963– American film director, *in the film* Pulp Fiction

All the business of war, and indeed all the business of life, is to endeavour to find out what you don't know by what you do; that's what I called 'guessing what was at the other side of the hill'.
Duke of Wellington 1769–1852 British general

Language see also **Meaning**, **Words**

One picture is worth ten thousand words.
Frederick R. Barnard

A word fitly spoken is like apples of gold in pictures of silver.
Bible

A definition is the enclosing a wilderness of idea within a wall of words.
Samuel Butler 1835–1902 English novelist

Take care of the sense, and the sounds will take care of themselves.
Lewis Carroll 1832–98 English writer

Colourless green ideas sleep furiously.
Noam Chomsky 1928– American linguist, *illustrating that grammatical structure is independent of meaning*

This is the sort of English up with which I will not put.
Winston Churchill 1874–1965 British statesman, *on prepositions*

He who understands baboon would do more towards metaphysics than Locke.
Charles Darwin 1809–82 English naturalist

Language is fossil poetry.
Ralph Waldo Emerson 1803–82 American writer

My pedantry is your scholarship, his reasonable accuracy, her irreducible minimum of education, and someone else's ignorance.
H. W. Fowler 1858–1933 English lexicographer

Language

Merely corroborative detail, intended to give artistic verisimilitude to an otherwise bald and unconvincing narrative.

W. S. Gilbert 1836–1911 English writer

The only person entitled to use the imperial 'we' in speaking of himself is a king, an editor, and a man with a tapeworm.

Robert G. Ingersoll 1833–99 American agnostic

Language is the dress of thought.

Samuel Johnson 1709–84 English lexicographer

The mystery of language was revealed to me. I knew then that 'w-a-t-e-r' meant the wonderful cool something that was flowing over my hand. That living word awakened my soul, gave it light, joy, set it free!

Helen Keller 1880–1968 American writer

All that is not prose is verse; and all that is not verse is prose.

Molière 1622–73 French comic dramatist

Good heavens! For more than forty years I have been speaking prose without knowing it.

Molière 1622–73 French comic dramatist

Slang is a language that rolls up its sleeves, spits on its hands and goes to work.

Carl Sandburg 1878–1967 American poet

You taught me language; and my profit on't
Is, I know how to curse.

William Shakespeare 1564–1616 English dramatist

A language is a dialect with an army and a navy.

Max Weinreich 1894–1969 American Yiddish scholar

The limits of my language mean the limits of my world.

Ludwig Wittgenstein 1889–1951 Austrian-born philosopher

Languages

The inherited and permanent fact that North America speaks English.
> **Otto von Bismarck** 1815-98 German statesman, *when asked what was the greatest political fact of modern times*

If I'm selling to you, I speak your language; if I'm buying *dann mussen Sie Deutsch sprechen* [then you must speak German].
> **Willy Brandt** 1913-92 German statesman

To God I speak Spanish, to women Italian, to men French, and to my horse—German.
> **Charles V** 1500-58 Holy Roman emperor

I like to be beholden to the great metropolitan English speech, the sea which receives tributaries from every region under heaven.
> **Ralph Waldo Emerson** 1803-82 American writer

My English text is chaste, and all licentious passages are left in the obscurity of a learned language.
> **Edward Gibbon** 1737-94 English historian, *parodied as 'decent obscurity' in the* Anti-Jacobin

He who does not know foreign languages knows nothing of his own.
> **Johann Wolfgang von Goethe** 1749-1832 German writer

I am always sorry when any language is lost, because languages are the pedigree of nations.
> **Samuel Johnson** 1709-84 English lexicographer

What is not clear is not French.
> **Antoine de Rivarol** 1753-1801 French man of letters

The Law

It is impossible for an Englishman to open his mouth without making some other Englishman hate or despise him.
George Bernard Shaw 1856–1950 Irish dramatist

England and America are two countries divided by a common language.
George Bernard Shaw 1856–1950 Irish dramatist

The English language is nobody's special property. It is the property of the imagination: it is the property of the language itself.
Derek Walcott 1930–2017 West Indian writer

 The Law see also **Crime**, **Justice**

Written laws are like spider's webs; they will catch, it is true, the weak and poor, but would be torn in pieces by the rich and powerful.
Anacharsis Scythian prince of the 6th century BC

Law is a bottomless pit.
Dr Arbuthnot 1667–1735 Scottish physician

Bad laws are the worst sort of tyranny.
Edmund Burke 1729–97 Irish-born politician

The good of the people is the chief law.
Cicero 106–43 BC Roman statesman

Cui bono?
To whose profit?
Cicero 106–43 BC Roman statesman

If the law supposes that…the law is a ass—a idiot.
Charles Dickens 1812–70 English novelist

'You must not tell us what the soldier, or any other man, said, sir,' interposed the judge; 'it's not evidence.'
Charles Dickens 1812–70 English novelist

Be you never so high, the law is above you.
Thomas Fuller 1654–1734 English physician

No poet ever interpreted nature as freely as a lawyer interprets the truth.
Jean Giraudoux 1882–1944 French dramatist

Laws grind the poor, and rich men rule the law.
Oliver Goldsmith 1728–74 Irish writer

A verbal contract isn't worth the paper it is written on.
Sam Goldwyn 1882–1974 American film producer

I know no method to secure the repeal of bad or obnoxious laws so effective as their stringent execution.
Ulysses S. Grant 1822–85 American statesman

English law does not permit good persons, as such, to strangle bad persons, as such.
T. H. Huxley 1825–95 English biologist

The more laws and orders are made prominent,
The more thieves and bandits there will be.
Lao Tzu c.604–c.531 BC Chinese philosopher

I don't know as I want a lawyer to tell me what I cannot do. I hire him to tell me how to do what I want to do.
John Pierpont Morgan 1837–1913 American financier

Laws were made to be broken.
Christopher North 1785–1854 Scottish critic

A lawyer with his briefcase can steal more than a hundred men with guns.
Mario Puzo 1920–99 American novelist

Leadership

Ignorance of the law excuses no man; not that all men know the law, but because 'tis an excuse every man will plead, and no man can tell how to confute him.
John Selden 1584–1654 English historian

The first thing we do, let's kill all the lawyers.
William Shakespeare 1564–1616 English dramatist

The big print giveth, and the fine print taketh away.
Fulton J. Sheen 1895–1979 American bishop

Everything not forbidden is compulsory.
T. H. White 1906–64 English novelist

Asking the ignorant to use the incomprehensible to decide the unknowable.
Hiller B. Zobel 1932– American judge, *on the jury system*

 # Leadership

By the structure of the world we often want, at the sudden occurrence of a grave tempest, to change the helmsman—to replace the pilot of the calm by the pilot of the storm.
Walter Bagehot 1826–77 English economist

If the blind lead the blind, both shall fall into the ditch.
Bible

The art of leadership is saying no, not yes. It is very easy to say yes.
Tony Blair 1953– British statesman

If you desire what is good, the people will be good. The character of a ruler is like wind and that of the people is like grass. In whatever direction the wind blows the grass always bends.
Confucius 551–479 BC Chinese philosopher

Leadership

The art of leadership…consists in consolidating the attention of the people against a single adversary and taking care that nothing will split up that attention.
Adolf Hitler 1889–1945 German dictator

Ultimately a genuine leader is not a searcher for consensus, but a moulder of consensus.
Martin Luther King 1929–68 American civil rights leader

A leader is best when people barely know he exists…He acts without unnecessary speech, and when the work is done the people say 'We did it ourselves'.
Lao Tzu c.604–c.531 BC Chinese philosopher

The final test of a leader is that he leaves behind him in other men the conviction and the will to carry on.
Walter Lippmann 1889–1974 American journalist

The first method for estimating the intelligence of a ruler is to look at the men he has around him.
Niccolò Machiavelli 1469–1527 Italian political philosopher

A leader who doesn't hesitate before he sends his nation into battle is not fit to be a leader.
Golda Meir 1898–1978 Israeli stateswoman

I don't mind how much my Ministers talk, so long as they do what I say.
Margaret Thatcher 1925–2013 British stateswoman

The buck stops here.
Harry S. Truman 1884–1972 American statesman

You can't lead the people if you don't love the people, and you can't save the people if you won't serve the people.
Cornel West 1953– American academic

Leisure

We are closer to the ants than to the butterflies. Very few people can endure much leisure.
   Gerald Brenan 1894–1987 British writer

There's sand in the porridge and sand in the bed,
And if this is pleasure we'd rather be dead.
   Noël Coward 1899–1973 English dramatist

What is this life if, full of care,
We have no time to stand and stare.
   W. H. Davies 1871–1940 Welsh poet

Man is so made that he can only find relaxation from one kind of labour by taking up another.
   Anatole France 1844–1924 French man of letters

Take rest; a field that has rested gives a bountiful crop.
   Ovid 43 BC–C.AD 17 Roman poet

To be able to fill leisure intelligently is the last product of civilization.
   Bertrand Russell 1872–1970 British philosopher

If all the year were playing holidays,
To sport would be as tedious as to work;
But when they seldom come, they wished for come.
   William Shakespeare 1564–1616 English dramatist

Repose is a good thing, but boredom is its brother.
   Voltaire 1694–1778 French writer

We're all going on a summer holiday,
No more worries for a week or two.
   Bruce Welch 1941– and **Brian Bennett** 1940– English musicians

The world is too much with us; late and soon,
Getting and spending, we lay waste our powers.
   William Wordsworth 1770–1850 English poet

Letters

Letters of thanks, letters from banks,
Letters of joy from girl and boy.
   W. H. Auden 1907–73 English poet

She'll vish there wos more, and that's the great art o' letter
writin'.
   Charles Dickens 1812–70 English novelist

Sir, more than kisses, letters mingle souls.
   John Donne 1572–1631 English poet

It is wonderful how much news there is when people write
every other day; if they wait for a month, there is nothing
that seems worth telling.
   O. Douglas 1877–1948 Scottish writer

All letters, methinks, should be free and easy as one's
discourse, not studied as an oration, nor made up of hard
words like a charm.
   Dorothy Osborne 1627–95

Don't think that this is a letter. It is only a small eruption of
a disease called friendship.
   Jean Renoir 1894–1979 French film director

A woman seldom writes her mind but in her postscript.
   Richard Steele 1672–1729 Irish-born essayist

The humane art which owes its origin to the love of friends.
   Virginia Woolf 1882–1941 English novelist, *on letter-writing*

Liberty

Liberty is always unfinished business.
> **Anonymous**

Real freedom is freedom from fear, and unless you can live free from fear you cannot live a dignified human life.
> **Aung San Suu Kyi** 1945– Burmese political leader

Liberty is liberty, not equality or fairness or justice or human happiness or a quiet conscience.
> **Isaiah Berlin** 1909–97 British philosopher

The people never give up their liberties except under some delusion.
> **Edmund Burke** 1729–97 Irish-born politician

The condition upon which God hath given liberty to man is eternal vigilance.
> **John Philpot Curran** 1750–1817 Irish judge

The cost of liberty is less than the price of repression.
> **W. E. B. Du Bois** 1868–1963 American political activist

I know not what course others may take; but as for me, give me liberty, or give me death!
> **Patrick Henry** 1736–99 American statesman

It is better to die on your feet than to live on your knees.
> **Dolores Ibarruri** 1895–1989 Spanish communist leader

The enemies of Freedom do not argue; they shout and they shoot.
> **Dean Inge** 1860–1954 English writer

We shall pay any price, bear any burden, meet any hardship, support any friend, oppose any foe to assure the survival and the success of liberty.
> **John F. Kennedy** 1917–63 American statesman

Liberty is precious—so precious that it must be rationed.
Lenin 1870–1924 Russian revolutionary

Stone walls do not a prison make,
Nor iron bars a cage.
Richard Lovelace 1618–58 English poet

Freedom is always and exclusively freedom for the one who thinks differently.
Rosa Luxemburg 1871–1919 German revolutionary

If men are to wait for liberty till they become wise and good in slavery, they may indeed wait for ever.
Lord Macaulay 1800–59 English historian

The liberty of the individual must be thus far limited;
he must not make himself a nuisance to other people.
John Stuart Mill 1806–73 English philosopher

Freedom is the freedom to say that two plus two make four.
If that is granted, all else follows.
George Orwell 1903–50 English novelist

O liberty! what crimes are committed in thy name!
Mme Roland 1754–93 French revolutionary

Man was born free, and everywhere he is in chains.
Jean-Jacques Rousseau 1712–78 French philosopher

What is freedom of expression? Without the freedom to offend, it ceases to exist.
Salman Rushdie 1947–   Indian-born British novelist

Liberty means responsibility. That is why most men dread it.
George Bernard Shaw 1856–1950 Irish dramatist

A free society is a society where it is safe to be unpopular.
Adlai Stevenson 1900–65 American politician

Libraries see also **Books**, **Reading**

I have always imagined Paradise as a kind of library.
Jorge Luis Borges 1899–1986 Argentinian writer

The true University of these days is a collection of books.
Thomas Carlyle 1795–1881 Scottish historian

A man should keep his little brain attic stocked with all the furniture that he is likely to use, and the rest he can put away in the lumber room of his library, where he can get it if he wants it.
Arthur Conan Doyle 1859–1930 Scottish-born writer

No place affords a more striking conviction of the vanity of human hopes, than a public library.
Samuel Johnson 1709–84 English lexicographer

Your *borrowers of books*—those mutilators of collections, spoilers of the symmetry of shelves, and creators of odd volumes.
Charles Lamb 1775–1834 English writer

A library is thought in cold storage.
Lord Samuel 1870–1963 British politician

Come, and take choice of all my library,
And so beguile thy sorrow.
William Shakespeare 1564–1616 English dramatist

 # Lies see also **Deceit**, **Truth**

An abomination unto the Lord, but a very present help in time of trouble.
Anonymous, *definition of a lie, an amalgamation of two biblical verses*

Truth, like light, blinds. Falsehood, on the contrary, is a beautiful twilight, that enhances every object.
Albert Camus 1913–60 French writer

Great is the power of steady misrepresentation.
Charles Darwin 1809–82 English naturalist

There are three kinds of lies: lies, damned lies and statistics.
Benjamin Disraeli 1804–81 British statesman

Without lies humanity would perish of despair and boredom.
Anatole France 1844–1924 French man of letters

In human relations kindness and lies are worth a thousand truths.
Graham Greene 1904–91 English novelist

Whoever would lie usefully should lie seldom.
Lord Hervey 1696–1743 English politician

The broad mass of a nation…will more easily fall victim to a big lie than to a small one.
Adolf Hitler 1889–1945 German dictator

There is no worse lie than a truth misunderstood by those who hear it.
William James 1842–1910 American philosopher

He would, wouldn't he?
Mandy Rice-Davies 1944–2014 English model, *on hearing that Lord Astor denied her allegations*

It is well said in the old proverb, 'a lie will go round the world while truth is pulling its boots on'.
C. H. Spurgeon 1834–92 English preacher

The cruellest lies are often told in silence.
Robert Louis Stevenson 1850–94 Scottish novelist

Life

One of the most striking differences between a cat and a lie is that a cat has only nine lives.
Mark Twain 1835–1910 American writer

 Life see also **Life Sciences**, **Lifestyles**

The Answer to the Great Question Of…Life, the Universe and Everything…[is] Forty-two.
Douglas Adams 1952–2001 English writer

'Such,' he said, 'O King, seems to me the present life of men on earth, in comparison with that time which to us is uncertain, as if when on a winter's night you sit feasting with your ealdormen and thegns,—a single sparrow should fly swiftly into the hall, and coming in at one door, instantly fly out through another'.
The Venerable Bede AD 673–735 English historian

Man that is born of a woman is of few days, and full of trouble.
Bible

All that a man hath will he give for his life.
Bible

Life is just a bowl of cherries.
Lew Brown 1893–1958 American songwriter

Life is a tragedy when seen in close-up, but a comedy in long-shot.
Charlie Chaplin 1889–1977 English film actor

W. C. FIELDS: It's a funny old world—a man's lucky if he gets out of it alive.
Walter de Leon and **Paul M. Jones** American screenwriters, *in the film* You're Telling Me

All that matters is love and work.
Sigmund Freud 1856–1939 Austrian psychoanalyst

No arts; no letters; no society; and which is worst of all, continual fear and danger of violent death; and the life of man, solitary, poor, nasty, brutish, and short.
Thomas Hobbes 1588–1679 English philosopher

Life is just one damned thing after another.
Elbert Hubbard 1859–1915 American writer

As far as we can discern, the sole purpose of human existence is to kindle a light in the darkness of mere being.
Carl Gustav Jung 1875–1961 Swiss psychologist

Life is either a daring adventure or nothing.
Helen Keller 1880–1968 American writer

Life must be understood backwards; but…it must be lived forwards.
Sören Kierkegaard 1813–55 Danish philosopher

Life is first boredom, then fear.
Philip Larkin 1922–85 English poet

Life is like a sewer. What you get out of it depends on what you put into it.
Tom Lehrer 1928–   American humorist

Life is just what happens to you,
while you're busy making other plans.
John Lennon 1940–80 English pop singer

Life well spent is long.
Leonardo da Vinci 1452–1519 Italian painter

Life is real! Life is earnest!
And the grave is not its goal;

Life

Dust thou art, to dust returnest,
Was not spoken of the soul.
Henry Wadsworth Longfellow 1807–82 American poet

What, knocked a tooth out? Never mind, dear, laugh it off,
laugh it off; it's all part of life's rich pageant.
Arthur Marshall 1910–89 British journalist

We live, not as we wish to, but as we can.
Menander 342–c.292 BC Greek comic dramatist

I've looked at life from both sides now,
From win and lose and still somehow
It's life's illusions I recall;
I really don't know life at all.
Joni Mitchell 1945– Canadian singer

Man is born to live, not to prepare for life.
Boris Pasternak 1890–1960 Russian novelist

Real life is elsewhere.
Arthur Rimbaud 1854–91 French poet

TOM HANKS: My momma always said life was like a box of
chocolates…you never know what you're gonna get.
Eric Roth 1945– American screenwriter, *in the film* Forrest
Gump

All the world's a stage,
And all the men and women merely players:
They have their exits and their entrances;
And one man in his time plays many parts,
His acts being seven ages.
William Shakespeare 1564–1616 English dramatist

Life is not meant to be easy, my child; but take courage:
it can be delightful.
George Bernard Shaw 1856–1950 Irish dramatist

Not to be born is, past all prizing, best.
Sophocles c.496–406 BC Greek dramatist

The same stream of life that runs through my veins night and day runs through the world and dances in rhythmic measures.

It is the same life that shoots in joy through the dust of the earth into numberless blades of grass and breaks into tumultuous waves of leaves and flowers.
Rabindranath Tagore 1861–1941 Bengali poet

Our life is frittered away by detail…Simplify, simplify.
Henry David Thoreau 1817–62 American writer

Expect nothing. Live frugally
on surprise.
Alice Walker 1944–   American poet

This world is a comedy to those that think, a tragedy to those that feel.
Horace Walpole 1717–97 English connoisseur

Never to have lived is best, ancient writers say;
Never to have drawn the breath of life, never to have looked
into the eye of day;
The second best's a gay goodnight and quickly turn away.
W. B. Yeats 1865–1939 Irish poet

Life Sciences see also **Science**

The Microbe is so very small
You cannot make him out at all.
Hilaire Belloc 1870–1953 British writer

Men will not be content to manufacture life: they will want to improve on it.
J. D. Bernal 1901–71 Irish-born physicist

Life Sciences

It has, I believe, been often remarked that a hen is only an egg's way of making another egg.

Samuel Butler 1835–1902 English novelist

We have discovered the secret of life!

Francis Crick 1916–2004 English biophysicist, *on the discovery of the structure of DNA*

Almost all aspects of life are engineered at the molecular level, and without understanding molecules we can only have a very sketchy understanding of life itself.

Francis Crick 1916–2004 English biophysicist

I have called this principle, by which each slight variation, if useful, is preserved, by the term of Natural Selection.

Charles Darwin 1809–82 English naturalist

From so simple a beginning endless forms most beautiful and most wonderful have been, and are being, evolved.

Charles Darwin 1809–82 English naturalist

I'd lay down my life for two brothers or eight cousins.

J. B. S. Haldane 1892–1964 Scottish mathematical biologist

Life exists in the universe only because the carbon atom possesses certain exceptional properties.

James Jeans 1877–1946 Scottish astronomer

The biologist passes, the frog remains.

Jean Rostand 1894–1977 French biologist, *sometimes quoted as 'Theories pass. The frog remains'*

So, naturalists observe, a flea
Hath smaller fleas that on him prey;
And these have smaller fleas to bite 'em,
And so proceed *ad infinitum*.

Jonathan Swift 1667–1745 Irish poet and satirist

Water is life's *mater* and *matrix*, mother and medium. There is no life without water.

Albert von Szent-Györgyi 1893–1986 Hungarian-born biochemist

Biology is the search for the chemistry that works.

R. J. P. Williams 1926–2015 British chemist

Lifestyles see also **Life**

What is the secret of my long life? I really don't know—cigarettes, whisky and wild, wild women!

Henry Allingham 1896–2009, *the oldest British survivor of the First World War*

I've lived a life that's full, I've travelled each and ev'ry highway
And more, much more than this. I did it my way.

Paul Anka 1941–   Canadian singer

Love and do what you will.

St Augustine of Hippo AD 354–430 Roman theologian

A man hath no better thing under the sun, than to eat, and to drink, and to be merry.

Bible

Thou shalt love thy neighbour as thyself.

Bible

The hippies wanted peace and love. We wanted Ferraris, blondes and switchblades.

Alice Cooper 1948–   American rock singer

Dream as if you'll live forever. Live as if you'll die today.

James Dean 1931–55 American actor

Lifestyles

Live in the sunshine, swim the sea,
Drink the wild air's salubrity.
Ralph Waldo Emerson 1803–82 American writer

RUSSELL CROWE: What we do in life echoes in eternity.
David Franzoni 1947– American screenwriter, *in the film*
Gladiator

Just trust yourself and you'll learn the art of living.
Johann Wolfgang von Goethe 1749–1832 German writer

If I had but two loaves of bread I would sell one of them,
and buy White Hyacinths to feed my soul.
Elbert Hubbard 1859–1915 American writer

Live all you can; it's a mistake not to. It doesn't so much
matter what you do in particular, so long as you have your
life. If you haven't had that, what *have* you had?
Henry James 1843–1916 American novelist

Your time is limited, so don't waste it living someone else's
life…Stay hungry. Stay foolish.
Steve Jobs 1955–2011 American computer executive

Turn on, tune in and drop out.
Timothy Leary 1920–96 American psychologist

Believe me! The secret of reaping the greatest fruitfulness
and the greatest enjoyment from life is *to live dangerously*!
Friedrich Nietzsche 1844–1900 German philosopher

To live at all is miracle enough.
Mervyn Peake 1911–68 British novelist

Fais ce que voudras.
Do what you like.
François Rabelais c.1494–c.1553 French humanist

You only live once, and the way I live, once is enough.
Frank Sinatra 1915–98 American singer and actor

Take short views, hope for the best, and trust in God.
Sydney Smith 1771–1845 English essayist

Keep your eyes open and your mouth shut.
John Steinbeck 1902–68 American novelist

It's better to burn out
Than to fade away.
Neil Young 1945– Canadian singer

Literature see also **Writing**

A losing trade, I assure you, sir: literature is a drug.
George Borrow 1803–81 English writer

All tragedies are finished by a death,
All comedies are ended by a marriage;
The future states of both are left to faith.
Lord Byron 1788–1824 English poet

Literature is a luxury; fiction is a necessity.
G. K. Chesterton 1874–1936 English writer

The greatest masterpiece in literature is only a dictionary out of order.
Jean Cocteau 1889–1963 French film director

Yes—oh dear yes—the novel tells a story.
E. M. Forster 1879–1970 English novelist

Works of serious purpose and grand promises often have a purple patch or two stitched on, to shine far and wide.
Horace 65–8 BC Roman poet

It takes a great deal of history to produce a little literature.
Henry James 1843–1916 American novelist

London

Never trust the artist. Trust the tale.
D. H. Lawrence 1885–1930 English writer

Literature is news that STAYS news.
Ezra Pound 1885–1972 American poet

'Thou shalt not' might reach the head, but it takes 'Once upon a time' to reach the heart.
Philip Pullman 1946– English writer

Remarks are not literature.
Gertrude Stein 1874–1946 American writer

A novel is a mirror which passes over a highway. Sometimes it reflects to your eyes the blue of the skies, at others the churned-up mud of the road.
Stendhal 1783–1842 French novelist

The good ended happily, and the bad unhappily. That is what fiction means.
Oscar Wilde 1854–1900 Irish dramatist

 # London

Was für Plunder!
What rubbish!
Gebhard Lebrecht Blücher 1742–1819 Prussian field marshal,
often misquoted as 'Was für plündern [*What a place to plunder*]!'

The great wen of all.
William Cobbett 1762–1835 English political reformer

Crowds without company, and dissipation without pleasure.
Edward Gibbon 1737–94 English historian

Maybe it's because I'm a Londoner
That I love London so.
Hubert Gregg 1914–2004 English songwriter

When a man is tired of London, he is tired of life.
Samuel Johnson 1709–84 English lexicographer

I thought of London spread out in the sun,
Its postal districts packed like squares of wheat.
Philip Larkin 1922–85 English poet

Earth has not anything to show more fair:
Dull would he be of soul who could pass by
A sight so touching in its majesty.
William Wordsworth 1770–1850 English poet

Love see also **Lovers, Marriage, Sex**

Love is, above all, the gift of oneself!
Jean Anouilh 1910–87 French dramatist

With love, you see, even too much is not enough.
Pierre-Augustin Caron de Beaumarchais 1732–99 French
dramatist

Love is free; it is not practised as a way of achieving
other ends.
Benedict XVI 1927– German pope

Many waters cannot quench love, neither can the floods
drown it.
Bible

Greater love hath no man than this, that a man lay down his
life for his friends.
Bible

Though I speak with the tongues of men and of angels,
and have not charity, I am become as sounding brass,
or a tinkling cymbal…

Love

And though I have all faith; so that I could remove mountains; and have not charity, I am nothing.
> **Bible**

And now abideth faith, hope, charity, these three; but the greatest of these is charity.
> **Bible**

There is no fear in love; but perfect love casteth out fear.
> **Bible**

Love seeketh not itself to please,
Nor for itself hath any care;
But for another gives its ease,
And builds a Heaven in Hell's despair.
> **William Blake** 1757–1827 English poet

When love is not madness, it is not love.
> **Pedro Calderón de La Barca** 1600–81 Spanish dramatist

Say what you will, 'tis better to be left than never to have been loved.
> **William Congreve** 1670–1729 English dramatist

The love that moves the sun and the other stars.
> **Dante Alighieri** 1265–1321 Italian poet

Much love much trial, but what an utter desert is life without love.
> **Charles Darwin** 1809–82 English naturalist

Selfhood begins with a walking away,
And love is proved in the letting go.
> **C. Day-Lewis** 1904–72 English poet

Love itself is what is left over when being in love has burned away.
> **Louis de Bernières** 1954– British novelist

Love built on beauty, soon as beauty, dies.
John Donne 1572–1631 English poet

I am the Love that dare not speak its name.
Lord Alfred Douglas 1870–1945 English poet

Oh, if only we could lean over the soul we love and see as in a mirror the image we cast there!
André Gide 1869–1951 French novelist

If I love you, what does that matter to you!
Johann Wolfgang von Goethe 1749–1832 German writer

There is no disguise which can hide love for long where it exists, or feign it where it does not.
Duc de la Rochefoucauld 1613–80 French moralist

Only the flow matters; live and let live, love and let love. There is no point to love.
D. H. Lawrence 1885–1930 English writer

Where both deliberate, the love is slight;
Who ever loved that loved not at first sight?
Christopher Marlowe 1564–93 English dramatist

The love that lasts longest is the love that is never returned.
W. Somerset Maugham 1874–1965 English novelist

Love is the triumph of imagination over intelligence.
H. L. Mencken 1880–1956 American journalist

If I am pressed to say why I loved him, I feel it can only be explained by replying: 'Because it was he; because it was me.'
Montaigne 1533–92 French moralist

No, there's nothing half so sweet in life
As love's young dream.
Thomas Moore 1779–1852 Irish musician

Love is so short, forgetting is so long.
Pablo Neruda 1904–73 Chilean poet

Love

I find no peace, and I am not at war,
I fear and hope, and burn and I am ice.
> **Petrarch** 1304–74 Italian poet

Birds do it, bees do it,
Even educated fleas do it.
Let's do it, let's fall in love.
> **Cole Porter** 1891–1964 American songwriter

Love consists in this, that two solitudes protect and touch and greet each other.
> **Rainer Maria Rilke** 1875–1926 German poet

Life has taught us that love does not consist in gazing at each other but in looking together in the same direction.
> **Antoine de Saint-Exupéry** 1900–44 French novelist

Love rules the court, the camp, the grove
And men below and saints above
For love is heaven, and heaven is love.
> **Sir Walter Scott** 1771–1832 Scottish novelist

Love means never having to say you're sorry.
> **Erich Segal** 1937–2010 American writer

The course of true love never did run smooth.
> **William Shakespeare** 1564–1616 English dramatist

Then, must you speak
Of one that loved not wisely but too well.
> **William Shakespeare** 1564–1616 English dramatist

For stony limits cannot hold love out,
And what love can do that dares love attempt.
> **William Shakespeare** 1564–1616 English dramatist

To be wise, and love,
Exceeds man's might.
> **William Shakespeare** 1564–1616 English dramatist

Let me not to the marriage of true minds
Admit impediments. Love is not love
Which alters when it alteration finds.
William Shakespeare 1564–1616 English dramatist

We cease loving ourselves if no one loves us.
Mme de Staël 1766–1817 French writer

'Tis better to have loved and lost
Than never to have loved at all.
Alfred, Lord Tennyson 1809–92 English poet

Love conquers all things: let us too give in to Love.
Virgil 70–19 BC Roman poet

Yet each man kills the thing he loves,
By each let this be heard,
Some do it with a bitter look,
Some with a flattering word.
The coward does it with a kiss,
The brave man with a sword!
Oscar Wilde 1854–1900 Irish dramatist

A pity beyond all telling,
Is hid in the heart of love.
W. B. Yeats 1865–1939 Irish poet

Lovers

If equal affection cannot be,
Let the more loving one be me.
W. H. Auden 1907–73 English poet

One is never too old for romance.
Ingrid Bergman 1915–82 Swedish actress

A man chases a girl (until she catches him).
Irving Berlin 1888–1989 American songwriter

Lovers

To fall in love is to create a religion that has a fallible god.
   Jorge Luis Borges 1899–1986 Argentinian writer

He's more myself than I am. Whatever our souls are made of his and mine are the same.
   Emily Brontë 1818–48 English writer

If thou must love me, let it be for nought
Except for love's sake only.
   Elizabeth Barrett Browning 1806–61 English poet

How do I love thee? Let me count the ways.
   Elizabeth Barrett Browning 1806–61 English poet

O, my Luve's like a red, red rose
That's newly sprung in June;
O my Luve's like the melodie
That's sweetly play'd in tune.
   Robert Burns 1759–96 Scottish poet

My heart has made its mind up
And I'm afraid it's you.
   Wendy Cope 1945–   English poet

My soul is so knit to yours that it is but a divided life I live without you.
   George Eliot 1819–80 English novelist

BILLY CRYSTAL: When you realize you want to spend the rest of your life with somebody, you want the rest of your life to start as soon as possible.
   Nora Ephron 1941–2012 American screenwriter, *in the film* When Harry Met Sally

Stay, little Valentine, stay,
Each day is Valentine's day.
   Lorenz Hart 1895–1943 American songwriter

I was more pleased with possessing your heart than with any other happiness.

Héloise c.1098–1164 French abbess

All you need is love.

John Lennon 1940–80 and **Paul McCartney** 1942– English pop singers

The life that I have
Is all that I have
And the life that I have
Is yours.

The love that I have
Of the life that I have
Is yours and yours and yours.

Leo Marks 1920–2001 English cryptographer, *given to the British secret agent Violette Szabo (1921–45), for use with the Special Operations Executive*

Difficult or easy, pleasant or bitter, you are the same you: I cannot live with you—or without you.

Martial c.AD 40–c.104 Roman epigrammatist

Love is never any better than the lover. Wicked people love wickedly, violent people love violently, weak people love weakly, stupid people love stupidly, but the love of a free man is never safe. There is no gift for the beloved.

Toni Morrison 1931– American novelist

I want to do with you
what spring does with the cherry trees.

Pablo Neruda 1904–73 Chilean poet

It were all one
That I should love a bright particular star
And think to wed it, he is so above me.

William Shakespeare 1564–1616 English dramatist

Luck

The fickleness of the women I love is only equalled by the infernal constancy of the women who love me.
George Bernard Shaw 1856–1950 Irish dramatist

Why so pale and wan, fond lover?
Prithee, why so pale?
Will, when looking well can't move her,
Looking ill prevail?
John Suckling 1609–42 English poet

Why is it that the most unoriginal thing we can say to one another is still the thing we long to hear? 'I love you' is always a quotation.
Jeanette Winterson 1959– English novelist

Luck

What we call luck is the inner man externalized. We make things happen to us.
Robertson Davies 1913–95 Canadian novelist

The best mascot is a good mechanic.
Amelia Earhart 1898–1937 American aviator

There is much good luck in the world, but it is luck. We are none of us safe. We are children, playing or quarrelling on the line.
E. M. Forster 1879–1970 English novelist

Care and diligence bring luck.
Thomas Fuller 1654–1734 English physician

Some folk want their luck buttered.
Thomas Hardy 1840–1928 English novelist

Watch out w'en you'er gittin all you want. Fattenin' hogs ain't in luck.
Joel Chandler Harris 1848–1908 American writer

All you know about it [luck] for certain is that it's bound to change.

Bret Harte 1836–1902 American poet

Is he lucky?

Cardinal Mazarin 1602–61 Italian-born French statesman, *first question on being requested to take anyone into his service, later associated with Napoleon*

Miracles do happen, but one has to work very hard for them.

Chaim Weizmann 1874–1952 Russian-born Israeli statesman

Luck is preparation meeting opportunity.

Oprah Winfrey 1954– American talk show hostess

Madness

Babylon in all its desolation is a sight not so awful as that of the human mind in ruins.

Scrope Davies c.1783–1852 English conversationalist

Whom God would destroy He first sends mad.

James Duport 1606–79 English scholar, *summarizing a Greek original*

Mad, is he? Then I hope he will *bite* some of my other generals.

George II 1683–1760 British monarch, *replying to the Duke of Newcastle, who had complained that General Wolfe was a madman*

There was only one catch and that was Catch-22…Orr would be crazy to fly more missions and sane if he didn't, but if he was sane he had to fly them. If he flew them he was crazy and didn't have to; but if he didn't want to he was sane and had to.

Joseph Heller 1923–99 American novelist

Management

Every one is more or less mad on one point.
Rudyard Kipling 1865–1936 English writer

Madness need not be all breakdown. It may also be break-through.
R. D. Laing 1927–89 Scottish psychiatrist

They called me mad, and I called them mad, and damn them, they outvoted me.
Nathaniel Lee c.1653–92 English dramatist

Is there no way out of the mind?
Sylvia Plath 1932–63 American poet

Though this be madness, yet there is method in't.
William Shakespeare 1564–1616 English dramatist

O! let me not be mad, not mad, sweet heaven;
Keep me in temper; I would not be mad!
William Shakespeare 1564–1616 English dramatist

 # Management see also **Careers**, **Planning**

Committee—a group of men who individually can do nothing but as a group decide that nothing can be done.
Fred Allen 1894–1956 American humorist

A place for everything and everything in its place.
Mrs Beeton 1836–65 English cookery writer

You're either part of the solution or you're part of the problem.
Eldridge Cleaver 1935–98 American political activist

Meetings are a great trap…However, they are indispensable when you don't want to do anything.
J. K. Galbraith 1908–2006 American economist

If you want people motivated to do a good job, give them a good job to do.

Frederick Herzberg 1923–2000 American management researcher

A camel is a horse designed by a committee.

Alec Issigonis 1906–88 British engineer

There cannot be a crisis next week. My schedule is already full.

Henry Kissinger 1923– American politician

If it ain't broke, don't fix it.

Bert Lance 1931–2013 American government official

Every time I create an appointment, I create a hundred malcontents and one ingrate.

Louis XIV 1638–1715 French monarch

There is always a well-known solution to every human problem—neat, plausible, and wrong.

H. L. Mencken 1880–1956 American journalist

Time spent on any item of the agenda will be in inverse proportion to the sum involved.

C. Northcote Parkinson 1909–93 English writer

In a hierarchy every employee tends to rise to his level of incompetence.

Laurence Peter 1919–90 Canadian writer

Surround yourself with the best people you can find, delegate authority, and don't interfere.

Ronald Reagan 1911–2004 American statesman

There is nothing in the world which does not have its decisive moment, and the masterpiece of good management is to recognize and grasp this moment.

Cardinal de Retz 1613–79 French cardinal

Manners

A problem left to itself dries up or goes rotten. But fertilize a problem with a solution—you'll hatch out dozens.
N. F. Simpson 1919–2011 English dramatist

The shortest way to do many things is to do only one thing at once.
Samuel Smiles 1812–1904 English writer

Dans ce pays-ci il est bon de tuer de temps en temps un amiral pour encourager les autres.

In this country [England] it is thought well to kill an admiral from time to time to encourage the others.
Voltaire 1694–1778 French writer

 Manners see also **Behaviour**, **Punctuality**

Evil communications corrupt good manners.
Bible

Curtsey while you're thinking what to say. It saves time.
Lewis Carroll 1832–98 English writer

Take the tone of the company that you are in.
Lord Chesterfield 1694–1773 English writer

It is wise to apply the oil of refined politeness to the mechanism of friendship.
Colette 1873–1954 French novelist

It's not a slam at *you* when people are rude—it's a slam at the people they've met before.
F. Scott Fitzgerald 1896–1940 American novelist

The art of pleasing consists in being pleased.
William Hazlitt 1778–1830 English essayist

An insolent reply from a polite person is a bad sign.
Hippocrates c.460–357 BC Greek physician

To Americans, English manners are far more frightening than none at all.
Randall Jarrell 1914–65 American poet

THUMPER: If you can't say something nice…don't say nothing at all.
Larry Morey 1905–71, *in the film* Bambi

Manners maketh man.
Proverb, *motto of William of Wykeham (1324–1404)*

Stand not upon the order of your going.
William Shakespeare 1564–1616 English dramatist

He is the very pineapple of politeness!
Richard Brinsley Sheridan 1751–1816 Irish dramatist

Manners are especially the need of the plain. The pretty can get away with anything.
Evelyn Waugh 1903–66 English novelist

Marriage see also **Love, Weddings**

It is a truth universally acknowledged, that a single man in possession of a good fortune, must be in want of a wife.
Jane Austen 1775–1817 English novelist

Wives are young men's mistresses, companions for middle age, and old men's nurses.
Francis Bacon 1561–1626 English courtier

Being a husband is a whole-time job. That is why so many husbands fail. They cannot give their entire attention to it.
Arnold Bennett 1867–1931 English novelist

What therefore God hath joined together, let not man put asunder.
Bible

Marriage

To have and to hold from this day forward, for better for worse, for richer for poorer, in sickness and in health, to love, cherish, and to obey, till death us do part.

Book of Common Prayer 1662

The deep, deep peace of the double-bed after the hurly-burly of the chaise-longue.

Mrs Patrick Campbell 1865–1940 English actress, *on her recent marriage*

Oh! how many torments lie in the small circle of a wedding-ring!

Colley Cibber 1671–1757 English dramatist

I learnt a long time ago that the only people who count in any marriage are the two that are in it.

Hillary Rodham Clinton 1947– American lawyer

Marriage is a wonderful invention; but, then again, so is a bicycle repair kit.

Billy Connolly 1942– Scottish comedian

The heart of marriage is memories.

Bill Cosby 1937– American actor

I would be married, but I'd have no wife,
I would be married to a single life.

Richard Crashaw c.1612–49 English poet

The chains of marriage are so heavy that it takes two to bear them, and sometimes three.

Alexandre Dumas 1824–95 French writer

Man's best possession is a sympathetic wife.

Euripides c.485–c.406 BC Greek dramatist

Keep your eyes wide open before marriage, half shut afterwards.

Benjamin Franklin 1706–90 American statesman and scientist

Always remember that the most important thing in a good marriage is not happiness, but stability.

Gabriel García Márquez 1927–2014 Colombian novelist

Do you think your mother and I should have lived comfortably so long together, if ever we had been married?

John Gay 1685–1732 English writer

You shall be together when the white wings of death scatter your days.
Ay, you shall be together even in the silent memory of God.
But let there be spaces in your togetherness,
And let the winds of the heavens dance between you.

Kahlil Gibran 1883–1931 Lebanese-born American writer

The triumph of hope over experience.

Samuel Johnson 1709–84 English lexicographer, *of a man who remarried immediately after the death of a wife with whom he had been unhappy*

Marriage is one long fit of compromise, deep and wide.

Barbara Kingsolver 1955– American writer

I am your clay.
You are my clay.
In life we share a single quilt.
In death we will share one coffin.

Kuan Tao-sheng 1262–1319 Chinese poet

A happy marriage is a long conversation that always seems too short.

André Maurois 1885–1967 French writer

One doesn't have to get anywhere in a marriage. It's not a public conveyance.

Iris Murdoch 1919–99 English novelist

The great secret of a successful marriage is to treat all disasters as incidents and none of the incidents as disasters.

Harold Nicolson 1886–1968 English diplomat

Tolerance is the one essential ingredient.
Philip, Duke of Edinburgh 1921– Greek-born husband of
Elizabeth II, *his recipe for a successful marriage*

It doesn't much signify whom one marries, for one is sure to
find next morning that it was someone else.
Samuel Rogers 1763–1855 English poet

A young man married is a man that's marred.
William Shakespeare 1564–1616 English dramatist

Marriage is popular because it combines the maximum of
temptation with the maximum of opportunity.
George Bernard Shaw 1856–1950 Irish dramatist

Chains do not hold a marriage together. It is threads,
hundreds of tiny threads which sew people together
through the years. That is what makes a marriage last—
more than passion or even sex!
Simone Signoret 1921–85 French actress

Marriage is like life in this—that it is a field of battle,
and not a bed of roses.
Robert Louis Stevenson 1850–94 Scottish novelist

Marriage isn't a word…it's a *sentence*!
King Vidor 1895–1982 American film director

In married life three is company and two none.
Oscar Wilde 1854–1900 Irish dramatist

 # Mathematics

Let no one enter who does not know geometry
[mathematics].
Anonymous, *inscription on Plato's door, probably at the Academy
at Athens*

Mathematics

If in other sciences we should arrive at certainty without doubt and truth without error, it behoves us to place the foundations of knowledge in mathematics.
   Roger Bacon *c.*1220–*c.*92 English philosopher and friar

They are neither finite quantities, or quantities infinitely small, nor yet nothing. May we not call them the ghosts of departed quantities?
   Bishop George Berkeley 1685–1753 Irish philosopher, *on Newton's infinitesimals*

I never could make out what those damned dots meant.
   Lord Randolph Churchill 1849–94 British politician, *on decimal points*

Equations are more important to me, because politics is for the present, but an equation is something for eternity.
   Albert Einstein 1879–1955 German-born theoretical physicist

There is no 'royal road' to geometry.
   Euclid fl. 300 BC Greek mathematician

This book is written in mathematical language and its characters are triangles, circles and other geometrical figures, without whose help…one wanders in vain through a dark labyrinth.
   Galileo Galilei 1564–1642 Italian astronomer, *often quoted as 'The book of nature is written…'*

Prime numbers are what is left when you have taken all the patterns away. I think prime numbers are like life.
   Mark Haddon 1962– British novelist

Beauty is the first test: there is no permanent place in the world for ugly mathematics.
   Godfrey Harold Hardy 1877–1947 English mathematician

Meaning

Someone told me that each equation I included in the book would halve the sales.
Stephen Hawking 1942– English theoretical physicist

God made the integers, all the rest is the work of man.
Leopold Kronecker 1823–91 German mathematician

In mathematics you don't understand things. You just get used to them.
John von Neumann 1903–57 American mathematician

There are 10 types of people in the country: those who understand binary and those who don't.
Jeremy Paxman 1950– British journalist

God is always doing geometry.
Plato 429–347 BC Greek philosopher

An equation for me has no meaning unless it expresses a thought of God.
Srinivasa Ramanujan 1887–1920 Indian mathematician

What would life be without arithmetic, but a scene of horrors?
Sydney Smith 1771–1845 English essayist

 # Meaning see also **Words**

No one means all he says, and yet very few say all they mean, for words are slippery and thought is viscous.
Henry Brooks Adams 1838–1918 American historian

'Then you should say what you mean,' the March Hare went on. 'I do,' Alice hastily replied; 'at least—at least I mean what I say—that's the same thing, you know.' 'Not the same thing a bit!' said the Hatter. 'Why, you might just as well say that "I see what I eat" is the same thing as "I eat what I see!" '
Lewis Carroll 1832–98 English writer

It depends on what the meaning of 'is' is.
Bill Clinton 1946– American statesman

The meaning doesn't matter if it's only idle chatter of a
transcendental kind.
W. S. Gilbert 1836–1911 English writer

It all depends what you mean by...
C. E. M. Joad 1891–1953 English philosopher, *characteristic
response to questions*

God and I both knew what it meant once; now God alone
knows.
Friedrich Klopstock 1724–1803 German poet

I pray thee, understand a plain man in his plain meaning.
William Shakespeare 1564–1616 English dramatist

The little girl had the making of a poet in her who, being
told to be sure of her meaning before she spoke, said,
'How can I know what I think till I see what I say?'
Graham Wallas 1858–1932 British political scientist

Medicine see also **Health**, **Sickness**

Cure the disease and kill the patient.
Francis Bacon 1561–1626 English courtier

The remedy is worse than the disease.
Francis Bacon 1561–1626 English courtier

Physician, heal thyself.
Bible

He that sinneth before his Maker, let him fall into the hand
of the physician.
Bible (Apocrypha)

Medicine

We all labour against our own cure, for death is the cure of all diseases.
Sir Thomas Browne 1605–82 English writer

Every day, in every way, I am getting better and better.
Émile Coué 1857–1926 French psychologist, *to be said 15 to 20 times, morning and evening*

Life is short, the art long.
Hippocrates c.460–357 BC Greek physician, *often quoted as 'Ars longa, vita brevis'*

As to diseases, make a habit of two things—to help, or at least to do no harm.
Hippocrates c.460–357 BC Greek physician

It may seem a strange principle to enunciate as the very first requirement in a Hospital that it should do the sick no harm.
Florence Nightingale 1820–1910 English nurse

One finger in the throat and one in the rectum makes a good diagnostician.
William Osler 1849–1919 Canadian-born physician

By medicine life may be prolonged, yet death
Will seize the doctor too.
William Shakespeare 1564–1616 English dramatist

Throw physic to the dogs; I'll none of it.
William Shakespeare 1564–1616 English dramatist

Formerly, when religion was strong and science weak, men mistook magic for medicine; now, when science is strong and religion weak, men mistake medicine for magic.
Thomas Szasz 1920–2012 Hungarian-born psychiatrist

Meeting see also **Parting**

Gin a body meet a body
Comin thro' the rye,
Gin a body kiss a body
Need a body cry?

Robert Burns 1759–96 Scottish poet

'Is there anybody there?' said the Traveller,
Knocking on the moonlit door.

Walter de la Mare 1873–1956 English poet

HUMPHREY BOGART: Of all the gin joints in all the towns in
all the world, she walks into mine.

Julius J. Epstein 1909–2001 and **others** American
screenwriters, *in the film* Casablanca

Some enchanted evening,
You may see a stranger,
You may see a stranger,
Across a crowded room.

Oscar Hammerstein II 1895–1960 American songwriter

Not many sounds in life, and I include all urban and all
rural sounds, exceed in interest a knock at the door.

Charles Lamb 1775–1834 English writer

How d'ye do, and how is the old complaint?

Lord Palmerston 1784–1865 British statesman, *reputed to be his
greeting to all those he did not know*

We'll meet again, don't know where,
Don't know when,
But I know we'll meet again some sunny day.

Ross Parker 1914–74 and **Hugh Charles** 1907–95 British
songwriters

Memory

When shall we three meet again
In thunder, lightning, or in rain?
William Shakespeare 1564–1616 English dramatist

Ill met by moonlight, proud Titania.
William Shakespeare 1564–1616 English dramatist

Dr Livingstone, I presume?
Henry Morton Stanley 1841–1904 British explorer

Why don't you come up sometime, and see me?
Mae West 1892–1980 American film actress

 Memory

And we forget because we must
And not because we will.
Matthew Arnold 1822–88 English poet

Someone said that God gave us memory so that we might
have roses in December.
J. M. Barrie 1860–1937 Scottish writer

Nobody can remember more than seven of anything.
St Robert Bellarmine 1542–1621 Italian cardinal, *reason for
omitting the eight beatitudes from his catechism*

We'll tak a cup o' kindness yet,
For auld lang syne.
Robert Burns 1759–96 Scottish poet

Our memories are card-indexes consulted, and then put
back in disorder by authorities whom we do not control.
Cyril Connolly 1903–74 English writer

Memory

Everyone seems to remember with great clarity what they were doing on November 22nd, 1963, at the precise moment they heard President Kennedy was dead.
Frederick Forsyth 1938– English novelist

The heart's memory eliminates the bad and magnifies the good, and…thanks to this artifice we manage to endure the burden of the past.
Gabriel García Márquez 1927–2014 Colombian novelist

What are those blue remembered hills,
What spires, what farms are those?
A. E. Housman 1859–1936 English poet

The true art of memory is the art of attention.
Samuel Johnson 1709–84 English lexicographer

A cigarette that bears a lipstick's traces,
An airline ticket to romantic places;
And still my heart has wings
These foolish things
Remind me of you.
Holt Marvell 1901–69 English songwriter

You may break, you may shatter the vase, if you will,
But the scent of the roses will hang round it still.
Thomas Moore 1779–1852 Irish musician

Better by far you should forget and smile
Than that you should remember and be sad.
Christina Rossetti 1830–94 English poet

There's rosemary, that's for remembrance; pray, love, remember.
William Shakespeare 1564–1616 English dramatist

Men

Are all men in disguise except those crying?
Dannie Abse 1923–2014 Welsh-born poet

ANTHONY QUINN: Am I not a man? And is not a man stupid? I'm a man, so I married. Wife, children, house, everything, the full catastrophe.
Michael Cacoyannis 1922–2011 Cypriot-born film director, *in the film* Zorba the Greek

Older men treat women like possessions, which is why I like younger men.
Joan Collins 1933– British actress

A man…is *so* in the way in the house!
Elizabeth Gaskell 1810–65 English novelist

Man is Nature's sole mistake!
W. S. Gilbert 1836–1911 English writer

Years ago, manhood was an opportunity for achievement, and now it is a problem to be overcome.
Garrison Keillor 1942– American writer

Why can't a woman be more like a man?
Men are so honest, so thoroughly square;
Eternally noble, historically fair.
Alan Jay Lerner 1918–86 American songwriter

Give me macho, or give me death.
Madonna 1958– American pop singer

Somehow a bachelor never quite gets over the idea that he is a thing of beauty and a boy forever.
Helen Rowland 1875–1950 American writer

Sigh no more, ladies, sigh no more,
Men were deceivers ever.
William Shakespeare 1564–1616 English dramatist

It's not the men in my life that counts—it's the life in
my men.
Mae West 1892–1980 American film actress

Men and Women see also **Woman's Role**

Women are really much nicer than men:
No wonder we like them.
Kingsley Amis 1922–95 English novelist

In societies where men are truly confident of their own
worth, women are not merely tolerated but valued.
Aung San Suu Kyi 1945– Burmese political leader

Men look at women. Women watch themselves being
looked at.
John Berger 1926–2017 British writer

Man's love is of man's life a thing apart,
'Tis woman's whole existence.
Lord Byron 1788–1824 English poet

The man's desire is for the woman; but the woman's desire is
rarely other than for the desire of the man.
Samuel Taylor Coleridge 1772–1834 English poet

Any woman who is sure of her own wits is a match at any
time for a man who is not sure of his own temper.
Wilkie Collins 1824–89 English novelist

There is more difference within the sexes than between
them.
Ivy Compton-Burnett 1884–1969 English novelist

Men and Women

In the sex-war thoughtlessness is the weapon of the male, vindictiveness of the female.
Cyril Connolly 1903–74 English writer

[Woman] is defined and differentiated with reference to man and not he with reference to her; she is the incidental, the inessential as opposed to the essential.
Simone de Beauvoir 1908–86 French novelist

A woman needs a man like a fish needs a bicycle.
Irina Dunn 1948– Australian writer and politician

Men are from Mars, women are from Venus.
John Gray 1951– American writer

Women have very little idea of how much men hate them.
Germaine Greer 1939– Australian feminist

The female of the species is more deadly than the male.
Rudyard Kipling 1865–1936 English writer

A woman can forgive a man for the harm he does her, but she can never forgive him for the sacrifices he makes on her account.
W. Somerset Maugham 1874–1965 English novelist

He for God only, she for God in him.
John Milton 1608–74 English poet

I admit it is better fun to punt than to be punted, and that a desire to have all the fun is nine-tenths of the law of chivalry.
Dorothy L. Sayers 1893–1957 English writer

'Tis strange what a man may do, and a woman yet think him an angel.
William Makepeace Thackeray 1811–63 English novelist

After all these years, I see that I was mistaken about Eve in the beginning; it is better to live outside the Garden with her than inside it without her.
> **Mark Twain** 1835–1910 American writer

Me Tarzan, you Jane.
> **Johnny Weissmuller** 1904–84 American film actor

Whatever women do they must do twice as well as men to be thought half as good.
> **Charlotte Whitton** 1896–1975 Canadian writer

All women become like their mothers. That is their tragedy. No man does. That's his.
> **Oscar Wilde** 1854–1900 Irish dramatist

Middle Age

Years ago we discovered the exact point, the dead centre of middle age. It occurs when you are too young to take up golf and too old to rush up to the net.
> **Franklin P. Adams** 1881–1960 American journalist

You are living in a land you no longer recognize. You don't know the language.
> **Martin Amis** 1949– English novelist

I am past thirty, and three parts iced over.
> **Matthew Arnold** 1822–88 English poet

Nel mezzo del cammin di nostra vita.

Midway along the path of our life.
> **Dante Alighieri** 1265–1321 Italian poet

At eighteen our convictions are hills from which we look; at forty-five they are caves in which we hide.
> **F. Scott Fitzgerald** 1896–1940 American novelist

Middle Age

The afternoon of human life must also have a significance of its own and cannot be merely a pitiful appendage to life's morning.
Carl Gustav Jung 1875–1961 Swiss psychologist

Men at forty
Learn to close softly
The doors to rooms they will not be
Coming back to.
Donald Justice 1925–2004 American poet

At forty-five,
What next, what next?
At every corner,
I meet my Father,
my age, still alive.
Robert Lowell 1917–77 American poet

The lovely thing about being forty is that you can appreciate twenty-five-year-old men more.
Colleen McCullough 1937–2015 Australian writer

Middle age is when you've met so many people that every new person you meet reminds you of someone else.
Ogden Nash 1902–71 American humorist

Do you think my mind is maturing late,
Or simply rotted early?
Ogden Nash 1902–71 American humorist, *on facing forty*

One of the pleasures of middle age is to *find out* that one WAS right, and that one was much righter than one knew at say 17 or 23.
Ezra Pound 1885–1972 American poet

One's prime is elusive. You little girls, when you grow up, must be on the alert to recognise your prime at whatever time of your life it may occur.
Muriel Spark 1918–2006 British novelist

By the time you hit 50, I reckon you've earned your
wrinkles, so why not be proud of them?

Twiggy 1949– English model

The Mind

Our modern skulls house a Stone Age mind.

Leda Cosmides 1957– and **John Tooby** – American
psychologist and American anthropologist

It is not enough to have a good mind; the main thing is to
use it well.

René Descartes 1596–1650 French philosopher

On earth there is nothing great but man; in man there is
nothing great but mind.

William Hamilton 1788–1856 Scottish metaphysician

O the mind, mind has mountains; cliffs of fall
Frightful, sheer, no-man-fathomed.

Gerard Manley Hopkins 1844–89 English poet

Everyone complains of his memory, and no one complains
of his judgement.

Duc de la Rochefoucauld 1613–80 French moralist

The mind loves the unknown. It loves images whose
meaning is unknown, since the meaning of the mind itself
is unknown.

René Magritte 1898–1967 Belgian surrealist painter

The mind of man is capable of anything.

Guy de Maupassant 1850–93 French writer

The mind is its own place, and in itself
Can make a heaven of hell, a hell of heaven.

John Milton 1608–74 English poet

Misfortune

Those who are caught in mental cages can often picture freedom, it just has no attractive power.
Iris Murdoch 1919–99 English novelist

That's the classical mind at work, runs fine inside but looks dingy on the surface.
Robert M. Pirsig 1928–2017 American writer

Why waste money on psychotherapy when you can listen to the B Minor Mass?
Michael Torke 1961– American composer

 # Misfortune

Prosperity doth best discover vice, but adversity doth best discover virtue.
Francis Bacon 1561–1626 English courtier

And always keep a-hold of Nurse
For fear of finding something worse.
Hilaire Belloc 1870–1953 British writer

Man is born unto trouble, as the sparks fly upward.
Bible

There is no greater pain than to remember a happy time when one is in misery.
Dante Alighieri 1265–1321 Italian poet

In the words of one of my more sympathetic correspondents, it has turned out to be an 'annus horribilis'.
Elizabeth II 1926– British monarch

I left the room with silent dignity, but caught my foot in the mat.
George Grossmith 1847–1912 and **Weedon Grossmith** 1854–1919 English writers

Man needs difficulties; they are necessary for health.
    Carl Gustav Jung 1875–1961 Swiss psychologist

In the misfortune of our best friends, we always find
something which is not displeasing to us.
    Duc de la Rochefoucauld 1613–80 French moralist

Into each life some rain must fall,
Some days must be dark and dreary.
    Henry Wadsworth Longfellow 1807–82 American poet

When fortune empties her chamberpot on your head,
smile—and say 'we are going to have a summer shower'.
    John A. Macdonald 1815–91 Canadian statesman

now and then
there is a person born
who is so unlucky
that he runs into accidents
which started to happen
to somebody else.
    Don Marquis 1878–1937 American poet

All the misfortunes of men derive from one single thing,
which is their inability to be at ease in a room.
    Blaise Pascal 1623–62 French scientist and philosopher

I had never had a piece of toast
Particularly long and wide,
But fell upon the sanded floor,
And always on the buttered side.
    James Payn 1830–98 English writer

Sweet are the uses of adversity,
Which like the toad, ugly and venomous,
Wears yet a precious jewel in his head.
    William Shakespeare 1564–1616 English dramatist

Mistakes

One likes people much better when they're battered down by a prodigious siege of misfortune than when they triumph.

Virginia Woolf 1882–1941 English novelist

 # Mistakes

Truth lies within a little and certain compass, but error is immense.

Henry St John, 1st Viscount Bolingbroke 1678–1751 English politician

It is worse than a crime, it is a blunder.

Antoine Boulay de la Meurthe 1761–1840 French statesman, *on hearing of the execution of the Duc d'Enghien*

I would rather be wrong, by God, with Plato…than be correct with those men.

Cicero 106–43 BC Roman statesman, *of Pythagoreans*

I beseech you, in the bowels of Christ, think it possible you may be mistaken.

Oliver Cromwell 1599–1658 English statesman

If all else fails, immortality can always be assured by adequate error.

J. K. Galbraith 1908–2006 American economist

Mistakes are a fact of life
It is the response to error that counts.

Nikki Giovanni 1943– American poet

An expert is someone who knows some of the worst mistakes that can be made in his subject and who manages to avoid them.

Werner Heisenberg 1901–76 German mathematical physicist

Sometimes even excellent Homer nods.
> **Horace** 65–8 BC Roman poet

Crooked things may be as stiff and unflexible as straight:
and men may be as positive in error as in truth.
> **John Locke** 1632–1704 English philosopher

I don't like people who have never fallen or stumbled.
Their virtue is lifeless and it isn't of much value. Life hasn't
revealed its beauty to them.
> **Boris Pasternak** 1890–1960 Russian novelist

To err is human, but it feels divine.
> **Dolly Parton** 1946– American singer

The man who makes no mistakes does not usually make
anything.
> **Edward John Phelps** 1822–1900 American lawyer

One Galileo in two thousand years is enough.
> **Pius XII** 1876–1958 Italian pope, *on being asked to proscribe the works of Teilhard de Chardin*

A man should never be ashamed to own he has been in the
wrong, which is but saying, in other words, that he is wiser
to-day than he was yesterday.
> **Alexander Pope** 1688–1744 English poet

It is better to be vaguely right than exactly wrong.
> **Carveth Read** 1848–1931 English philosopher

'Forward, the Light Brigade!'
Was there a man dismayed?
Not though the soldier knew
Some one had blundered.
> **Alfred, Lord Tennyson** 1809–92 English poet

Moderation

To lose one parent, Mr Worthing, may be regarded as a misfortune; to lose both looks like carelessness.
Oscar Wilde 1854–1900 Irish dramatist

 # Moderation

Nothing in excess.
Anonymous, *inscribed on the temple of Apollo at Delphi*

To many, total abstinence is easier than perfect moderation.
St Augustine of Hippo AD 354–430 Roman theologian

We know what happens to people who stay in the middle of the road. They get run down.
Aneurin Bevan 1897–1960 British politician

There's nothing in the middle of the road but yellow stripes and dead armadillos.
Jim Hightower 1943–   American writer

There is moderation in everything.
Horace 65–8 BC Roman poet

You will go most safely by the middle way.
Ovid 43 BC–c.AD 17 Roman poet

To gild refinèd gold, to paint the lily…
Is wasteful and ridiculous excess.
William Shakespeare 1564–1616 English dramatist

Above all, gentlemen, not the slightest zeal.
Charles-Maurice de Talleyrand 1754–1838 French statesman

Use, do not abuse…Neither abstinence nor excess ever renders man happy.
Voltaire 1694–1778 French writer

Too much of a good thing can be wonderful.
Mae West 1892–1980 American film actress

Money see also **Poverty**, **Wealth**

Nothing that costs only a dollar is worth having.
Elizabeth Arden 1876–1966 American businesswoman

Money is like muck, not good except it be spread.
Francis Bacon 1561–1626 English courtier

Money, it turned out, was exactly like sex, you thought of nothing else if you didn't have it and thought of other things if you did.
James Baldwin 1924–87 American writer

Money speaks sense in a language all nations understand.
Aphra Behn 1640–89 English writer

The love of money is the root of all evil.
Bible

The sinews of war, unlimited money.
Cicero 106–43 BC Roman statesman

MR MICAWBER: Annual income twenty pounds, annual expenditure nineteen nineteen six, result happiness. Annual income twenty pounds, annual expenditure twenty pounds ought and six, result misery.
Charles Dickens 1812–70 English novelist

Money doesn't talk, it swears.
Bob Dylan 1941– American singer

Money makes the world go around.
Fred Ebb 1932–2004 American songwriter

Money without brains is always dangerous.
Napoleon Hill 1883–1970 American writer

Put not your trust in money, but put your money in trust.
Oliver Wendell Holmes 1809–94 American physician

Money

A bank is a place that will lend you money if you can prove that you don't need it.
> **Bob Hope** 1903–2003 American comedian

If possible honestly, if not, somehow, make money.
> **Horace** 65–8 BC Roman poet

When a feller says, 'It hain't the money, but th' principle o' th' thing,' it's the money.
> **Frank McKinney ('Kin') Hubbard** 1868–1930 American humorist

Economy does not lie in sparing money, but in spending it wisely.
> **T. H. Huxley** 1825–95 English biologist

For I don't care too much for money,
For money can't buy me love.
> **John Lennon** 1940–80 and **Paul McCartney** 1942– English pop singers

Take care of the pence, and the pounds will take care of themselves.
> **William Lowndes** 1652–1724 English politician

Money is like a sixth sense without which you cannot make a complete use of the other five.
> **W. Somerset Maugham** 1874–1965 English novelist

Money couldn't buy friends but you got a better class of enemy.
> **Spike Milligan** 1918–2002 Irish comedian

I want to spend, and spend, and spend.
> **Vivian Nicholson** 1936–2015 British pools winner, *said to reporters on arriving to collect her winnings of £152,000*

Expenditure rises to meet income.
> **C. Northcote Parkinson** 1909–93 English writer

'My boy,' he says, 'always try to rub up against money, for if you rub up against money long enough, some of it may rub off on you.'
   Damon Runyon 1884–1946 American writer

Money is always there but the pockets change.
   Gertrude Stein 1874–1946 American writer

Pennies don't fall from heaven. They have to be earned on earth.
   Margaret Thatcher 1925–2013 British stateswoman

You can be young without money but you can't be old without it.
   Tennessee Williams 1911–83 American dramatist

Morality

Morality is a private and costly luxury.
   Henry Brooks Adams 1838–1918 American historian

Waste no more time arguing what a good man should be. Be one.
   Marcus Aurelius AD 121–180 Roman emperor

Standards are always out of date. That is what makes them standards.
   Alan Bennett 1934–   English writer

Food comes first, then morals.
   Bertolt Brecht 1898–1956 German dramatist

The end justifies the means.
   Hermann Busenbaum 1600–68 German theologian

What I know most surely about morality and the duty of man I owe to sport.
   Albert Camus 1913–60 French writer, *often quoted as '…I owe to football'*

Morality

The last temptation is the greatest treason:
To do the right deed for the wrong reason.
   T. S. Eliot 1888–1965 American-born British poet

I know only that what is moral is what you feel good after
and what is immoral is what you feel bad after.
   Ernest Hemingway 1899–1961 American novelist

State a moral case to a ploughman and a professor. The
former will decide it as well, and often better than the latter,
because he has not been led astray by artificial rules.
   Thomas Jefferson 1743–1826 American statesman

Two things fill the mind with ever new and increasing
wonder and awe, the more often and the more seriously
reflection concentrates upon them: the starry heaven above
me and the moral law within me.
   Immanuel Kant 1724–1804 German philosopher

We know no spectacle so ridiculous as the British public in
one of its periodical fits of morality.
   Lord Macaulay 1800–59 English historian

If people want a sense of purpose, they should get it from
their archbishops. They should not hope to receive it from
their politicians.
   Harold Macmillan 1894–1986 British statesman

The most useful thing about a principle is that it can always
be sacrificed to expediency.
   W. Somerset Maugham 1874–1965 English novelist

Morality is the herd-instinct in the individual.
   Friedrich Nietzsche 1844–1900 German philosopher

There is no good or evil, there is only power, and those too
weak to seek it.
   J. K. Rowling 1965– English novelist

There is nothing either good or bad, but thinking makes it so.
    William Shakespeare 1564–1616 English dramatist

We know that a man can read Goethe or Rilke in the evening, that he can play Bach and Schubert, and go to his day's work at Auschwitz in the morning.
    George Steiner 1929– American critic

If your morals make you dreary, depend upon it they are wrong.
    Robert Louis Stevenson 1850–94 Scottish novelist

The more things are forbidden, the more popular they become.
    Mark Twain 1835–1910 American writer

Moral indignation is jealousy with a halo.
    H. G. Wells 1866–1946 English novelist

Mothers

What *do* girls do who haven't any mothers to help them through their troubles?
    Louisa May Alcott 1832–88 American novelist

I have reached the age when a woman begins to perceive that she is growing into the person she least plans to resemble: her mother.
    Anita Brookner 1928–2016 British novelist

The mother's yearning, that completest type of the life in another life which is the essence of real human love, feels the presence of the cherished child even in the debased, degraded man.
    George Eliot 1819–80 English novelist

Mountains

A mother's arms are made of tenderness, and children sleep soundly in them.
Victor Hugo 1802–85 French writer

If I were damned of body and soul,
I know whose prayers would make me whole,
Mother o' mine, O mother o' mine.
Rudyard Kipling 1865–1936 English writer

Here's to the happiest years of our lives
Spent in the arms of other men's wives.
Gentlemen!—Our mothers!
Edwin Lutyens 1869–1944 English architect, *proposing a toast*

My mother had a good deal of trouble with me, but I think she enjoyed it.
Mark Twain 1835–1910 American writer

The hand that rocks the cradle
Is the hand that rules the world.
William Ross Wallace 1819–81 American poet

Guilt is to motherhood as grapes are to wine.
Fay Weldon 1931– British novelist

 # Mountains

The Alps, the Rockies and all other mountains are related to the earth, the Himalayas to the heavens.
J. K. Galbraith 1908–2006 American economist

There are other Annapurnas in the lives of men.
Maurice Herzog 1919–2012 French mountaineer

Well, we knocked the bastard off!
Edmund Hillary 1919–2008 New Zealand mountaineer, *on conquering Mount Everest, 1953*

It is a fine thing to be out on the hills alone. A man can hardly be a beast or a fool alone on a great mountain.
Francis Kilvert 1840–79 English clergyman

Because it's there.
George Leigh Mallory 1886–1924 British mountaineer, *on being asked why he wanted to climb Mount Everest*

Climb the mountains and get their good tidings.
John Muir 1838–1914 Scottish-born American naturalist

My mountain did not seem to me a lifeless thing of rock and ice, but warm and friendly and living. She was a mother hen, and the other mountains were chicks under her wings.
Tenzing Norgay 1914–86 Sherpa mountaineer, *on Everest*

Mountains are the beginning and the end of all natural scenery.
John Ruskin 1819–1900 English critic

Do nothing in haste, look well to each step, and from the beginning think what may be the end.
Edward Whymper 1840–1911 English mountaineer

Murder ✳

Thou shalt not kill.
Bible

Mordre wol out; that se we day by day.
Geoffrey Chaucer c.1343–1400 English poet

Thou shalt not kill; but need'st not strive
Officiously to keep alive.
Arthur Hugh Clough 1819–61 English poet

Murder considered as one of the fine arts.
Thomas De Quincey 1785–1859 English essayist

Music

Kill a man, and you are an assassin. Kill millions of men, and you are a conqueror. Kill everyone, and you are a god.

Jean Rostand 1894–1977 French biologist

Murder most foul, as in the best it is;
But this most foul, strange, and unnatural.

William Shakespeare 1564–1616 English dramatist

I don't think a man who has watched the sun going down could walk away and commit a murder.

Laurens van der Post 1906–96 South African explorer

 # Music see also **Singing**

Beethoven tells you what it's like to be Beethoven and Mozart tells you what it's like to be human. Bach tells you what it's like be the universe.

Douglas Adams 1952–2001 English writer

Please do not shoot the pianist. He is doing his best.

Anonymous, *printed notice in a dancing saloon, c.1882*

If you still have to ask…shame on you.

Louis Armstrong 1901–71 American jazz musician, *when asked what jazz is; sometimes quoted as 'Man, if you gotta ask you'll never know'*

All music is folk music, I ain't never heard no horse sing a song.

Louis Armstrong 1901–71 American jazz musician

There are two golden rules for an orchestra: start together and finish together. The public doesn't give a damn what goes on in between.

Thomas Beecham 1879–1961 English conductor

Music is a higher revelation than all wisdom and philosophy.

Ludwig van Beethoven 1770–1827 German composer

Music…can name the unnameable, and communicate the unknowable.
Leonard Bernstein 1918–90 American composer

Music has charms to sooth a savage breast.
William Congreve 1670–1729 English dramatist

Extraordinary how potent cheap music is.
Noël Coward 1899–1973 English dramatist

It is only that which cannot be expressed otherwise that is worth expressing in music.
Frederick Delius 1862–1934 English composer

There is music in the air.
Edward Elgar 1857–1934 English composer

The hills are alive with the sound of music,
With songs they have sung for a thousand years.
Oscar Hammerstein II 1895–1960 American songwriter

Music is the pleasure the human mind experiences from counting without being aware that it is counting.
Gottfried Wilhelm Leibniz 1646–1716 German philosopher

Down the road someone is practising scales,
The notes like little fishes vanish with a wink of tails.
Louis MacNeice 1907–63 British poet

Fortissimo at last!
Gustav Mahler 1860–1911 Austrian composer, *on seeing Niagara Falls*

The symphony must be like the world. It must embrace everything.
Gustav Mahler 1860–1911 Austrian composer

Art is not national. It is international. Music is not written in red, white and blue; it is written with the heart's blood of the composer.
Nellie Melba 1861–1931 Australian operatic soprano

Music

Music is spiritual. The music business is not.
Van Morrison 1945- Irish musician

Melody is the essence of music. I compare a good melodist to a fine racer, and counterpoints to hack post-horses.
Wolfgang Amadeus Mozart 1756-91 Austrian composer

If I don't practise for one day, I know it; if I don't practise for two days, the critics know it; if I don't practise for three days, the audience knows it.
Ignacy Jan Paderewski 1860-1941 Polish pianist and statesman

Music is your own experience, your thoughts, your wisdom. If you don't live it, it won't come out of your horn.
Charlie Parker 1920-55 American jazz saxophonist

Music begins to atrophy when it departs too far from the dance…poetry begins to atrophy when it gets too far from music.
Ezra Pound 1885-1972 American poet

Applause is a receipt, not a note of demand.
Artur Schnabel 1882-1951 Austrian-born pianist

If music be the food of love, play on.
William Shakespeare 1564-1616 English dramatist

Hell is full of musical amateurs: music is the brandy of the damned.
George Bernard Shaw 1856-1950 Irish dramatist

Music is feeling, then, not sound.
Wallace Stevens 1879-1955 American poet

A good composer does not imitate; he steals.
Igor Stravinsky 1882-1971 Russian composer

You just pick a chord, go twang, and you've got music.
Sid Vicious 1957-79 British rock musician

Names

Proper names are poetry in the raw. Like all poetry they are untranslatable.
W. H. Auden 1907–73 English poet

With a name like yours, you might be any shape, almost.
Lewis Carroll 1832–98 English writer, *Humpty Dumpty to Alice*

Colin is the sort of name you give your goldfish for a joke.
Colin Firth 1960– British actor

A self-made man may prefer a self-made name.
Learned Hand 1872–1961 American judge, *on Samuel Goldfish changing his name to Samuel Goldwyn*

A nickname is the heaviest stone that the devil can throw at a man.
William Hazlitt 1778–1830 English essayist

What's in a name? that which we call a rose
By any other name would smell as sweet.
William Shakespeare 1564–1616 English dramatist

JAQUES: I do not like her name.
ORLANDO: There was no thought of pleasing you when she was christened.
William Shakespeare 1564–1616 English dramatist

Nature

KATHARINE HEPBURN: Nature, Mr Allnutt, is what we are put into this world to rise above.
James Agee 1909–55 American writer, *in the film* The African Queen

Nature does nothing without purpose or uselessly.
Aristotle 384–322 BC Greek philosopher

Nature

A culture is no better than its woods.
W. H. Auden 1907–73 English poet

The subtlety of nature is greater many times over than the subtlety of the senses and understanding.
Francis Bacon 1561–1626 English courtier

The tree which moves some to tears of joy is in the eyes of others only a green thing that stands in the way.
William Blake 1757–1827 English poet

All things are artificial, for nature is the art of God.
Sir Thomas Browne 1605–82 English writer

I love not man the less, but nature more.
Lord Byron 1788–1824 English poet

What a book a devil's chaplain might write on the clumsy, wasteful, blundering, low, and horridly cruel works of nature!
Charles Darwin 1809–82 English naturalist

You may drive out nature with a pitchfork, yet she'll be constantly running back.
Horace 65–8 BC Roman poet

In her [Nature's] inventions nothing is lacking, and nothing is superfluous.
Leonardo da Vinci 1452–1519 Italian painter

It is far from easy to judge whether she [Nature] has proved a kind parent to man or a harsh step-mother.
Pliny the Elder AD 23–79 Roman senator

And this our life, exempt from public haunt,
Finds tongues in trees, books in the running brooks,
Sermons in stones, and good in everything.
William Shakespeare 1564–1616 English dramatist

Nature, red in tooth and claw.
Alfred, Lord Tennyson 1809–92 English poet

Nature is not a temple, but a workshop, and man's the workman in it.
Ivan Turgenev 1818–83 Russian novelist

One impulse from a vernal wood
May teach you more of man,
Of moral evil and of good,
Than all the sages can.
William Wordsworth 1770–1850 English poet

News see also **Journalism**

Tell it not in Gath, publish it not in the streets of Askelon.
Bible

How beautiful upon the mountains are the feet of him that bringeth good tidings.
Bible

If a dog bites a man it is not news, but if a man bites a dog it is.
Charles A. Dana 1819–97 American newspaper editor, *often attributed to the American journalist John B. Bogart*

Ill news hath wings, and with the wind doth go,
Comfort's a cripple and comes ever slow.
Michael Drayton 1563–1631 English poet

News is something which somebody wants suppressed—all the rest is advertising.
William Randolph Hearst 1863–1951 American newspaper publisher

What news on the Rialto?
William Shakespeare 1564–1616 English dramatist

Night

The nature of bad news infects the teller.
William Shakespeare 1564–1616 English dramatist

A squirrel dying in front of your house may be more relevant to your interests right now than people dying in Africa.
Mark Zuckerberg 1984– American computer entrepreneur

 # Night see also **Day**

Lighten our darkness, we beseech thee, O Lord; and by thy great mercy defend us from all perils and dangers of this night.
Book of Common Prayer 1662

I cannot walk through the suburbs in the solitude of the night without thinking that the night pleases us because it suppresses idle details, just as our memory does.
Jorge Luis Borges 1899–1986 Argentinian writer

The Sun's rim dips; the stars rush out;
At one stride comes the dark.
Samuel Taylor Coleridge 1772–1834 English poet

The curfew tolls the knell of parting day,
The lowing herd wind slowly o'er the lea,
The ploughman homeward plods his weary way,
And leaves the world to darkness and to me.
Thomas Gray 1716–71 English poet

The cares that infest the day
Shall fold their tents, like the Arabs,
And as silently steal away.
Henry Wadsworth Longfellow 1807–82 American poet

Night came down, and enfolded the earth in her dusky wings.
Virgil 70–19 BC Roman poet

Old Age �֍

Age is whatever you think it is. You are as old as you think you are.

Muhammad Ali 1942–2016 American boxer

Age will not be defied.

Francis Bacon 1561–1626 English courtier

To me old age is always fifteen years older than I am.

Bernard Baruch 1870–1965 American financier

The days of our age are threescore years and ten; and though men be so strong that they come to fourscore years: yet is their strength then but labour and sorrow; so soon passeth it away, and we are gone.

Bible

If I'd known I was gonna live this long, I'd have taken better care of myself.

Eubie Blake 1883–1983 American ragtime pianist, *on reaching the age of 100*

What is called the serenity of age is only perhaps a euphemism for the fading power to feel the sudden shock of joy or sorrow.

Arthur Bliss 1891–1975 English composer

The man who works and is not bored is never old.

Pablo Casals 1876–1973 Spanish cellist

Considering the alternative, it's not too bad at all.

Maurice Chevalier 1888–1972 French actor, *when asked what he felt about the advancing years on his 72nd birthday*

Oh, to be seventy again!

Georges Clemenceau 1841–1929 French statesman, *on seeing a pretty girl on his eightieth birthday*

Old Age

It's a good thing to be old, because that means you haven't died yet, right?
Penelope Cruz 1974– Spanish actress

We turn not older with years, but newer every day.
Emily Dickinson 1830–86 American poet

While there's snow on the roof, it doesn't mean the fire has gone out in the furnace.
John G. Diefenbaker 1895–1979 Canadian statesman, *approaching his 80th birthday*

As Groucho Marx once said, 'Anyone can get old—all you have to do is to live long enough.'
Elizabeth II 1926– British monarch

Age does not make us childish, as men tell,
It merely finds us children still at heart.
Johann Wolfgang von Goethe 1749–1832 German writer

You will recognize, my boy, the first sign of old age: it is when you go out into the streets of London and realize for the first time how young the policemen look.
Seymour Hicks 1871–1949 English actor-manager

A person is always startled when he hears himself seriously called an old man for the first time.
Oliver Wendell Holmes 1809–94 American physician

When I am an old woman I shall wear purple
With a red hat which doesn't go, and doesn't suit me.
Jenny Joseph 1932– English poet

Perhaps being old is having lighted rooms
Inside your head, and people in them, acting.
People you know, yet can't quite name.
Philip Larkin 1922–85 English poet

Will you still need me, will you still feed me,
When I'm sixty four?
>   **John Lennon** 1940–80 and **Paul McCartney** 1942– English
>   pop singers

Growing old is no more than a bad habit which a busy man
has no time to form.
>   **André Maurois** 1885–1967 French writer

The unending problem of growing old was not how he
changed, but how things did.
>   **Toni Morrison** 1931– American novelist

Growing old is like being increasingly penalized for a crime
you haven't committed.
>   **Anthony Powell** 1905–2000 English novelist

In a dream you are never eighty.
>   **Anne Sexton** 1928–74 American poet

Second childishness, and mere oblivion,
Sans teeth, sans eyes, sans taste, sans everything.
>   **William Shakespeare** 1564–1616 English dramatist

Every man desires to live long; but no man would be old.
>   **Jonathan Swift** 1667–1745 Irish poet and satirist

Do not go gentle into that good night,
Old age should burn and rave at close of day;
Rage, rage against the dying of the light.
>   **Dylan Thomas** 1914–53 Welsh poet

Old age is the most unexpected of all things that happen to
a man.
>   **Leon Trotsky** 1879–1940 Russian revolutionary

When you are old and grey and full of sleep,
And nodding by the fire, take down this book

Opinion

And slowly read and dream of the soft look
Your eyes had once, and of their shadows deep.
   W. B. Yeats 1865–1939 Irish poet

Opinion

Why should you mind being wrong if someone can show
you that you are?
   A. J. Ayer 1910–89 English philosopher

I've never had a humble opinion. If you've got an opinion,
why be humble about it?
   Joan Baez 1941–   American singer

He that complies against his will,
Is of his own opinion still.
   Samuel Butler 1612–80 English poet

People seem not to see that their opinion of the world is
also a confession of character.
   Ralph Waldo Emerson 1803–82 American writer

Every man has a right to utter what he thinks truth, and
every other man has a right to knock him down for it.
Martyrdom is the test.
   Samuel Johnson 1709–84 English lexicographer

There are nine and sixty ways of constructing tribal lays,
And—every—single—one—of—them—is—right!
   Rudyard Kipling 1865–1936 English writer

Thank God, in these days of enlightenment and
establishment, everyone has a right to his own opinions,
and chiefly to the opinion that nobody else has a right to
theirs.
   Ronald Knox 1888–1957 English writer

New opinions are always suspected, and usually opposed, without any other reason but because they are not already common.
John Locke 1632–1704 English philosopher

There never were in the world two opinions alike, no more than two hairs or two grains; the most universal quality is diversity.
Montaigne 1533–92 French moralist

Some praise at morning what they blame at night;
But always think the last opinion right.
Alexander Pope 1688–1744 English poet

Optimism see also **Hope, Pessimism**

The lark's on the wing;
The snail's on the thorn:
God's in his heaven—
All's right with the world!
Robert Browning 1812–89 English poet

In the depths of winter, I finally learned that within me there lay an invincible summer.
Albert Camus 1913–60 French writer

I have known him come home to supper with a flood of tears, and a declaration that nothing was now left but a jail; and go to bed making a calculation of the expense of putting bow-windows to the house, 'in case anything turned up,' which was his favourite expression.
Charles Dickens 1812–70 English novelist, *of Mr Micawber*

Grab your coat, and get your hat,
Leave your worry on the doorstep,
Just direct your feet

Originality

To the sunny side of the street.
Dorothy Fields 1905-74 American songwriter

Cheer up! the worst is yet to come!
Philander Chase Johnson 1866-1939

Sin is behovely, but all shall be well and all shall be well and all manner of thing shall be well.
Julian of Norwich 1343-after 1416 English anchoress

an optimist is a guy
that has never had
much experience.
Don Marquis 1878-1937 American poet

You've got to ac-cent-tchu-ate the positive
Elim-my-nate the negative
Latch on to the affirmative
Don't mess with Mister In-between.
Johnny Mercer 1909-76 American songwriter

In this best of possible worlds…all is for the best.
Voltaire 1694-1778 French writer

 # Originality

Be daring, be different, be impractical, be anything that will assert integrity of purpose and imaginative vision against the play-it-safers, the creatures of the commonplace, the slaves of the ordinary.
Cecil Beaton 1904-80 English photographer

The original writer is not he who refrains from imitating others, but he who can be imitated by none.
François-René Chateaubriand 1768-1848 French writer

What is originality? Undetected plagiarism.
Dean Inge 1860-1954 English writer

If you steal from one author, it's plagiarism; if you steal from many, it's research.
>   **Wilson Mizner** 1876–1933 American dramatist

It could be said of me that in this book I have only made up a bunch of other men's flowers, providing of my own only the string that ties them together.
>   **Montaigne** 1533–92 French moralist

Posterity weaves no garlands for imitators.
>   **Friedrich von Schiller** 1759–1805 German poet

Painting

Good painters imitate nature, bad ones spew it up.
>   **Cervantes** 1547–1616 Spanish novelist

The sound of water escaping from mill-dams, etc., willows, old rotten planks, slimy posts, and brickwork…those scenes made me a painter and I am grateful.
>   **John Constable** 1776–1837 English painter

Remark all these roughnesses, pimples, warts, and everything as you see me; otherwise I will never pay a farthing for it.
>   **Oliver Cromwell** 1599–1658 English statesman, *to Lely, on the painting of his portrait; commonly quoted as 'warts and all'*

I don't want justice, I want mercy.
>   **William Morris 'Billy' Hughes** 1862–1952 British-born Australian statesman, *on having his portrait painted*

Art does not reproduce the visible; rather, it makes visible.
>   **Paul Klee** 1879–1940 German-Swiss painter

This is not a pipe.
>   **René Magritte** 1898–1967 Belgian surrealist painter, *on a painting of a tobacco pipe*

Parents

I paint objects as I think them, not as I see them.
> **Pablo Picasso** 1881–1973 Spanish painter

No, painting is not made to decorate apartments. It's an offensive and defensive weapon against the enemy.
> **Pablo Picasso** 1881–1973 Spanish painter

I have seen, and heard, much of Cockney impudence before now; but never expected to hear a coxcomb ask two hundred guineas for flinging a pot of paint in the public's face.
> **John Ruskin** 1819–1900 English critic, *on Whistler's* Nocturne in Black and Gold

Every time I paint a portrait I lose a friend.
> **John Singer Sargent** 1856–1925 American painter

A good picture is equivalent to a good deed.
> **Vincent Van Gogh** 1853–90 Dutch painter

No, I ask it for the knowledge of a lifetime.
> **James McNeill Whistler** 1834–1903 American-born painter, *in his case against Ruskin, replying to the question: 'For two days' labour, you ask two hundred guineas?'*

 Parents see also **Children, Family**

The joys of parents are secret, and so are their griefs and fears.
> **Francis Bacon** 1561–1626 English courtier

Honour thy father and thy mother.
> **Bible**

A wise son maketh a glad father: but a foolish son is the heaviness of his mother.
> **Bible**

Having one child makes you a parent; having two you are a referee.

David Frost 1939–2013 English broadcaster

The father is always a Republican toward his son, and his mother's always a Democrat.

Robert Frost 1874–1963 American poet

Your children are not your children.
They are the sons and daughters of Life's longing for itself.
They came through you but not from you
And though they are with you yet they belong not to you.

Kahlil Gibran 1883–1931 Lebanese-born American writer

They fuck you up, your mum and dad.
They may not mean to, but they do.
They fill you with the faults they had
And add some extra, just for you.

Philip Larkin 1922–85 English poet

Parents can plant magic in a child's mind through certain words spoken with some thrilling quality of voice, some uplift of the heart and spirit.

Robert MacNeil 1931– Canadian writer

Love crawls with the baby, walks with the toddler, runs with the child, then stands aside to let the youth walk into adulthood.

Jo Ann Merrell

Children aren't happy with nothing to ignore,
And that's what parents were created for.

Ogden Nash 1902–71 American humorist

If you bungle raising your children I don't think whatever else you do well matters very much.

Jacqueline Kennedy Onassis 1929–94 American First Lady

Parties

No matter how old a mother is she watches her middle-aged children for signs of improvement.
Florida Scott-Maxwell 1883–1979 American writer

Parentage is a very important profession, but no test of fitness for it is ever imposed in the interest of the children.
George Bernard Shaw 1856–1950 Irish dramatist

The natural term of the affection of the human animal for its offspring is six years.
George Bernard Shaw 1856–1950 Irish dramatist

Parents learn a lot from their children about coping with life.
Muriel Spark 1918–2006 British novelist

You shouldn't sit in judgment of your parents. We did the best we could while being people too.
John Updike 1932–2009 American writer

Parents are the bones on which children sharpen their teeth.
Peter Ustinov 1921–2004 British actor

My children are ungrateful: they don't care. That is my great reward. They are free.
Fay Weldon 1931– British novelist

Children begin by loving their parents; after a time they judge them; rarely, if ever, do they forgive them.
Oscar Wilde 1854–1900 Irish dramatist

 # Parties

The sooner every party breaks up the better.
Jane Austen 1775–1817 English novelist

Like other parties of the kind, it was first silent, then talky, then argumentative, then disputatious, then unintelligible, then altogethery, then inarticulate, and then drunk.
Lord Byron 1788–1824 English poet

Parting

At every party there are two kinds of people—those who want to go home and those who don't. The trouble is, they are usually married to each other.
Ann Landers 1918–2002 American advice columnist

At a dinner party one should eat wisely but not too well, and talk well but not too wisely.
W. Somerset Maugham 1874–1965 English novelist

He showed me his bill of fare to tempt me to dine with him; poh, said I, I value not your bill of fare, give me your bill of company.
Jonathan Swift 1667–1745 Irish poet and satirist

If one plays good music, people don't listen and if one plays bad music people don't talk.
Oscar Wilde 1854–1900 Irish dramatist

Parting see also **Meeting**

CORBETT: It's goodnight from me.
BARKER: And it's goodnight from him.
Ronnie Barker 1929–2005 and **Ronnie Corbett** 1930–2016 English comedians

I wish everyone, friend or foe, well. That is that. The end.
Tony Blair 1953– British statesman, *leaving the House of Commons*

ARNOLD SCHWARZENEGGER: I'll be back.
James Cameron 1954– Canadian film director, *in the film* The Terminator

Atque in perpetuum, frater, ave atque vale.
And so, my brother, hail, and farewell evermore!
Catullus c.84–c.54 BC Roman poet

Parting

You have sat too long here for any good you have been doing. Depart, I say, and let us have done with you. In the name of God, go!

Oliver Cromwell 1599–1658 English statesman, *addressing the Rump Parliament*

Parting is all we know of heaven,
And all we need of hell.

Emily Dickinson 1830–86 American poet

Since there's no help, come let us kiss and part,
Nay, I have done: you get no more of me.

Michael Drayton 1563–1631 English poet

And ever has it been that love knows not its own depth until the hour of separation.

Kahlil Gibran 1883–1931 Lebanese-born American writer

GROUCHO MARX: If you can't leave in a taxi you can leave in a huff. If that's too soon, you can leave in a minute and a huff.

Bert Kalmar 1884–1947 and **others** American screenwriters, *in the film* Duck Soup

Leave them while you're looking good.

Anita Loos 1893–1981 American writer

Fare well my dear child and pray for me, and I shall for you and all your friends that we may merrily meet in heaven.

Thomas More 1478–1535 English scholar and saint

Good-night, good-night! parting is such sweet sorrow
That I shall say good-night till it be morrow.

William Shakespeare 1564–1616 English dramatist

The Past ✻

Even a god cannot change the past.
Agathon b. c.445 BC Greek tragic poet

Nostalgia isn't what it used to be.
Anonymous

In every age 'the good old days' were a myth. No one ever
thought they were good at the time. For every age has
consisted of crises that seemed intolerable to the people
who lived through them.
Brooks Atkinson 1894–1984 American writer

Think only of the past as its remembrance gives you
pleasure.
Jane Austen 1775–1817 English novelist

Stands the Church clock at ten to three?
And is there honey still for tea?
Rupert Brooke 1887–1915 English poet

The moving finger writes; and, having writ,
Moves on: nor all thy piety nor wit
Shall lure it back to cancel half a line,
Nor all thy tears wash out a word of it.
Edward Fitzgerald 1809–83 English poet

The past is a foreign country: they do things differently
there.
L. P. Hartley 1895–1972 English novelist

O God! Put back Thy universe and give me yesterday.
Henry Arthur Jones 1851–1929 and **Henry Herman** 1832–94
English dramatists

Yesterday, all my troubles seemed so far away,
Now it looks as though they're here to stay.

Patience

Oh I believe in yesterday.
John Lennon 1940–80 and **Paul McCartney** 1942– English
pop singers

Think of it, soldiers; from the summit of these pyramids,
forty centuries look down upon you.
Napoleon I 1769–1821 French emperor

Things ain't what they used to be.
Ted Persons

I tell you the past is a bucket of ashes.
Carl Sandburg 1878–1967 American poet

Those who cannot remember the past are condemned to
repeat it.
George Santayana 1863–1952 Spanish-born philosopher

What's gone and what's past help
Should be past grief.
William Shakespeare 1564–1616 English dramatist

O! call back yesterday, bid time return.
William Shakespeare 1564–1616 English dramatist

The past is the only dead thing that smells sweet.
Edward Thomas 1878–1917 English poet

But where are the snows of yesteryear?
François Villon c.1431–after 63 French poet

 # Patience

We had better wait and see.
Herbert Asquith 1852–1928 British statesman

Our patience will achieve more than our force.
Edmund Burke 1729–97 Irish-born politician

Beware the fury of a patient man.
John Dryden 1631–1700 English poet

All human wisdom is contained in these two words, Wait and Hope.
Alexandre Dumas 1802–70 French novelist

They also serve who only stand and wait.
John Milton 1608–74 English poet

Patience is a bitter thing, but its fruit is sweet.
Sadi c.1213–c.91 Persian poet

Let nothing trouble you, nothing frighten you. All things are passing; God never changes. Patient endurance attains all things.
St Teresa of Ávila 1512–82 Spanish mystic

I am extraordinarily patient, provided I get my own way in the end.
Margaret Thatcher 1925–2013 British stateswoman

The strongest of all warriors are these two—time and patience.
Leo Tolstoy 1828–1910 Russian novelist

Patriotism

What pity is it
That we can die but once to serve our country!
Joseph Addison 1672–1719 English writer

Patriotism is a lively sense of collective responsibility. Nationalism is a silly cock crowing on its own dunghill.
Richard Aldington 1892–1962 English writer

A steady patriot of the world alone,
The friend of every country but his own.
George Canning 1770–1827 British statesman

Patriotism

Patriotism is not enough. I must have no hatred or bitterness towards anyone.

Edith Cavell 1865–1915 English nurse, *on the eve of her execution*

> Be England what she will,
With all her faults, she is my country still.

Charles Churchill 1731–64 English poet

Our country! In her intercourse with foreign nations, may she always be in the right; but our country, right or wrong.

Stephen Decatur 1779–1820 American naval officer

If I had to choose between betraying my country and betraying my friend, I hope I should have the guts to betray my country.

E. M. Forster 1879–1970 English novelist

That this House will in no circumstances fight for its King and Country.

D. M. Graham 1911–99 British broadcaster, *motion for a debate at the Oxford Union, 1933*

I only regret that I have but one life to lose for my country.

Nathan Hale 1755–76 American revolutionary, *prior to his execution by the British for spying*

Dulce et decorum est pro patria mori.

Lovely and honourable it is to die for one's country.

Horace 65–8 BC Roman poet

Patriotism is the last refuge of a scoundrel.

Samuel Johnson 1709–84 English lexicographer

And so, my fellow Americans: ask not what your country can do for you—ask what you can do for your country.

John F. Kennedy 1917–63 American statesman

I fell in love with my country when I was a prisoner in someone else's.

John McCain 1936– American politician

My country, right or wrong; if right, to be kept right; and if wrong, to be set right!
Carl Schurz 1829–1906 American soldier

Breathes there the man, with soul so dead,
Who never to himself hath said,
This is my own, my native land!
Sir Walter Scott 1771–1832 Scottish novelist

You'll never have a quiet world till you knock the patriotism out of the human race.
George Bernard Shaw 1856–1950 Irish dramatist

I vow to thee, my country—all earthly things above—
Entire and whole and perfect, the service of my love.
Cecil Spring-Rice 1859–1918 British diplomat

The cricket test—which side do they cheer for?…Are you still looking back to where you came from or where you are?
Norman Tebbit 1931– British politician, *on the loyalties of Britain's immigrant population*

Peace

They shall beat their swords into plowshares, and their spears into pruninghooks: nation shall not lift up sword against nation, neither shall they learn war any more.
Bible

The peace of God, which passeth all understanding, shall keep your hearts and minds through Christ Jesus.
Bible

Give peace in our time, O Lord.
Book of Common Prayer 1662

Peace

This is the second time in our history that there has come back from Germany to Downing Street peace with honour. I believe it is peace for our time.

Neville Chamberlain 1869–1940 British statesman

In His will is our peace.

Dante Alighieri 1265–1321 Italian poet

Lord Salisbury and myself have brought you back peace— but a peace I hope with honour.

Benjamin Disraeli 1804–81 British statesman

Go placidly amid the noise and the haste, and remember what peace there may be in silence.

Max Ehrmann 1872–1945 American writer

I think that people want peace so much that one of these days governments had better get out of the way and let them have it.

Dwight D. Eisenhower 1890–1969 American statesman

If we are to reach real peace in this world, and if we are to carry on a real war against war, we shall have to begin with the children.

Mahatma Gandhi 1869–1948 Indian statesman

Give peace a chance.

John Lennon 1940–80 and **Paul McCartney** 1942– English pop singers

A war can perhaps be won single-handedly. But peace— lasting peace—cannot be secured without the support of all.

Luiz Inácio Lula da Silva 1945– Brazilian statesman

War appears to be as old as mankind, but peace is a modern invention.

Henry Maine 1822–88 English jurist

You can't separate peace from freedom because no one can be at peace unless he has his freedom.
Malcolm X 1925-65 American civil rights campaigner

…Peace hath her victories
No less renowned than war.
John Milton 1608-74 English poet

Enough of blood and tears. Enough.
Yitzhak Rabin 1922-95 Israeli statesman

They make a wilderness and call it peace.
Tacitus c.AD 56-after 117 Roman historian

Shantih, shantih, shantih.
Peace! Peace! Peace!
The Upanishads 800-200 BC Hindu sacred treatises

Let him who desires peace, prepare for war.
Vegetius fl. AD 379-395 Roman military writer

Perfection

The pursuit of perfection, then, is the pursuit of sweetness and light.
Matthew Arnold 1822-88 English poet

Pictures of perfection as you know make me sick and wicked.
Jane Austen 1775-1817 English novelist

Faultless to a fault.
Robert Browning 1812-89 English poet

Forget your perfect offering
There is a crack in everything
That's how the light gets in.
Leonard Cohen 1934-2016 Canadian singer

Persistence

Trifles make perfection, and perfection is no trifle.
Michelangelo 1475–1564 Italian artist

The best is the best, though a hundred judges have declared it so.
Arthur Quiller-Couch 1863–1944 English critic

Perfection is finally attained not when there is no longer anything to add but when there is no longer anything to take away, when a body has been stripped down to its nakedness.
Antoine de Saint-Exupéry 1900–44 French novelist

How many things by season seasoned are
To their right praise and true perfection!
William Shakespeare 1564–1616 English dramatist

Finality is death. Perfection is finality.
Nothing is perfect. There are lumps in it.
James Stephens 1882–1950 Irish poet

The best is the enemy of the good.
Voltaire 1694–1778 French writer

The intellect of man is forced to choose
Perfection of the life, or of the work.
W. B. Yeats 1865–1939 Irish poet

 Persistence see also **Determination**

Nothing in the world can take the place of persistence. Talent will not; nothing is more common than unsuccessful men with talent. Genius will not; unrewarded genius is almost a proverb. Education will not; the world is full of educated derelicts. Persistence and determination are

omnipotent. The slogan 'press on' has solved and always will solve the problems of the human race.
Calvin Coolidge 1872–1933 American statesman

There must be a beginning of any great matter, but the continuing unto the end until it be thoroughly finished yields the true glory.
Francis Drake c.1540–96 English sailor

Pick yourself up,
Dust yourself off,
Start all over again.
Dorothy Fields 1905–74 American songwriter

The drop of rain maketh a hole in the stone, not by violence, but by oft falling.
Hugh Latimer c.1485–1555 English martyr

Keep right on to the end of the road,
Keep right on to the end.
Tho' the way be long, let your heart be strong,
Keep right on round the bend.
Harry Lauder 1870–1950 Scottish music-hall entertainer

Either don't attempt it, or carry it through to the end.
Ovid 43 BC–c.AD 17 Roman poet

Perseverance, dear my lord,
Keeps honour bright.
William Shakespeare 1564–1616 English dramatist

'Tis known by the name of perseverance in a good cause,— and of obstinacy in a bad one.
Laurence Sterne 1713–68 English novelist

What is the victory of a cat on a hot tin roof?—I wish I knew…Just staying on it, I guess, as long as she can.
Tennessee Williams 1911–83 American dramatist

Pessimism see also **Despair**, **Optimism**

WOODY ALLEN: I feel that life is—is divided up into the horrible and the miserable.

> **Woody Allen** 1935- and **Marshall Brickman** 1941-
> American film director and American screenwriter, *in the film*
> Annie Hall

The optimist proclaims that we live in the best of all possible worlds; and the pessimist fears this is true.

> **James Branch Cabell** 1879–1958 American writer

I don't consider myself a pessimist. I think of a pessimist as someone who is waiting for it to rain. And I feel soaked to the skin.

> **Leonard Cohen** 1934–2016 Canadian singer

If way to the Better there be, it exacts a full look at the worst.

> **Thomas Hardy** 1840–1928 English novelist

Man hands on misery to man.
It deepens like a coastal shelf.
Get out as early as you can,
And don't have any kids yourself.

> **Philip Larkin** 1922–85 English poet

If we see light at the end of the tunnel,
It's the light of the oncoming train.

> **Robert Lowell** 1917–77 American poet

The nice part about being a pessimist is that you are constantly being either proven right or pleasantly surprised.

> **George F. Will** 1941- American columnist

'Twixt the optimist and pessimist
The difference is droll:

The optimist sees the doughnut
But the pessimist sees the hole.
McLandburgh Wilson b. 1892

Philosophy ✳

Metaphysics is the finding of bad reasons for what we
believe upon instinct.
F. H. Bradley 1846–1924 English philosopher

If it was so, it might be; and if it were so, it would be: but as
it isn't, it ain't. That's logic.
Lewis Carroll 1832–98 English writer

There is nothing so absurd but some philosopher has said it.
Cicero 106–43 BC Roman statesman

I refute it *thus*.
Samuel Johnson 1709–84 English lexicographer, *kicking a
large stone by way of refuting Bishop Berkeley's theory of the non-
existence of matter*

The philosophers have only interpreted the world in various
ways; the point is to change it.
Karl Marx 1818–83 German philosopher

No more things should be presumed to exist than are
absolutely necessary.
William of Occam c.1285–1349 English philosopher, *'Occam's
razor', not found in this form in his writings, although he frequently
used similar expressions*

The point of philosophy is to start with something so simple
as not to seem worth stating, and to end with something so
paradoxical that no one will believe it.
Bertrand Russell 1872–1970 British philosopher

The unexamined life is not worth living.
Socrates 469–399 BC Greek philosopher

Photography

The safest general characterization of the European philosophical tradition is that it consists of a series of footnotes to Plato.
Alfred North Whitehead 1861–1947 English philosopher

Philosophy is a battle against the bewitchment of our intelligence by means of language.
Ludwig Wittgenstein 1889–1951 Austrian-born philosopher

 # Photography

There are always two people in every picture: the photographer and the viewer.
Ansel Adams 1902–84 American photographer

A photograph is a secret about a secret. The more it tells you the less you know.
Diane Arbus 1923–71 American photographer

Most things in life are moments of pleasure and a lifetime of embarrassment; photography is a moment of embarrassment and a lifetime of pleasure.
Tony Benn 1925–2014 British politician

In photography you've got to be quick, quick, quick, like an animal and a prey.
Henri Cartier-Bresson 1908–2004 French photographer

You press the button, we do the rest.
George Eastman 1854–1932 American inventor, *advertising slogan to launch the Kodak camera, 1888*

The important thing is not the camera but the eye.
Alfred Eisenstaedt 1898–1995 American photographer

Photography deals exquisitely with appearances, but nothing is what it appears to be.
Duane Michals 1932– American photographer

The photographer is like the cod which produces a million eggs in order that one may reach maturity.
George Bernard Shaw 1856–1950 Irish dramatist

My idea of a good picture is one that's in focus and of a famous person doing something unfamous. It's being in the right place at the wrong time.
Andy Warhol 1927–87 American artist

Planning ✳

Be prepared.
Lord Baden-Powell 1857–1941 English soldier, *motto of the Scout Association*

We are ready for any unforeseen event which may or may not happen.
George W. Bush 1946– American statesman

Probability is the very guide of life.
Joseph Butler 1692–1752 English bishop

First things first, second things never.
Shirley Conran 1932– English writer

In preparing for battle I have always found that plans are useless, but planning is indispensable.
Dwight D. Eisenhower 1890–1969 American statesman

No plan of operations reaches with any certainty beyond the first encounter with the enemy's main force.
Helmuth von Moltke 1800–91 Prussian military commander, *often quoted as 'no plan survives first contact with the enemy'*

A good plan violently executed *Now* is better than a perfect plan next week.
George S. Patton 1885–1945 American general

Pleasure

There are no small steps in great affairs.
Cardinal de Retz 1613–79 French cardinal

The thing that is important is the thing that is not seen.
Antoine de Saint-Exupéry 1900–44 French novelist

If we had had more time for discussion we should probably
have made a great many more mistakes.
Leon Trotsky 1879–1940 Russian revolutionary

 # Pleasure

One half of the world cannot understand the pleasures of
the other.
Jane Austen 1775–1817 English novelist

The great pleasure in life is doing what people say you
cannot do.
Walter Bagehot 1826–77 English economist

I'm tired of Love: I'm still more tired of Rhyme.
But Money gives me pleasure all the time.
Hilaire Belloc 1870–1953 British writer

Let us have wine and women, mirth and laughter,
Sermons and soda-water the day after.
Lord Byron 1788–1824 English poet

The essence of pleasure is spontaneity.
Germaine Greer 1939– Australian feminist

Speed, it seems to me, provides the one genuinely modern
pleasure.
Aldous Huxley 1894–1963 English novelist

The less we indulge our pleasures the more we enjoy them.
Juvenal c.AD 60–c.140 Roman satirist

Ever let the fancy roam,
Pleasure never is at home.
>**John Keats** 1795–1821 English poet

The greatest pleasure I know, is to do a good action by
stealth, and to have it found out by accident.
>**Charles Lamb** 1775–1834 English writer

Who loves not woman, wine, and song
Remains a fool his whole life long.
>**Martin Luther** 1483–1546 German theologian

Pleasure is nothing else but the intermission of pain.
>**John Selden** 1584–1654 English historian

Life would be very pleasant if it were not for its enjoyments.
>**R. S. Surtees** 1805–64 English novelist

All the things I really like to do are either illegal, immoral,
or fattening.
>**Alexander Woollcott** 1887–1943 American writer

Poetry

A poet's hope: to be,
like some valley cheese,
local, but prized elsewhere.
>**W. H. Auden** 1907–73 English poet

Prose is when all the lines except the last go on to the end.
Poetry is when some of them fall short of it.
>**Jeremy Bentham** 1748–1832 English philosopher

The reason Milton wrote in fetters when he wrote of
Angels and God, and at liberty when of Devils and Hell, is
because he was a true Poet, and of the Devil's party without
knowing it.
>**William Blake** 1757–1827 English poet

Poetry

All poets are mad.
Robert Burton 1577–1640 English clergyman

That willing suspension of disbelief for the moment, which constitutes poetic faith.
Samuel Taylor Coleridge 1772–1834 English poet

Prose = words in their best order;—poetry = the *best* words in the best order.
Samuel Taylor Coleridge 1772–1834 English poet

I used to think all poets were Byronic.
They're mostly wicked as a ginless tonic
And wild as pension plans.
Wendy Cope 1945-   English poet

If I read a book [and] it makes my whole body so cold no fire can ever warm me, I know *that* is poetry. If I feel physically as if the top of my head were taken off, I know *that* is poetry. These are the only way I know it. Is there any other way.
Emily Dickinson 1830–86 American poet

Immature poets imitate; mature poets steal.
T. S. Eliot 1888–1965 American-born British poet

Poetry is a subject as precise as geometry.
Gustave Flaubert 1821–80 French novelist

Like a piece of ice on a hot stove the poem must ride on its own melting.
Robert Frost 1874–1963 American poet

As soon as war is declared it will be impossible to hold the poets back. Rhyme is still the most effective drum.
Jean Giraudoux 1882–1944 French dramatist

Skilled or unskilled, we all scribble poems.
Horace 65–8 BC Roman poet

[BOSWELL:] Sir, what is poetry?
[JOHNSON:] Why Sir, it is much easier to say what it is not. We all *know* what light is; but it is not easy to *tell* what it is.
Samuel Johnson 1709–84 English lexicographer

If poetry comes not as naturally as the leaves to a tree it had better not come at all.
John Keats 1795–1821 English poet

A poem should not mean
But be.
Archibald MacLeish 1892–1982 American poet

Writing a book of poetry is like dropping a rose petal down the Grand Canyon and waiting for the echo.
Don Marquis 1878–1937 American poet

Rhyme being…but the invention of a barbarous age, to set off wretched matter and lame metre.
John Milton 1608–74 English poet

Most people ignore most poetry
because
most poetry ignores most people.
Adrian Mitchell 1932–2008 English writer

All a poet can do today is warn.
Wilfred Owen 1893–1918 English poet

Poets are the unacknowledged legislators of the world.
Percy Bysshe Shelley 1792–1822 English poet

Poetry is the spontaneous overflow of powerful feelings: it takes its origin from emotion recollected in tranquillity.
William Wordsworth 1770–1850 English poet

We make out of the quarrel with others, rhetoric, but of the quarrel with ourselves, poetry.
W. B. Yeats 1865–1939 Irish poet

Politicians see also **Politics**

A constitutional statesman is in general a man of common opinion and uncommon abilities.
Walter Bagehot 1826–77 English economist

I am not going to spend any time whatsoever in attacking the Foreign Secretary…If we complain about the tune, there is no reason to attack the monkey when the organ grinder is present.
Aneurin Bevan 1897–1960 British politician

Your representative owes you, not his industry only, but his judgement; and he betrays, instead of serving you, if he sacrifices it to your opinion.
Edmund Burke 1729–97 Irish-born politician

An honest politician is one who when he's bought stays bought.
Simon Cameron 1799–1889 American politician

A minister who moves about in society is in a position to read the signs of the times even in a festive gathering, but one who remains shut up in his office learns nothing.
Duc de Choiseul 1719–85 French politician

It is the ability to foretell what is going to happen tomorrow, next week, next month, and next year. And to have the ability afterwards to explain why it didn't happen.
Winston Churchill 1874–1965 British statesman, *on the qualifications for becoming a politician*

There are no true friends in politics. We are all sharks circling, and waiting, for traces of blood to appear in the water.
Alan Clark 1928–99 British politician

Definition of an independent Member of Parliament, viz. one that could not be depended upon.

Edward Stanley, 14th Earl of Derby 1799–1869 British Conservative statesman

'Do you pray for the senators, Dr Hale?' 'No, I look at the senators and I pray for the country.'

Edward Everett Hale 1822–1909 American clergyman

Politicians are the same all over. They promise to build a bridge where there is no river.

Nikita Khrushchev 1894–1971 Soviet statesman

Forever poised between a cliché and an indiscretion.

Harold Macmillan 1894–1986 British statesman, *on the life of a Foreign Secretary*

What I want is men who will support me when I am in the wrong.

Lord Melbourne 1779–1848 British statesman, *replying to a politician who said 'I will support you as long as you are in the right'*

A statesman is a politician who places himself at the service of the nation. A politician is a statesman who places the nation at his service.

Georges Pompidou 1911–74 French statesman

A statesman is a politician who's been dead 10 or 15 years.

Harry S. Truman 1884–1972 American statesman

If you want a friend in Washington, get a dog.

Harry S. Truman 1884–1972 American statesman

All those men have their price.

Robert Walpole 1676–1745 English statesman, *of fellow parliamentarians*

Politics see also **Democracy**, **Government**

In politics the middle way is none at all.
John Adams 1735–1826 American statesman

Man is by nature a political animal.
Aristotle 384–322 BC Greek philosopher

Politics is the art of looking for trouble, finding it
everywhere, diagnosing it wrongly and applying unsuitable
remedies.
Ernest Benn 1875–1954 English publisher

Politics is the art of the possible.
Otto von Bismarck 1815–98 German statesman

A statesman…must wait until he hears the steps of God
sounding through events; then leap up and grasp the hem
of his garment.
Otto von Bismarck 1815–98 German statesman

Magnanimity in politics is not seldom the truest wisdom;
and a great empire and little minds go ill together.
Edmund Burke 1729–97 Irish-born politician

In politics, there is no use looking beyond the next
fortnight.
Joseph Chamberlain 1836–1914 British politician

In politics, what begins in fear usually ends in folly.
Samuel Taylor Coleridge 1772–1834 English poet

You campaign in poetry. You govern in prose.
Mario Cuomo 1932–2015 American politician

International life is right-wing, like nature. The social
contract is left-wing, like humanity.
Régis Debray 1940– French Marxist theorist

'Two nations; between whom there is no intercourse and no sympathy; who are as ignorant of each other's habits, thoughts, and feelings, as if they were dwellers in different zones, or inhabitants of different planets...' 'You speak of—' said Egremont, hesitatingly, 'THE RICH AND THE POOR.'
Benjamin Disraeli 1804–81 British statesman

Damn your principles! Stick to your party.
Benjamin Disraeli 1804–81 British statesman

I never dared be radical when young
For fear it would make me conservative when old.
Robert Frost 1874–1963 American poet

Politics is not the art of the possible. It consists in choosing between the disastrous and the unpalatable.
J. K. Galbraith 1908–2006 American economist

If I could not go to Heaven but with a party, I would not go there at all.
Thomas Jefferson 1743–1826 American statesman

The great nations have always acted like gangsters, and the small nations like prostitutes.
Stanley Kubrick 1928–99 American film director

Who? Whom?
Lenin 1870–1924 Russian revolutionary, *definition of political science, meaning 'Who will outstrip whom?'*

Politics is a marathon, not a sprint.
Ken Livingstone 1945– British politician

If you want to succeed in politics, you must keep your conscience well under control.
David Lloyd George 1863–1945 British statesman

The opposition of events.
Harold Macmillan 1894–1986 British statesman, *on his biggest problem; popularly quoted as 'Events, dear boy. Events'*

Pollution

Politics is war without bloodshed while war is politics with bloodshed.

Mao Zedong 1893–1976 Chinese statesman

Never doubt that a small group of thoughtful committed citizens can change the world. In fact, it's the only thing that ever has.

Margaret Mead 1901–78 American anthropologist

Political language…is designed to make lies sound truthful and murder respectable, and to give an appearance of solidity to pure wind.

George Orwell 1903–50 English novelist

Socialism can only arrive by bicycle.

José Antonio Viera Gallo 1943– Chilean politician

A week is a long time in politics.

Harold Wilson 1916–95 British statesman

A liberal is a conservative who's been arrested.

Tom Wolfe 1931– American writer

 # Pollution see also **Environment**

Woe to her that is filthy and polluted, to the oppressing city!
Bible

NOISE, *n*. A stench in the ear…The chief product and authenticating sign of civilization.
Ambrose Bierce 1842–c.1914 American writer

Over increasingly large areas of the United States, spring now comes unheralded by the return of the birds, and the early mornings are strangely silent where once they were filled with the beauty of bird song.
Rachel Carson 1907–64 American zoologist

Pollution

Man has been endowed with reason, with the power to create, so that he can add to what he's been given. But up to now he hasn't been a creator, only a destroyer. Forests keep disappearing, rivers dry up, wild life's become extinct, the climate's ruined and the land grows poorer and uglier every day.

Anton Chekhov 1860–1904 Russian writer

The river Rhine, it is well known,
Doth wash your city of Cologne;
But tell me, Nymphs, what power divine
Shall henceforth wash the river Rhine?

Samuel Taylor Coleridge 1772–1834 English poet

The sea is the universal sewer.

Jacques Cousteau 1910–97 French underwater explorer

Clear the air! clean the sky! wash the wind!

T. S. Eliot 1888–1965 American-born British poet

The sanitary and mechanical age we are now entering makes up for the mercy it grants to our sense of smell by the ferocity with which it assails our sense of hearing. As usual, what we call 'progress' is the exchange of one nuisance for another nuisance.

Havelock Ellis 1859–1939 English sexologist

And all is seared with trade; bleared, smeared with toil;
And wears man's smudge and shares man's smell.

Gerard Manley Hopkins 1844–89 English poet

It goes so heavily with my disposition that this goodly frame, the earth, seems to me a sterile promontory; this most excellent canopy, the air, look you, this brave o'erhanging firmament, this majestical roof fretted with golden fire, why, it appears no other thing to me but a foul and pestilent congregation of vapours.

William Shakespeare 1564–1616 English dramatist

Poverty

Make poverty history.
> **Anonymous**, *campaign slogan, 2005*

The poor have the sufferings to which they are fairly
accustomed.
> **W. H. Auden** 1907–73 English poet

Anyone who has ever struggled with poverty knows how
extremely expensive it is to be poor.
> **James Baldwin** 1924–87 American writer

The poor always ye have with you.
> **Bible**

When I give food to the poor they call me a saint. When
I ask why the poor have no food they call me a communist.
> **Helder Camara** 1909–99 Brazilian priest

There is no scandal like rags, nor any crime so shameful as
poverty.
> **George Farquhar** 1678–1707 Irish dramatist

I want there to be no peasant in my kingdom so poor that
he is unable to have a chicken in his pot every Sunday.
> **Henri IV** 1553–1610 French monarch

Oh! God! that bread should be so dear,
And flesh and blood so cheap!
> **Thomas Hood** 1799–1845 English poet

It's easy to be independent when you've got money. But to
be independent when you haven't got a thing—that's the
Lord's test.
> **Mahalia Jackson** 1911–72 American singer

Resolve not to be poor: whatever you have, spend less.
Poverty is a great enemy to human happiness; it certainly

destroys liberty, and it makes some virtues impracticable, and others extremely difficult.
Samuel Johnson 1709–84 English lexicographer

The misfortunes of poverty carry with them nothing harder to bear than that it makes men ridiculous.
Juvenal c.AD 60–c.140 Roman satirist

Overcoming poverty is not a gesture of charity. It is an act of justice.
Nelson Mandela 1918–2013 South African statesman

The greatest of evils and the worst of crimes is poverty.
George Bernard Shaw 1856–1950 Irish dramatist

Poverty is no disgrace to a man, but it is confoundedly inconvenient.
Sydney Smith 1771–1845 English essayist

A hungry man is not a free man.
Adlai Stevenson 1900–65 American politician

Sixteen tons, what do you get?
Another day older and deeper in debt.
Say brother, don't you call me 'cause I can't go
I owe my soul to the company store.
Merle Travis 1917–83 American singer

Power

Power tends to corrupt and absolute power corrupts absolutely.
Lord Acton 1834–1902 British historian

Every dictator uses religion as a prop to keep himself in power.
Benazir Bhutto 1953–2007 Pakistani stateswoman

Power

The most potent weapon in the hands of the oppressor is the mind of the oppressed.

Steve Biko 1946–77 South African anti-apartheid campaigner

A man may build himself a throne of bayonets, but he cannot sit on it.

Dean Inge 1860–1954 English writer, *quoted by Boris Yeltsin at the time of the failed military coup in Russia, 1991*

Power without love is reckless and abusive, and love without power is sentimental and anaemic. Power at its best is love implementing the demands of justice, and justice at its best is power correcting everything that stands against love.

Martin Luther King 1929–68 American civil rights leader

Power is the great aphrodisiac.

Henry Kissinger 1923– American politician

Power? It's like a Dead Sea fruit. When you achieve it, there is nothing there.

Harold Macmillan 1894–1986 British statesman

Political power grows out of the barrel of a gun.

Mao Zedong 1893–1976 Chinese statesman

On the highest throne in the world, we still sit only on our bottom.

Montaigne 1533–92 French moralist

Who controls the past controls the future: who controls the present controls the past.

George Orwell 1903–50 English novelist

You only have power over people as long as you don't take *everything* away from them. But when you've robbed a man of *everything* he's no longer in your power—he's free again.

Alexander Solzhenitsyn 1918–2008 Russian novelist

The Pope! How many divisions has *he* got?
Joseph Stalin 1879–1953 Soviet dictator, *on being asked to encourage Catholicism in Russia by way of conciliating the Pope*

Practicality

Put your trust in God, my boys, and keep your powder dry.
Valentine Blacker 1728–1823 Irish soldier, *'Oliver's Advice', often attributed to Oliver Cromwell himself*

The colour of the cat doesn't matter as long as it catches the mice.
Deng Xiaoping 1904–97 Chinese statesman

Common sense is the best distributed commodity in the world, for every man is convinced that he is well supplied with it.
René Descartes 1596–1650 French philosopher

Common sense is nothing more than a deposit of prejudices laid down in the mind before you reach eighteen.
Albert Einstein 1879–1955 German-born theoretical physicist

Praise the Lord and pass the ammunition.
Howell Forgy 1908–83 American naval chaplain, *at Pearl Harbor, while sailors passed ammunition by hand to the deck*

So I really think that American gentlemen are the best after all, because kissing your hand may make you feel very very good but a diamond and safire bracelet lasts forever.
Anita Loos 1893–1981 American writer

Be nice to people on your way up because you'll meet 'em on your way down.
Wilson Mizner 1876–1933 American dramatist

Common sense is not so common.
Voltaire 1694–1778 French writer

Praise

The flattery of posterity is not worth much more than contemporary flattery, which is worth nothing.
Jorge Luis Borges 1899–1986 Argentinian writer

The advantage of doing one's praising for oneself is that one can lay it on so thick and exactly in the right places.
Samuel Butler 1835–1902 English novelist

Imitation is the sincerest of flattery.
Charles Caleb Colton c.1780–1832 English clergyman

How light, how small is the thing which casts down or restores a mind greedy for praise.
Horace 65–8 BC Roman poet

All censure of a man's self is oblique praise. It is in order to shew how much he can spare.
Samuel Johnson 1709–84 English lexicographer

And even the ranks of Tuscany
Could scarce forbear to cheer.
Lord Macaulay 1800–59 English historian

Damn with faint praise, assent with civil leer,
And without sneering, teach the rest to sneer.
Alexander Pope 1688–1744 English poet

But when I tell him he hates flatterers,
He says he does, being then most flattered.
William Shakespeare 1564–1616 English dramatist

I suppose flattery hurts no one, that is, if he doesn't inhale.
Adlai Stevenson 1900–65 American politician

Prayer

O Lord! thou knowest how busy I must be this day:
if I forget thee, do not thou forget me.
> **Jacob Astley** 1579–1652 English soldier, *before the Battle of Edgehill*

The wish for prayer is a prayer in itself.
> **Georges Bernanos** 1888–1948 French writer

Ask, and it shall be given you; seek, and ye shall find; knock, and it shall be opened unto you.
> **Bible**

And lips say, 'God be pitiful,'
Who ne'er said, 'God be praised.'
> **Elizabeth Barrett Browning** 1806–61 English poet

Prayer is translation. A man translates himself into a child asking for all there is in a language he has barely mastered.
> **Leonard Cohen** 1934–2016 Canadian singer

He prayeth best, who loveth best
All things both great and small.
> **Samuel Taylor Coleridge** 1772–1834 English poet

One single grateful thought raised to heaven is the most perfect prayer.
> **G. E. Lessing** 1729–81 German dramatist

Often when I pray I wonder if I am not posting letters to a non-existent address.
> **C. S. Lewis** 1898–1963 English literary scholar

The family that prays together stays together.
> **Al Scalpone** fl. 1947

Prejudice

My words fly up, my thoughts remain below:
Words without thoughts never to heaven go.
William Shakespeare 1564–1616 English dramatist

       More things are wrought by prayer
Than this world dreams of.
Alfred, Lord Tennyson 1809–92 English poet

Whatever a man prays for, he prays for a miracle. Every prayer reduces itself to this: Great God, grant that twice two be not four.
Ivan Turgenev 1818–83 Russian novelist

You can't pray a lie.
Mark Twain 1835–1910 American writer

 # Prejudice see also **Race**

Prejudices, it is well known, are most difficult to eradicate from the heart whose soil has never been loosened or fertilised by education.
Charlotte Brontë 1816–55 English novelist

Bigotry may be roughly defined as the anger of men who have no opinions.
G. K. Chesterton 1874–1936 English writer

Being a star has made it possible for me to get insulted in places where the average Negro could never *hope* to go and get insulted.
Sammy Davis Jnr. 1925–90 American entertainer

Minds are like parachutes. They only function when they are open.
James Dewar 1842–1923 Scottish physicist

Prejudice

Human diversity makes tolerance more than a virtue, it makes it a requirement for survival.

René Dubos 1901–82 French-born American microbiologist

If my theory of relativity is proven correct, Germany will claim me as a German and France will declare that I am a citizen of the world. Should my theory prove untrue, France will say that I am a German and Germany will declare that I am a Jew.

Albert Einstein 1879–1955 German-born theoretical physicist

Make hatred hated!

Anatole France 1844–1924 French man of letters

Drive out prejudices through the door, and they will return through the window.

Frederick the Great 1712–86 Prussian monarch

Without the aid of prejudice and custom, I should not be able to find my way across the room.

William Hazlitt 1778–1830 English essayist

The mind of the bigot [is like] the pupil of the eye; the more light you pour on it, the more it contracts.

Oliver Wendell Holmes 1809–94 American physician

Four legs good, two legs bad.

George Orwell 1903–50 English novelist

We should therefore claim, in the name of tolerance, the right not to tolerate the intolerant.

Karl Popper 1902–94 Austrian-born philosopher

The only good Indian is a dead Indian.

Philip Henry Sheridan 1831–88 American cavalry commander

Bigotry tries to keep truth safe in its hand
With a grip that kills it.

Rabindranath Tagore 1861–1941 Bengali poet

The Present

Can ye not discern the signs of the times?
Bible

Take therefore no thought for the morrow: for the morrow
shall take thought for the things of itself. Sufficient unto the
day is the evil thereof.
Bible

Few people can say: I am here. They look for themselves in
the past and see themselves in the future.
Georges Braque 1882–1963 French painter

Exhaust the little moment. Soon it dies.
And be it gash or gold it will not come
Again in this identical disguise.
Gwendolyn Brooks 1917–2000 American poet

The rule is, jam to-morrow and jam yesterday—but never
jam today.
Lewis Carroll 1832–98 English writer

Forever—is composed of nows.
Emily Dickinson 1830–86 American poet

Unborn TO-MORROW, and dead YESTERDAY,
Why fret about them if TO-DAY be sweet!
Edward Fitzgerald 1809–83 English poet

Carpe diem, quam minimum credula postero.
Seize the day, put no trust in the future.
Horace 65–8 BC Roman poet

Things are both more trivial than they ever were, and more
important than they ever were, and the difference between

the trivial and the important doesn't seem to matter. But the nowness of everything is absolutely wondrous.

> **Dennis Potter** 1935–94 English dramatist, *on his approaching death*

What is love? 'tis not hereafter;
Present mirth hath present laughter;
What's to come is still unsure.

> **William Shakespeare** 1564–1616 English dramatist

Our work is for today, yesterday has gone, tomorrow has not yet come. We have only today.

> **Mother Teresa** 1910–97 Roman Catholic nun

The Presidency

My country has in its wisdom contrived for me the most insignificant office that ever the invention of man contrived or his imagination conceived.

> **John Adams** 1735–1826 American statesman, *of the vice-presidency*

To those of you who received honours, awards and distinctions, I say well done. And to the C students, I say you, too, can be president of the United States.

> **George W. Bush** 1946– American statesman

When I was a boy I was told that anybody could become President. I'm beginning to believe it.

> **Clarence Darrow** 1857–1938 American lawyer

No easy problems ever come to the President of the United States. If they are easy to solve, somebody else has solved them.

> **Dwight D. Eisenhower** 1890–1969 American statesman

Pride

When the President does it, that means that it is not illegal.
Richard Nixon 1913–94 American statesman

I have got such a bully pulpit!
Theodore Roosevelt 1858–1919 American statesman

To announce that there must be no criticism of the
president, or that we are to stand by the president, right or
wrong, is not only unpatriotic and servile, but is morally
treasonable to the American public.
Theodore Roosevelt 1858–1919 American statesman

 # Pride

Pride goeth before destruction, and an haughty spirit before
a fall.
Bible

For whosoever exalteth himself shall be abased; and he that
humbleth himself shall be exalted.
Bible

Proud people breed sad sorrows for themselves.
Emily Brontë 1818–48 English writer

He that is down needs fear no fall,
He that is low no pride.
He that is humble ever shall
Have God to be his guide.
John Bunyan 1628–88 English writer

URIAH HEEP: We are so very 'umble.
Charles Dickens 1812–70 English novelist

Pride helps us; and pride is not a bad thing when it only
urges us to hide our own hurts, not to hurt others.
George Eliot 1819–80 English novelist

Progress

I can trace my ancestry back to a protoplasmal primordial atomic globule. Consequently, my family pride is something in-conceivable. I can't help it. I was born sneering.
W. S. Gilbert 1836–1911 English writer

PLEASE ACCEPT MY RESIGNATION. I DON'T WANT TO BELONG TO ANY CLUB THAT WILL ACCEPT ME AS A MEMBER.
Groucho Marx 1890–1977 American film comedian

No one can make you feel inferior without your consent.
Eleanor Roosevelt 1884–1962 American humanitarian

As for conceit, what man will do any good who is not conceited? Nobody holds a good opinion of a man who has a low opinion of himself.
Anthony Trollope 1815–82 English novelist

Progress

Want is one only of five giants on the road of reconstruction…the others are Disease, Ignorance, Squalor and Idleness.
William Henry Beveridge 1879–1963 British economist

The thing that hath been, it is that which shall be; and that which is done is that which shall be done: and there is no new thing under the sun.
Bible

pity this busy monster, manunkind,
not. Progress is a comfortable disease.
e. e. cummings 1894–1962 American poet

Progress doesn't come from early risers—progress is made by lazy men looking for easier ways to do things.
Robert Heinlein 1907–88 American science fiction writer

Progress

Is it progress if a cannibal uses knife and fork?
> **Stanislaw Lec** 1909–66 Polish writer

One step forward two steps back.
> **Lenin** 1870–1924 Russian revolutionary

Oui, cela était autrefois ainsi, mais nous avons changé tout cela.

Yes, in the old days that was so, but we have changed all that.
> **Molière** 1622–73 French comic dramatist

JOHN CLEESE: What have the Romans ever done for us?
> **Monty Python's Flying Circus** 1969–74 British television programme, *in the film* Monty Python's Life of Brian

If I have seen further it is by standing on the shoulders of giants.
> **Isaac Newton** 1642–1727 English mathematician

Forward ever, backward never.
> **Kwame Nkrumah** 1900–72 Ghanaian statesman

'Change' is scientific, 'progress' is ethical; change is indubitable, whereas progress is a matter of controversy.
> **Bertrand Russell** 1872–1970 British philosopher

The reasonable man adapts himself to the world: the unreasonable one persists in trying to adapt the world to himself. Therefore all progress depends on the unreasonable man.
> **George Bernard Shaw** 1856–1950 Irish dramatist

And he gave it for his opinion, that whoever could make two ears of corn or two blades of grass to grow upon a spot of ground where only one grew before, would deserve better of mankind, and do more essential service to his country than the whole race of politicians put together.

    Jonathan Swift 1667–1745 Irish poet and satirist

Without deviation from the norm, progress is not possible.

    Frank Zappa 1940–93 American rock musician

Promises

If [human life] depends on anything, it is on this frail cord, flung from the forgotten hills of yesterday to the invisible mountains of tomorrow.

    G. K. Chesterton 1874–1936 English writer, *on the promise*

My tongue swore, but my mind's unsworn.

    Euripides c.485–c.406 BC Greek dramatist, *lamenting the breaking of an oath*

I believe that it is better to light one candle than promise a million light bulbs.

    Stephen Harper 1959– Canadian statesman

You always pay too much. Particularly for promises. There ain't no such thing as a bargain promise.

    Cormac McCarthy 1933– American novelist

A promise made is a debt unpaid.

    Robert W. Service 1874–1958 Canadian poet

Promises and pie-crust are made to be broken.

    Jonathan Swift 1667–1745 Irish poet and satirist

To promise not to do a thing is the surest way in the world to make a body want to go and do that very thing.

    Mark Twain 1835–1910 American writer

Protest

'It's always best on these occasions to do what the mob do.'
'But suppose there are two mobs?' suggested Mr Snodgrass.
'Shout with the largest,' replied Mr Pickwick.
  Charles Dickens 1812–70 English novelist

Making noise is an effective means of opposition.
  Joseph Goebbels 1897–1945 German Nazi leader

The citizen's first duty is unrest.
  Günter Grass 1927–2015 German writer

Even a purely moral act that has no hope of any immediate
and visible political effect can gradually and indirectly, over
time, gain in political significance.
  Václav Havel 1936–2011 Czech statesman

Ev'rywhere I hear the sound of marching, charging feet, boy,
'Cause summer's here and the time is right for fighting in
  the street, boy.
  Mick Jagger 1943– and **Keith Richards** 1943– English rock
  musicians

One-fifth of the people are against everything all the time.
  Robert Kennedy 1925–68 American politician

A riot is at bottom the language of the unheard.
  Martin Luther King 1929–68 American civil rights leader

The lady doth protest too much, methinks.
  William Shakespeare 1564–1616 English dramatist

Minorities…are almost always in the right.
  Sydney Smith 1771–1845 English essayist

I've always had the impression that real militants are like
cleaning women, doing a thankless, daily but necessary job.
  François Truffaut 1932–84 French film director

Punctuality

I love deadlines. I love the whooshing noise they make as
they go by.
Douglas Adams 1952–2001 English writer

Punctuality is the politeness of kings.
Louis XVIII 1755–1824 French monarch

People who are late are often so much jollier than the people
who have to wait for them.
E. V. Lucas 1868–1938 English writer

We must leave exactly on time…From now on everything
must function to perfection.
Benito Mussolini 1883–1945 Italian dictator, *to a station-master*

You come most carefully upon your hour.
William Shakespeare 1564–1616 English dramatist

Punctuality is the virtue of the bored.
Evelyn Waugh 1903–66 English novelist

Punishment see also **Crime**

All punishment is mischief: all punishment in itself is evil.
Jeremy Bentham 1748–1832 English philosopher

He that spareth his rod hateth his son.
Bible

He that is without sin among you, let him first cast a stone
at her.
Bible

Hanging is too good for him, said Mr Cruelty.
John Bunyan 1628–88 English writer

Punishment

It is one thing to praise discipline, and another to submit to it.
Cervantes 1547–1616 Spanish novelist

Excessive bail shall not be required, nor excessive fines imposed, nor cruel and unusual punishment inflicted.
Constitution of the United States 1787

Punishment is not for revenge, but to lessen crime and reform the criminal.
Elizabeth Fry 1780–1845 English prison reformer

My object all sublime
I shall achieve in time—
To let the punishment fit the crime—
The punishment fit the crime.
W. S. Gilbert 1836–1911 English writer

Awaiting the sensation of a short, sharp shock,
From a cheap and chippy chopper on a big black block.
W. S. Gilbert 1836–1911 English writer

Men are not hanged for stealing horses, but that horses may not be stolen.
Lord Halifax 1633–95 English politician

If my life teaches the public that men are made mad by bad treatment, and if the police are taught that they may not exasperate to madness men they persecute and ill treat, my life will not be entirely thrown away.
Ned Kelly 1855–80 Australian outlaw

Society needs to condemn a little more and understand a little less.
John Major 1943– British statesman

I went out to Charing Cross, to see Major-general Harrison hanged, drawn, and quartered; which was done there, he looking as cheerful as any man could do in that condition.
Samuel Pepys 1633–1703 English diarist

Quotations

The surest way to make a monkey of a man is to quote him.
> **Robert Benchley** 1889–1945 American humorist

It is a good thing for an uneducated man to read books of quotations.
> **Winston Churchill** 1874–1965 British statesman

I hate quotation. Tell me what you know.
> **Ralph Waldo Emerson** 1803–82 American writer

When a thing has been said and well said, have no scruple: take it and copy it.
> **Anatole France** 1844–1924 French man of letters

I quote others only the better to express myself.
> **Montaigne** 1533–92 French moralist

I always have a quotation for everything—it saves original thinking.
> **Dorothy L. Sayers** 1893–1957 English writer

Famous remarks are very seldom quoted correctly.
> **Simeon Strunsky** 1879–1948 American writer

What a good thing Adam had. When he said a good thing he knew nobody had said it before.
> **Mark Twain** 1835–1910 American writer

OSCAR WILDE: How I wish I had said that.
WHISTLER: You will, Oscar, you will.
> **James McNeill Whistler** 1834–1903 American-born painter

Some for renown on scraps of learning dote,
And think they grow immortal as they quote.
> **Edward Young** 1683–1765 English poet

Race see also **Equality**, **Prejudice**

Black is beautiful.
>**Anonymous**, *slogan of American civil rights campaigners, mid-1960s*

You have seen how a man was made a slave; you shall see how a slave was made a man.
>**Frederick Douglass** c.1818–95 American former slave

I herewith commission you to carry out all preparations with regard to…a *total solution* of the Jewish question in those territories of Europe which are under German influence.
>**Hermann Goering** 1893–1946 German Nazi leader

Though it be a thrilling and marvellous thing to be merely young and gifted in such times, it is doubly so, doubly dynamic—to be young, gifted and *black*.
>**Lorraine Hansberry** 1930–65 American dramatist

When I look out at this convention, I see the face of America, red, yellow, brown, black, and white. We are all precious in God's sight—the real rainbow coalition.
>**Jesse Jackson** 1941– American clergyman

There are no 'white' or 'coloured' signs on the foxholes or graveyards of battle.
>**John F. Kennedy** 1917–63 American statesman

I have a dream that my four little children will one day live in a nation where they will not be judged by the colour of their skin but by the content of their character.
>**Martin Luther King** 1929–68 American civil rights leader

My son, your troubled eyes search mine,
Puzzled and hurt by colour line.

Your black skin as soft as velvet shine;
What can I tell you, son of mine?
Oodgeroo Noonuccal 1920–93 Australian poet

Our mistreatment was just not right, and I was tired of it.
Rosa Parks 1913–2005 American civil rights activist, *of her
refusal to surrender her seat on a segregated bus in Alabama to a
white man*

Where today are the Pequot? Where are the Narragansett,
the Mohican, the Pokanoket, and many other once powerful
tribes of our people? They have vanished before the avarice
and oppression of the white man, as snow before the
summer sun.
Tecumseh 1768–1813 Shawnee chief

Am I not a man and a brother.
Josiah Wedgwood 1730–95 English potter, *legend on
Wedgwood cameo, depicting a kneeling African slave in chains*

Remember, Christians, Negroes black as Cain
May be refined, and join th' angelic train.
Phillis Wheatley c.1753–84 American poet

Growing up, I came up with this name: I'm a Cablinasian.
Tiger Woods 1975– American golfer, *explaining his rejection
of 'African-American' as the term to describe his Caucasian,
Afro-American, Native American, Thai, and Chinese ancestry*

Railways

This is the Night Mail crossing the Border,
Bringing the cheque and the postal order,
Letters for the rich, letters for the poor,
The shop at the corner, the girl next door.
W. H. Auden 1907–73 English poet

Reading

Railways and the Church have their critics, but both are the best ways of getting a man to his ultimate destination.
Revd W. Awdry 1911–97 English writer

The only way of catching a train I have ever discovered is to miss the train before.
G. K. Chesterton 1874–1936 English writer

Railway termini. They are our gates to the glorious and the unknown. Through them we pass out into adventure and sunshine, to them, alas! we return.
E. M. Forster 1879–1970 English novelist

Sir, Saturday morning, although recurring at regular and well-foreseen intervals, always seems to take this railway by surprise.
W. S. Gilbert 1836–1911 English writer, *letter to the station-master at Baker Street, on the Metropolitan line*

That life-quickening atmosphere of a big railway station where everything is something trembling on the brink of something else.
Vladimir Nabokov 1899–1977 Russian novelist

 # Reading see also **Books**

In science, read, by preference, the newest works; in literature, the oldest.
Edward Bulwer-Lytton 1803–73 British novelist

Choose an author as you choose a friend.
Wentworth Dillon, Earl of Roscommon c.1633–85 Irish poet

What do we ever get nowadays from reading to equal the excitement and the revelation in those first fourteen years?
Graham Greene 1904–91 English novelist

A man ought to read just as inclination leads him; for what he reads as a task will do him little good.
  Samuel Johnson 1709–84 English lexicographer

Curiously enough, one cannot *read* a book: one can only reread it. A good reader, a major reader, an active and creative reader is a rereader.
  Vladimir Nabokov 1899–1977 Russian novelist

Much reading is an oppression of the mind, and extinguishes the natural candle, which is the reason of so many senseless scholars in the world.
  William Penn 1644–1718 English Quaker

The bookful blockhead, ignorantly read,
With loads of learned lumber in his head.
  Alexander Pope 1688–1744 English poet

POLONIUS: What do you read, my lord?
HAMLET: Words, words, words.
  William Shakespeare 1564–1616 English dramatist

People say that life is the thing, but I prefer reading.
  Logan Pearsall Smith 1865–1946 American writer

Reading is to the mind what exercise is to the body.
  Richard Steele 1672–1729 Irish-born essayist

Reality ✳

It's as large as life, and twice as natural!
  Lewis Carroll 1832–98 English writer

Reality is that which, when you stop believing in it, doesn't go away.
  Philip K. Dick 1928–82 American writer

Relationships

> Human kind
> Cannot bear very much reality.
>
> **T. S. Eliot** 1888–1965 American-born British poet

> All theory, dear friend, is grey, but the golden tree of actual life springs ever green.
>
> **Johann Wolfgang von Goethe** 1749–1832 German writer

> What is rational is actual and what is actual is rational.
>
> **G. W. F. Hegel** 1770–1831 German philosopher

> The camera makes everyone a tourist in other people's reality, and eventually in one's own.
>
> **Susan Sontag** 1933–2004 American writer

> They said, 'You have a blue guitar,
> You do not play things as they are.'
>
> The man replied, 'Things as they are
> Are changed upon the blue guitar.'
>
> **Wallace Stevens** 1879–1955 American poet

> The nineteenth century dislike of Realism is the rage of Caliban seeing his own face in the glass.
>
> **Oscar Wilde** 1854–1900 Irish dramatist

> BLANCHE: I don't want realism.
> MITCH: Naw, I guess not.
> BLANCHE: I'll tell you what I want. Magic!
>
> **Tennessee Williams** 1911–83 American dramatist

 # Relationships

> Love is like the wild rose-briar;
> Friendship like the holly-tree:
> The holly is dark when the rose-briar blooms,
> But which will bloom most constantly?
>
> **Emily Brontë** 1818–48 English writer

Men love women, women love children; children love hamsters—it's quite hopeless.
Alice Thomas Ellis 1932–2005 English novelist

The ones we choose to love become our anchor
when the hawser of the blood-tie's hacked, or frays.
Tony Harrison 1937– British poet

Three things in human life are important. The first is to be kind. The second is to be kind. And the third is to be kind.
Henry James 1843–1916 American novelist

Marriage may often be a stormy lake, but celibacy is almost always a muddy horsepond.
Thomas Love Peacock 1785–1866 English writer

Human relationships don't belong to engineering, mathematics, chess, which offer problems that can be perfectly solved. Human relationships grow, like trees.
J. B. Priestley 1894–1984 English writer

KATHARINE HEPBURN: The time to make up your mind about people is never.
Donald Ogden Stewart 1894–1980 American humorist, *in the film* The Philadelphia Story

By loving people without cause he discovered indubitable causes for loving them.
Leo Tolstoy 1828–1910 Russian novelist

Religion see also **Church**, **God**, **Prayer**

Render therefore unto Caesar the things which are Caesar's; and unto God the things that are God's.
Bible

One religion is as true as another.
Robert Burton 1577–1640 English clergyman

Religion

Christians have burnt each other, quite persuaded
That all the Apostles would have done as they did.
Lord Byron 1788–1824 English poet

Putting moral virtues at the highest, and religion at the
lowest, religion must still be allowed to be a collateral
security, at least, to virtue; and every prudent man will
sooner trust to two securities than to one.
Lord Chesterfield 1694–1773 English writer

Science without religion is lame, religion without science
is blind.
Albert Einstein 1879–1955 German-born theoretical physicist

The various modes of worship, which prevailed in the
Roman world, were all considered by the people as equally
true; by the philosopher, as equally false; and by the
magistrate, as equally useful. And thus toleration produced
not only mutual indulgence, but even religious concord.
Edward Gibbon 1737–94 English historian

In all ages of the world, priests have been enemies of liberty.
David Hume 1711–76 Scottish philosopher

I go into the Muslim mosque and the Jewish synagogue and
the Christian church and I see one altar.
Jalal ad-Din ar-Rumi 1207–73 Persian poet

Religion's in the heart, not in the knee.
Douglas Jerrold 1803–57 English writer

No compulsion is there in religion.
The Koran

I count religion but a childish toy,
And hold there is no sin but ignorance.
Christopher Marlowe 1564–93 English dramatist

Religion…is the opium of the people.
Karl Marx 1818–83 German philosopher

Things have come to a pretty pass when religion is allowed to invade the sphere of private life.
Lord Melbourne 1779–1848 British statesman, *on hearing an evangelical sermon*

My country is the world, and my religion is to do good.
Thomas Paine 1737–1809 English political theorist

Is that which is holy loved by the gods because it is holy, or is it holy because it is loved by the gods?
Plato 429–347 BC Greek philosopher

Religion to me has always been the wound, not the bandage.
Dennis Potter 1935–94 English dramatist

'Men of sense are really but of one religion.'…'Pray, my lord, what religion is that which men of sense agree in?' 'Madam,' says the earl immediately, 'men of sense never tell it.'
Lord Shaftesbury 1621–83 English statesman

We have just enough religion to make us hate, but not enough to make us love one another.
Jonathan Swift 1667–1745 Irish poet and satirist

India has 2,000,000 gods, and worships them all. In religion all other countries are paupers; India is the only millionaire.
Mark Twain 1835–1910 American writer

Orthodoxy is my doxy; heterodoxy is another man's doxy.
William Warburton 1698–1779 English theologian

I went to America to convert the Indians; but oh, who shall convert me?
John Wesley 1703–91 English preacher

Retirement

So many gods, so many creeds,
So many paths that wind and wind,
While just the art of being kind
Is all the sad world needs.

Ella Wheeler Wilcox 1855–1919 American poet

 # Retirement

Once I leave, I leave. I am not going to speak to the man on the bridge, and I am not going to spit on the deck.

Stanley Baldwin 1867–1947 British statesman, *on resigning*

If anything could have pulled me out of retirement, it would have been an Indiana Jones film. But in the end, retirement is just too damned much fun.

Sean Connery 1930– Scottish actor

The most horrifying thing in the world is to be without an adventure.

George Foreman 1948– American boxer, *considering a comeback at 55*

The transition from Who's Who to Who's He.

Eddie George 1938–2009 English banker

Learn to live well, or fairly make your will;
You've played, and loved, and ate, and drunk your fill:
Walk sober off; before a sprightlier age
Comes tittering on, and shoves you from the stage.

Alexander Pope 1688–1744 English poet

As to that leisure evening of life, I must say that I do not want it. I can conceive of no contentment of which toil is not to be the immediate parent.

Anthony Trollope 1815–82 English novelist

Revenge

Revenge is a kind of wild justice, which the more man's nature runs to, the more ought law to weed it out.
Francis Bacon 1561–1626 English courtier

Vengeance is mine; I will repay, saith the Lord.
Bible

Sweet is revenge—especially to women.
Lord Byron 1788–1824 English poet

It may be that vengeance is sweet, and that the gods forbade vengeance to men because they reserved for themselves so delicious and intoxicating a drink. But no one should drain the cup to the bottom. The dregs are often filthy-tasting.
Winston Churchill 1874–1965 British statesman

Heaven has no rage, like love to hatred turned,
Nor Hell a fury, like a woman scorned.
William Congreve 1670–1729 English dramatist

RUSSELL CROWE: And I will have my vengeance, in this life or the next.
David Franzoni 1947– American screenwriter, *in the film* Gladiator

The Germans…are going to be squeezed as a lemon is squeezed—until the pips squeak.
Eric Geddes 1875–1937 British politician

Nobody ever forgets where he buried a hatchet.
Frank McKinney ('Kin') Hubbard 1868–1930 American humorist

Get your retaliation in first.
Carwyn James 1929–83 Welsh rugby player

Revolution

Men should be either treated generously or destroyed,
because they take revenge for slight injuries—for heavy ones
they cannot.
Niccolò Machiavelli 1469–1527 Italian political philosopher

Don't get mad, get everything.
Ivana Trump 1949– Czech model, *advice to wronged wives*

 # Revolution

Better to abolish serfdom from above than to wait till it
begins to abolish itself from below.
Alexander II 1818–81 Russian tsar

The most radical revolutionary will become a conservative
on the day after the revolution.
Hannah Arendt 1906–75 American philosopher

Those who have served the cause of the revolution have
ploughed the sea.
Simón Bolívar 1783–1830 Venezuelan statesman

Revolutions are celebrated when they are no longer
dangerous.
Pierre Boulez 1925–2016 French composer

Rebellion to tyrants is obedience to God.
John Bradshaw 1602–59 English judge

Would it not be easier
In that case for the government
To dissolve the people
And elect another?
Bertolt Brecht 1898–1956 German dramatist, *on the 1953
uprising in East Germany*

Revolution

All modern revolutions have ended in a reinforcement of the State.
>**Albert Camus** 1913–60 French writer

A desperate disease requires a dangerous remedy.
>**Guy Fawkes** 1570–1606 English conspirator

I will die like a true-blue rebel. Don't waste any time in mourning—organize.
>**Joe Hill** 1879–1915 American labour leader, *farewell telegram prior to his death by firing squad*

The generation which commences a revolution can rarely complete it.
>**Thomas Jefferson** 1743–1826 American statesman

When smashing monuments, save the pedestals—they always come in handy.
>**Stanislaw Lec** 1909–66 Polish writer

Après nous le déluge.
After us the deluge.
>**Madame de Pompadour** 1721–64 French courtesan

J'ai vécu.
I survived.
>**Abbé Emmanuel Joseph Sieyès** 1748–1836 French politician, *when asked what he had done during the French Revolution*

I have seen the future; and it works.
>**Lincoln Steffens** 1866–1936 American journalist, *following a visit to the Soviet Union in 1919*

Bliss was it in that dawn to be alive,
But to be young was very heaven!
>**William Wordsworth** 1770–1850 English poet, *on the French revolution*

Royalty

[A king] is the fountain of honour.
Francis Bacon 1561–1626 English courtier

Its mystery is its life. We must not let in daylight upon magic.
Walter Bagehot 1826–77 English economist, *on royalty*

The Sovereign has, under a constitutional monarchy such as ours, three rights—the right to be consulted, the right to encourage, the right to warn.
Walter Bagehot 1826–77 English economist

To be Prince of Wales is not a position. It is a predicament.
Alan Bennett 1934– English writer

A subject and a sovereign are clean different things.
Charles I 1600–49 British monarch

I'd like to be a queen in people's hearts but I don't see myself being Queen of this country.
Diana, Princess of Wales 1961–97 British princess

Everyone likes flattery; and when you come to Royalty you should lay it on with a trowel.
Benjamin Disraeli 1804–81 British statesman

I have found it impossible to carry the heavy burden of responsibility and to discharge my duties as King as I would wish to do without the help and support of the woman I love.
Edward VIII 1894–1972 British monarch, *radio broadcast following his abdication*

I know I have the body of a weak and feeble woman, but I have the heart and stomach of a king, and of a king of England too.
Elizabeth I 1533–1603 English monarch

L'État c'est moi.
I am the State.
    Louis XIV 1638–1715 French monarch

Royalty is the gold filling in a mouthful of decay.
    John Osborne 1929– English dramatist

Uneasy lies the head that wears a crown.
    William Shakespeare 1564–1616 English dramatist

Monarchy is only the string that ties the robber's bundle.
    Percy Bysshe Shelley 1792–1822 English poet

I will be good.
    Queen Victoria 1819–1901 British monarch, *on being shown a chart of the line of succession*

Satisfaction see also Discontent

You never know what is enough unless you know what is more than enough.
    William Blake 1757–1827 English poet

He is a wise man who does not grieve for the things which he has not, but rejoices for those which he has.
    Epictetus C.AD 50–120 Phrygian philosopher

A book of verses underneath the bough,
A jug of wine, a loaf of bread—and Thou
Beside me singing in the wilderness—
And wilderness were paradise enow.
    Edward Fitzgerald 1809–83 English poet

I can't get no satisfaction.
    Mick Jagger 1943– and **Keith Richards** 1943– English rock musicians

Science

If one cannot catch the bird of paradise, better take a wet hen.
Nikita Khrushchev 1894–1971 Soviet statesman

So long as the great majority of men are not deprived of either property or honour, they are satisfied.
Niccolò Machiavelli 1469–1527 Italian political philosopher

He is well paid that is well satisfied.
William Shakespeare 1564–1616 English dramatist

As long as I have a want, I have a reason for living. Satisfaction is death.
George Bernard Shaw 1856–1950 Irish dramatist

Content is disillusioning to behold: what is there to be content about?
Virginia Woolf 1882–1941 English novelist

 # Science see also **Life Sciences**, **Technology**

When I find myself in the company of scientists, I feel like a shabby curate who has strayed by mistake into a drawing room full of dukes.
W. H. Auden 1907–73 English poet

Anybody who is not shocked by this subject has failed to understand it.
Niels Bohr 1885–1962 Danish physicist, *of quantum mechanics*

Basic research is what I am doing when I don't know what I am doing.
Wernher von Braun 1912–77 German-born rocket engineer

The aim of science is not to open the door to infinite wisdom, but to set a limit to infinite error.
Bertolt Brecht 1898–1956 German dramatist

The essence of science: ask an impertinent question, and you are on the way to a pertinent answer.
Jacob Bronowski 1908–74 Polish-born scientist

If an elderly but distinguished scientist says that something is possible he is almost certainly right, but if he says that it is impossible he is very probably wrong.
Arthur C. Clarke 1917–2008 English science fiction writer

In science the credit goes to the man who convinces the world, not to the man to whom the idea first occurs.
Francis Darwin 1848–1925 English botanist

It is more important to have beauty in one's equations than to have them fit experiment.
Paul Dirac 1902–84 British theoetical physicist

I ask you to look both ways. For the road to a knowledge of the stars leads through the atom; and important knowledge of the atom has been reached through the stars.
Arthur Eddington 1882–1944 British astrophysicist

The grand aim of all science [is] to cover the greatest number of empirical facts by logical deduction from the smallest possible number of hypotheses or axioms.
Albert Einstein 1879–1955 German-born theoretical physicist

It can scarcely be denied that the supreme goal of all theory is to make the irreducible basic elements as simple and as few as possible without having to surrender the adequate representation of a single datum of experience.
Albert Einstein 1879–1955 German-born theoretical physicist, *often quoted as 'Everything should be made as simple as possible, but not simpler'*

Nothing is too wonderful to be true, if it be consistent with the laws of nature, and in such things as these, experiment is the best test of such consistency.
Michael Faraday 1791–1867 English scientist

Science

The great tragedy of Science—the slaying of a beautiful hypothesis by an ugly fact.

T. H. Huxley 1825–95 English biologist

Where observation is concerned, chance favours only the prepared mind.

Louis Pasteur 1822–95 French chemist

Science knows no country, because knowledge belongs to humanity.

Louis Pasteur 1822–95 French chemist

I almost think it is the ultimate destiny of science to exterminate the human race.

Thomas Love Peacock 1785–1866 English writer

A new scientific truth does not triumph by convincing its opponents and making them see the light, but rather because its opponents eventually die, and a new generation grows up that is familiar with it.

Max Planck 1858–1947 German physicist

Science is built up of facts, as a house is built of stones; but an accumulation of facts is no more a science than a heap of stones is a house.

Henri Poincaré 1854–1912 French mathematician

Nature, and Nature's laws lay hid in night.
God said, *Let Newton be!* and all was light.

Alexander Pope 1688–1744 English poet

Aristotle maintained that women have fewer teeth than men; although he was twice married, it never occurred to him to verify this statement by examining his wives' mouths.

Bertrand Russell 1872–1970 British philosopher

All science is either physics or stamp collecting.

Ernest Rutherford 1871–1937 New Zealand physicist

We haven't got the money, so we've got to think!

Ernest Rutherford 1871–1937 New Zealand physicist

Science is always wrong; it is the very artifice of men.
Science can never solve one problem without raising ten
more problems.

George Bernard Shaw 1856–1950 Irish dramatist

It did not last: the Devil howling 'Ho!
Let Einstein be!' restored the status quo.

J. C. Squire 1884–1958 English man of letters, *responding to Pope's lines on Newton*

Scotland

There are few more impressive sights in the world than a
Scotsman on the make.

J. M. Barrie 1860–1937 Scottish writer

My heart's in the Highlands, my heart is not here;
My heart's in the Highlands a-chasing the deer.

Robert Burns 1759–96 Scottish poet

Scots, wha hae wi' Wallace bled,
Scots, wham Bruce has aften led,
Welcome to your gory bed,—
Or to victorie.

Robert Burns 1759–96 Scottish poet

From the lone shieling of the misty island
Mountains divide us, and the waste of seas—
Yet still the blood is strong, the heart is Highland,
And we in dreams behold the Hebrides!

John Galt 1779–1839 Scottish writer

The noblest prospect which a Scotchman ever sees, is the
high road that leads him to England!

Samuel Johnson 1709–84 English lexicographer

Sculpture

O Caledonia! stern and wild,
Meet nurse for a poetic child!
Sir Walter Scott 1771–1832 Scottish novelist

Stands Scotland where it did?
William Shakespeare 1564–1616 English dramatist

O flower of Scotland, when will we see your like again,
that fought and died for your wee bit hill and glen
and stood against him, proud Edward's army,
and sent him homeward tae think again.
Roy Williamson 1936–90 Scottish musician

It is never difficult to distinguish between a Scotsman with a
grievance and a ray of sunshine.
P. G. Wodehouse 1881–1975 English writer

 # Sculpture

Most statues seem sad and introspective,
they hold their breath between coming and going,
They lament their devoured, once shuddering stone.
Dannie Abse 1923–2014 Welsh-born poet

Carving is interrelated masses conveying an emotion: a
perfect relationship between the mind and the colour, light
and weight which is the stone, made by the hand which feels.
Barbara Hepworth 1903–75 English sculptor

It's amazing what you can do with an E in A-level art,
twisted imagination and a chainsaw.
Damien Hirst 1965– English artist, *after winning the 1995
Turner Prize*

The marble not yet carved can hold the form
Of every thought the greatest artist has.
Michelangelo 1475–1564 Italian artist

The first hole made through a piece of stone is a revelation.
Henry Moore 1898–1986 English sculptor

The Sea

A willing foe and sea room.
Anonymous, *naval toast in the time of Nelson*

They that go down to the sea in ships: and occupy their business in great waters.
Bible

Don't talk to me about naval tradition. It's nothing but rum, sodomy, and the lash.
Winston Churchill 1874–1965 British statesman

Water, water, everywhere,
And all the boards did shrink;
Water, water, everywhere,
Nor any drop to drink.
Samuel Taylor Coleridge 1772–1834 English poet

No man will be a sailor who has contrivance enough to get himself into a jail; for being in a ship is being in a jail, with the chance of being drowned…A man in a jail has more room, better food, and commonly better company.
Samuel Johnson 1709–84 English lexicographer

It is an interesting biological fact that all of us have in our veins the exact same percentage of salt in our blood that exists in the ocean, and therefore, we have salt in our blood, in our sweat, in our tears. We are tied to the ocean. And when we go back to the sea—whether it is to sail or to watch it—we are going back from whence we came.
John F. Kennedy 1917–63 American statesman

Secrecy

I must go down to the seas again, to the lonely sea and
   the sky,
And all I ask is a tall ship and a star to steer her by.
     John Masefield 1878–1967 English poet

Meditation and water are wedded for ever.
     Herman Melville 1819–91 American novelist

The sea hates a coward!
     Eugene O'Neill 1888–1953 American dramatist

Whosoever commands the sea commands the trade;
whosoever commands the trade of the world commands
the riches of the world, and consequently the world itself.
     Walter Ralegh c.1552–1618 English courtier

Full fathom five thy father lies;
Of his bones are coral made:
Those are pearls that were his eyes:
Nothing of him that doth fade,
But doth suffer a sea-change
Into something rich and strange.
     William Shakespeare 1564–1616 English dramatist

Rocked in the cradle of the deep.
     Emma Hart Willard 1787–1870 American educationist

 # Secrecy

I shall be but a short time tonight. I have seldom spoken
with greater regret, for my lips are not yet unsealed.
     Stanley Baldwin 1867–1947 British statesman, *usually quoted
as 'My lips are sealed'*

When thou doest alms, let not thy left hand know what thy
right hand doeth.
     Bible

The truth is out there.

Chris Carter 1957- American screenwriter, *catchphrase;*
The X Files

The small man said to the other: 'Where does a wise man
hide a pebble?' And the tall man answered in a low voice:
'On the beach.'

G. K. Chesterton 1874-1936 English writer

I would not open windows into men's souls.

Elizabeth I 1533-1603 English monarch

A secret in the Oxford sense: you may tell it to only one
person at a time.

Lord Franks 1905-92 British philosopher

We dance round in a ring and suppose,
But the Secret sits in the middle and knows.

Robert Frost 1874-1963 American poet

Once the toothpaste is out of the tube, it is awfully hard to
get it back in.

H. R. Haldeman 1929-93 American Presidential assistant,
comment on the Watergate affair

Love and a cough cannot be hid.

George Herbert 1593-1633 English poet

Nothing weighs so heavy as a secret; women find it difficult
to carry one far. And I know a lot of men who are just like
women about this.

Jean de la Fontaine 1621-95 French poet

It is wise to disclose what cannot be concealed.

Friedrich von Schiller 1759-1805 German poet

A secret may be sometimes best kept by keeping the secret
of its being a secret.

Henry Taylor 1800-86 British writer

The Self

Whatever you are is never enough; you must find a way to accept something however small from the other to make you whole.

Chinua Achebe 1930–2013 Nigerian novelist

Some thirty inches from my nose
The frontier of my Person goes,
And all the untilled air between
Is private *pagus* or demesne.

W. H. Auden 1907–73 English poet

Through the Thou a person becomes I.

Martin Buber 1878–1965 Austrian-born philosopher

Be who God meant you to be and you will set the world on fire.

St Catherine of Siena c.1347–80 Italian mystic

'You' your joys and your sorrows, your memories and ambitions, your sense of personal identity and free will, are in fact no more than the behaviour of a vast assembly of nerve cells and their associated molecules.

Francis Crick 1916–2004 English biophysicist

To study the self is to forget the self. To forget the self is to be authenticated by the myriad things.

Dogen Kigen 1200–53 Japanese Buddhist monk, *often quoted as '…to become one with the ten thousand things'*

If you have no confidence in self you are twice defeated in the race of life. With confidence you have won even before you have started.

Marcus Garvey 1887–1940 Jamaican political activist

I am the master of my fate:
I am the captain of my soul.

W. E. Henley 1849–1903 English poet

It is not contrary to reason to prefer the destruction of the whole world to the scratching of my finger.

David Hume 1711–76 Scottish philosopher

I am not a number, I am a free man!

Patrick McGoohan 1928–2009 English actor, *Number Six, in* The Prisoner

When a man points a finger at someone else, he should remember that four of his fingers are pointing to himself.

Louis Nizer 1902–94 American lawyer

The self is hateful.

Blaise Pascal 1623–62 French scientist and philosopher

Thus God and nature linked the gen'ral frame,
And bade self-love and social be the same.

Alexander Pope 1688–1744 English poet

Personal isn't the same as important.

Terry Pratchett 1948–2015 English novelist

Who is it that can tell me who I am?

William Shakespeare 1564–1616 English dramatist

It is easy—terribly easy—to shake a man's faith in himself. To take advantage of that to break a man's spirit is devil's work.

George Bernard Shaw 1856–1950 Irish dramatist

Whatever people think I am or say I am, that's what I'm not.

Alan Sillitoe 1928–2010 English writer

Rose is a rose is a rose is a rose, is a rose.

Gertrude Stein 1874–1946 American writer

If a man does not keep pace with his companions, perhaps it is because he hears a different drummer. Let him step to the music which he hears, however measured or far away.

Henry David Thoreau 1817–62 American writer

Self-Knowledge

Do I contradict myself?
Very well then I contradict myself,
(I am large, I contain multitudes.)
Walt Whitman 1819–92 American poet

 # Self-Knowledge

Know thyself.
Anonymous, *inscribed on the temple of Apollo at Delphi*

The image of myself which I try to create in my own mind
in order that I may love myself is very different from the
image which I try to create in the minds of others in order
that they may love me.
W. H. Auden 1907–73 English poet

Why beholdest thou the mote that is in thy brother's eye,
but considerest not the beam that is in thine own eye?
Bible

The one self-knowledge worth having is to know one's own
mind.
F. H. Bradley 1846–1924 English philosopher

O wad some Pow'r the giftie gie us
To see oursels as others see us!
It wad frae mony a blunder free us,
And foolish notion.
Robert Burns 1759–96 Scottish poet

How little do we know that which we are!
How less what we may be!
Lord Byron 1788–1824 English poet

I do not know whether I was then a man dreaming I was a
butterfly, or whether I am now a butterfly dreaming I am
a man.
Chuang-tzu (Zhuangzi) c.369–286 BC Chinese philosopher

I do not know myself, and God forbid that I should.
Johann Wolfgang von Goethe 1749–1832 German writer

He who knows others is wise;
He who knows himself is enlightened.
He who conquers others has physical strength.
He who conquers himself is strong.
Lao Tzu c.604–c.531 BC Chinese philosopher

All our knowledge is, ourselves to know.
Alexander Pope 1688–1744 English poet

This above all: to thine own self be true,
And it must follow, as the night the day,
Thou canst not then be false to any man.
William Shakespeare 1564–1616 English dramatist

Sex see also **Love**, **Marriage**

That [sex] was the most fun I ever had without laughing.
Woody Allen 1935– American film director

Don't knock masturbation. It's sex with someone I love.
Woody Allen 1935– American film director

On bisexuality: It immediately doubles your chances for a
date on Saturday night.
Woody Allen 1935– American film director

Give me chastity and continency—but not yet!
St Augustine of Hippo AD 354–430 Roman theologian

It doesn't matter what you do in the bedroom as long as you
don't do it in the street and frighten the horses.
Mrs Patrick Campbell 1865–1940 English actress

The pleasure is momentary, the position ridiculous, and the
expense damnable.
Lord Chesterfield 1694–1773 English writer

Sex

Licence my roving hands, and let them go,
Behind, before, above, between, below.
O my America, my new found land,
My kingdom, safeliest when with one man manned.
John Donne 1572–1631 English poet

I'll have what she's having.
Nora Ephron 1941–2012 American screenwriter, *said by woman to waiter, seeing Sally acting an orgasm, in the film* When Harry Met Sally

BILLY CRYSTAL: Women need a reason to have sex, men just need a place.
Lowell Ganz 1948– and **Babaloo Mandel** 1949– American screenwriters, *in the film* City Slickers

But did thee feel the earth move?
Ernest Hemingway 1899–1961 American novelist

When I hear his steps outside my door I lie down on my bed, close my eyes, open my legs, and think of England.
Lady Hillingdon 1857–1940

The only unnatural sex act is that which you cannot perform.
Alfred Kinsey 1894–1956 American sex researcher

'Tisn't beauty, so to speak, nor good talk necessarily. It's just It. Some women'll stay in a man's memory if they once walked down a street.
Rudyard Kipling 1865–1936 English writer

The Duke returned from the wars today and did pleasure me in his top-boots.
Sarah, Duchess of Marlborough 1660–1744

Not tonight, Josephine.
Napoleon I 1769–1821 French emperor

Love is two minutes fifty-two seconds of squishing noises.
Johnny Rotten 1957– English pop singer

Is it not strange that desire should so many years outlive
performance?
William Shakespeare 1564–1616 English dramatist

Someone asked Sophocles, 'How is your sex-life now?
Are you still able to have a woman?' He replied, 'Hush,
man; most gladly indeed am I rid of it all, as though I had
escaped from a mad and savage master.'
Sophocles c.496–406 BC Greek dramatist

Is that a gun in your pocket, or are you just glad to see me?
Mae West 1892–1980 American film actress

Sickness see also **Medicine**

A man's illness is his private territory and, no matter how
much he loves you and how close you are, you stay an
outsider. You are healthy.
Lauren Bacall 1924–2014 American actress

If a lot of cures are suggested for a disease, it means that the
disease is incurable.
Anton Chekhov 1860–1904 Russian writer

All diseases run into one, old age.
Ralph Waldo Emerson 1803–82 American writer

Did God who gave us flowers and trees,
Also provide the allergies?
E. Y. ('Yip') Harburg 1898–1981 American songwriter

It is a most extraordinary thing, but I never read a patent
medicine advertisement without being impelled to the

Sickness

conclusion that I am suffering from the particular disease therein dealt with in its most virulent form.

Jerome K. Jerome 1859–1927 English writer

I told you I was ill.

Spike Milligan 1918–2002 Irish comedian, *inscription on his gravestone*

The desire to take medicine is perhaps the greatest feature which distinguishes man from animals.

William Osler 1849–1919 Canadian-born physician

Cured yesterday of my disease,
I died last night of my physician.

Matthew Prior 1664–1721 English poet

Illness is the doctor to whom we pay most heed; to kindness, to knowledge, we make promise only; pain we obey.

Marcel Proust 1871–1922 French novelist

I now begin the journey that will lead me into the sunset of my life.

Ronald Reagan 1911–2004 American statesman, *statement to the American people revealing that he had Alzheimer's disease*

You matter because you are you, and you matter to the last moment of your life. We will do all that we can not only to help you die peacefully, but also to live until you die.

Cicely Saunders 1916–2005 English founder of hospice movement

Diseases desperate grown,
By desperate appliances are relieved
Or not at all.

William Shakespeare 1564–1616 English dramatist

Illness is the night-side of life, a more onerous citizenship.
Everyone who is born holds dual citizenship, in the
kingdom of the well and in the kingdom of the sick.

    Susan Sontag 1933–2004 American writer

The biggest disease today is not leprosy or tuberculosis,
but rather the feeling of being unwanted, uncared for and
deserted by everybody.

    Mother Teresa 1910–97 Roman Catholic nun

To know ourselves diseased, is half our cure.

    Edward Young 1683–1765 English poet

Silence

Silence is the virtue of fools.

    Francis Bacon 1561–1626 English courtier

Blessed is the man who, having nothing to say, abstains
from giving us wordy evidence of the fact.

    George Eliot 1819–80 English novelist

Thou still unravished bride of quietness,
Thou foster-child of silence and slow time.

    John Keats 1795–1821 English poet

People talking without speaking
People hearing without listening…
'Fools,' said I, 'You do not know
Silence like a cancer grows.'

    Paul Simon 1942– American singer

The sound of Brahman is OM. At the end of OM is silence.
It is a silence of joy.

    The Upanishads 800–200 BC Hindu sacred treatises

Singing see also **Music**

Nothing is capable of being well set to music that is not nonsense.

Joseph Addison 1672–1719 English writer

Today if something is not worth saying, people sing it.

Pierre-Augustin Caron de Beaumarchais 1732–99 French dramatist

The exercise of singing is delightful to Nature, and good to preserve the health of man. It doth strengthen all parts of the breast, and doth open the pipes.

William Byrd 1543–1623 English composer

Swans sing before they die: 'twere no bad thing
Should certain persons die before they sing.

Samuel Taylor Coleridge 1772–1834 English poet

Every tone [of the songs of the slaves] was a testimony against slavery, and a prayer to God for deliverance from chains.

Frederick Douglass c.1818–95 American former slave

In writing songs I've learned as much from Cézanne as I have from Woody Guthrie.

Bob Dylan 1941–   American singer

If a man were permitted to make all the ballads, he need not care who should make the laws of a nation.

Andrew Fletcher of Saltoun 1655–1716 Scottish patriot

Opera is when a guy gets stabbed in the back and, instead of bleeding, he sings.

Ed Gardner 1901–63 American comedian

Words make you think a thought. Music makes you feel a feeling. A song makes you feel a thought.

E. Y. ('Yip') Harburg 1898–1981 American songwriter

You think that's noise—you ain't heard nuttin' yet!
> **Al Jolson** 1886–1950 American singer, *in a café, competing with the din from a neighbouring building site*

The Skies

Beautiful! Beautiful! Magnificent desolation.
> **Buzz Aldrin** 1930– American astronaut, *on landing on the moon*

Looking up at the stars, I know quite well
That for all they care, I can go to hell.
> **W. H. Auden** 1907–73 English poet

The heavens declare the glory of God: and the firmament sheweth his handy-work.
> **Bible**

Slowly, silently, now the moon
Walks the night in her silver shoon.
> **Walter de la Mare** 1873–1956 English poet

Busy old fool, unruly sun,
Why dost thou thus,
Through windows, and through curtains call on us?
> **John Donne** 1572–1631 English poet

Eppur si muove.

But it does move.
> **Galileo Galilei** 1564–1642 Italian astronomer, *after his recantation, that the earth moves around the sun*

It may be that the stars of heaven appear to us fair and pure simply because we are at such a distance from them, and know nothing of their private life.
> **Heinrich Heine** 1797–1856 German poet

Sleep

Look at the stars! look, look up at the skies!
O look at all the fire-folk sitting in the air!
The bright boroughs, the circle-citadels there!
      Gerard Manley Hopkins 1844–89 English poet

…The evening star,
Love's harbinger.
      John Milton 1608–74 English poet

The eternal silence of these infinite spaces [the heavens]
terrifies me.
      Blaise Pascal 1623–62 French scientist and philosopher

        The moon's an arrant thief,
And her pale fire she snatches from the sun.
      William Shakespeare 1564–1616 English dramatist

I have loved the stars too truly to be fearful of the night.
      Sarah Williams 1837–68 British writer

 # Sleep see also **Dreams**

The sleep of a labouring man is sweet.
      Bible

…The cool kindliness of sheets, that soon
Smooth away trouble; and the rough male kiss
Of blankets.
      Rupert Brooke 1887–1915 English poet

When you're lying awake with a dismal headache, and
   repose is taboo'd by anxiety,
I conceive you may use any language you choose to indulge
   in, without impropriety.
      W. S. Gilbert 1836–1911 English writer

Sleep is when all the unsorted stuff comes flying out as from a dustbin upset in a high wind.
William Golding 1911–93 English novelist

What hath night to do with sleep?
John Milton 1608–74 English poet

Sleeping is no mean art: for its sake one must stay awake all day.
Friedrich Nietzsche 1844–1900 German philosopher

And so to bed.
Samuel Pepys 1633–1703 English diarist

Methought I heard a voice cry, 'Sleep no more!
Macbeth does murder sleep,' the innocent sleep,
Sleep that knits up the ravelled sleave of care.
William Shakespeare 1564–1616 English dramatist

In winter I get up at night
And dress by yellow candle-light.
In summer, quite the other way,—
I have to go to bed by day.
Robert Louis Stevenson 1850–94 Scottish novelist

Early to rise and early to bed makes a male healthy and wealthy and dead.
James Thurber 1894–1961 American humorist

Tired Nature's sweet restorer, balmy sleep!
Edward Young 1683–1765 English poet

Society

Hunger allows no choice
To the citizen or the police;
We must love one another or die.
W. H. Auden 1907–73 English poet

Society

We started off trying to set up a small anarchist community, but people wouldn't obey the rules.
> **Alan Bennett** 1934–   English writer

The greatest happiness of the greatest number is the foundation of morals and legislation.
> **Jeremy Bentham** 1748–1832 English philosopher

Society is indeed a contract…it becomes a partnership not only between those who are living, but between those who are living, those who are dead, and those who are to be born.
> **Edmund Burke** 1729–97 Irish-born politician

The Big Society is our big idea.
> **David Cameron** 1966–   British Conservative statesman

No man is an Island, entire of it self.
> **John Donne** 1572–1631 English poet

Economics is all about how people make choices. Sociology is all about why they don't have any choices to make.
> **James Stemble Duesenberry** 1918–2009 American economist

Only in the state does man have a rational existence…Man owes his entire existence to the state, and has his being within it alone.
> **G. W. F. Hegel** 1770–1831 German philosopher

In a consumer society there are inevitably two kinds of slaves: the prisoners of addiction and the prisoners of envy.
> **Ivan Illich** 1926–2002 American sociologist

From each according to his abilities, to each according to his needs.
> **Karl Marx** 1818–83 German philosopher

The city is not a concrete jungle, it is a human zoo.
> **Desmond Morris** 1928–   English anthropologist

There is no such thing as Society. There are individual men and women, and there are families.
Margaret Thatcher 1925–2013 British stateswoman

The Social Contract is nothing more or less than a vast conspiracy of human beings to lie to and humbug themselves and one another for the general Good. Lies are the mortar that bind the savage individual man into the social masonry.
H. G. Wells 1866–1946 English novelist

Solitude ✳

He who is unable to live in society, or who has no need because he is sufficient for himself, must be either a beast or a god.
Aristotle 384–322 BC Greek philosopher

It is not good that the man should be alone; I will make him an help meet for him.
Bible

I want to be alone.
Greta Garbo 1905–90 Swedish actress

Conversation enriches the understanding, but solitude is the school of genius.
Edward Gibbon 1737–94 English historian

If you are idle, be not solitary; if you are solitary, be not idle.
Samuel Johnson 1709–84 English lexicographer

Down to Gehenna or up to the Throne,
He travels the fastest who travels alone.
Rudyard Kipling 1865–1936 English writer

All the lonely people, where do they all come from?
John Lennon 1940–80 and **Paul McCartney** 1942–   English pop singers

Sorrow

Ships that pass in the night, and speak each other in
   passing;
Only a signal shown and a distant voice in the darkness;
So on the ocean of life we pass and speak one another,
Only a look and a voice; then darkness again and a silence.
Henry Wadsworth Longfellow 1807–82 American poet

Never less alone than when alone.
Samuel Rogers 1763–1855 English poet

Loneliness is the poverty of self; solitude is the richness
of self.
May Sarton 1912–95 American writer

Man goes into the noisy crowd to drown his own clamour
of silence.
Rabindranath Tagore 1861–1941 Bengali poet

One may have a blazing hearth in one's soul, and yet no one
ever comes to sit by it.
Vincent Van Gogh 1853–90 Dutch painter

We're born alone, we live alone, we die alone. Only through
our love and friendship can we create the illusion for the
moment that we're not alone.
Orson Welles 1915–85 American film director, *words added by
Welles to Henry Jaglom's script for the film* Someone to Love

 Sorrow see also **Bereavement**, **Suffering**

By the waters of Babylon we sat down and wept: when we
remembered thee, O Sion.
Bible

I tell you, hopeless grief is passionless.
Elizabeth Barrett Browning 1806–61 English poet

We do not expect people to be deeply moved by what is not unusual. That element of tragedy which lies in the very fact of frequency, has not yet wrought itself into the coarse emotion of mankind.

George Eliot 1819–80 English novelist

Yes, he thought, between grief and nothing I will take grief.

William Faulkner 1897–1962 American novelist

Now laughing friends deride tears I cannot hide,
So I smile and say 'When a lovely flame dies,
Smoke gets in your eyes.'

Otto Harbach 1873–1963 American songwriter

No one ever told me that grief felt so like fear.

C. S. Lewis 1898–1963 English literary scholar

Sorrow and silence are strong, and patient endurance is godlike.

Henry Wadsworth Longfellow 1807–82 American poet

The pain of grief is just as much a part of life as the joy of love; it is, perhaps, the price we pay for love, the cost of commitment .

Colin Murray Parkes 1928– English psychiatrist, *usually quoted as 'Grief is the price we pay for love'*

Small sorrows speak; great ones are silent.

Seneca ('the Younger') c.4 BC–AD 65 Roman philosopher

When sorrows come, they come not single spies,
But in battalions.

William Shakespeare 1564–1616 English dramatist

Give sorrow words: the grief that does not speak
Whispers the o'er-fraught heart, and bids it break.

William Shakespeare 1564–1616 English dramatist

Speechmaking

Tears, idle tears, I know not what they mean,
Tears from the depth of some divine despair.
Alfred, Lord Tennyson 1809–92 English poet

Pure and complete sorrow is as impossible as pure and
complete joy.
Leo Tolstoy 1828–1910 Russian novelist

Sunt lacrimae rerum et mentem mortalia tangunt.
There are tears shed for things and mortality touches the
heart.
Virgil 70–19 BC Roman poet

For of all sad words of tongue or pen,
The saddest are these: 'It might have been!'
John Greenleaf Whittier 1807–92 American poet

Laugh and the world laughs with you;
Weep, and you weep alone;
For the sad old earth must borrow its mirth,
But has trouble enough of its own.
Ella Wheeler Wilcox 1855–1919 American poet

 # Speechmaking see also **Conversation**

I do not object to people looking at their watches when
I am speaking. But I strongly object when they start shaking
them to make certain they are still going.
Lord Birkett 1883–1962 English judge

Grasp the subject, the words will follow.
Cato the Elder 234–149 BC Roman statesman

He [Lord Charles Beresford] is one of those orators of
whom it was well said, 'Before they get up, they do not
know what they are going to say; when they are speaking,

they do not know what they are saying; and when they have sat down, they do not know what they have said.'

Winston Churchill 1874–1965 British statesman

When you have nothing to say, say nothing.

Charles Caleb Colton c.1780–1832 English clergyman

When asked what was first in oratory, [he] replied to his questioner, 'action,' what second, 'action,' and again third, 'action'.

Demosthenes c.384–c.322 BC Greek statesman

Human speech is like a cracked kettle on which we tap crude rhythms for bears to dance to, while we long to make music that will melt the stars.

Gustave Flaubert 1821–80 French novelist

But all was false and hollow; though his tongue
Dropped manna, and could make the worse appear
The better reason.

John Milton 1608–74 English poet

Be silent, unless your speech is better than silence.

Salvator Rosa 1615–73 Italian painter, *inscription on self portrait*

I do not much dislike the matter, but
The manner of his speech.

William Shakespeare 1564–1616 English dramatist

Friends, Romans, countrymen, lend me your ears.

William Shakespeare 1564–1616 English dramatist

If I reprehend any thing in this world, it is the use of my oracular tongue, and a nice derangement of epitaphs!

Richard Brinsley Sheridan 1751–1816 Irish dramatist

Do you remember that in classical times when Cicero had finished speaking, the people said, 'How well he spoke',

Sport

but when Demosthenes had finished speaking, they said, 'Let us march.'

Adlai Stevenson 1900–65 American politician

What can be said at all can be said clearly; and whereof one cannot speak thereof one must be silent.

Ludwig Wittgenstein 1889–1951 Austrian-born philosopher

The reason why we have two ears and only one mouth is that we may listen the more and talk the less.

Zeno c.335–c.263 BC Greek philosopher

 # Sport see also **Baseball, Cricket, Football, Golf, Tennis**

Citius, altius, fortius.
Swifter, higher, stronger.

Anonymous, *motto of the Olympic Games*

This is a hard tour and hard work wins it. Vive Le Tour.

Lance Armstrong 1971– American cyclist, *on winning his seventh consecutive Tour de France*

I just blew my mind. And I blew the world's mind.

Usain Bolt 1986– Jamaican athlete, *on winning the 200m at the Beijing Olympics*

Sports do not build character. They reveal it.

Heywood Hale Broun 1918–2001 American sports commentator

The important thing in life is not the victory but the contest; the essential thing is not to have won but to have fought well.

Baron Pierre de Coubertin 1863–1937 French sportsman, *on the Olympic Games*

There is plenty of time to win this game, and to thrash the Spaniards too.

Francis Drake c.1540–96 English sailor, *receiving news of the Armada while playing bowls on Plymouth Hoe*

Nice guys. Finish last.

Leo Durocher 1906–91 American baseball coach, *usually quoted as 'Nice guys finish last'*

He shoots! He scores!

Foster William Hewitt 1902–85 Canadian broadcaster, *catchphrase used at ice-hockey games*

Only two things does he [the modern citizen] anxiously wish for—bread and circuses.

Juvenal c.AD 60–c.140 Roman satirist

The flannelled fools at the wicket or the muddied oafs at the goals.

Rudyard Kipling 1865–1936 English writer

A royal sport for the natural kings of earth.

Jack London 1876–1916 American novelist, *on surfing*

> Chaos umpire sits,
> And by decision more embroils the fray.

John Milton 1608–74 English poet

Play up! play up! and play the game!

Henry Newbolt 1862–1938 English writer

Eclipse first, the rest nowhere.

Dennis O'Kelly c.1720–87 Irish racehorse-owner, *comment on a horse race*

Serious sport has nothing to do with fair play. It is bound up with hatred, jealousy, boastfulness, and disregard of all the rules.

George Orwell 1903–50 English novelist

Spring

For when the One Great Scorer comes to mark against
your name,
He writes—not that you won or lost—but how you played
the Game.
Grantland Rice 1880–1954 American sports writer

To play billiards well is a sign of an ill-spent youth.
Charles Roupell British lawyer

Sure, winning isn't everything. It's the only thing.
Henry 'Red' Sanders 1905–58 American football coach

Ka mate! Ka mate! Ka ora! Ka ora!
I die! I die! I live! I live!
Te Rauparaha –d. 1849 Maori chief, *haka, now particularly
associated with the New Zealand All Blacks rugby union team*

 # Spring

In fact, it is about five o'clock in an evening that the
first hour of spring strikes—autumn arrives in the early
morning, but spring at the close of a winter day.
Elizabeth Bowen 1899–1973 Anglo-Irish novelist

Whan that Aprill with his shoures soote
The droghte of March hath perced to the roote.
Geoffrey Chaucer c.1343–1400 English poet

April is the cruellest month, breeding
Lilacs out of the dead land.
T. S. Eliot 1888–1965 American-born British poet

And since to look at things in bloom
Fifty springs are little room,
About the woodlands I will go
To see the cherry hung with snow.
A. E. Housman 1859–1936 English poet

Work seethes in the hands of spring,
That strapping dairymaid.
   Boris Pasternak 1890–1960 Russian novelist

Statistics

Statistics are the triumph of the quantitative method, and
the quantitative method is the victory of sterility and death.
   Hilaire Belloc 1870–1953 British writer

All models are wrong but some are useful.
   George Box 1919–2013 English statistician

A witty statesman said, you might prove anything by
figures.
   Thomas Carlyle 1795–1881 Scottish historian

Long and painful experience has taught me one great
principle in managing business for other people, viz., if you
want to inspire confidence, *give plenty of statistics*.
   Lewis Carroll 1832–98 English writer

There are three kinds of lies: lies, damned lies and statistics.
   Benjamin Disraeli 1804–81 British statesman

From the fact that there are 400,000 species of beetles
on this planet, but only 8,000 species of mammals, he
[Haldane] concluded that the Creator, if He exists, has a
special preference for beetles.
   J. B. S. Haldane 1892–1964 Scottish mathematical biologist

We are just statistics, born to consume resources.
   Horace 65–8 BC Roman poet

He uses statistics as a drunken man uses lampposts—for
support rather than for illumination.
   Andrew Lang 1844–1912 Scottish man of letters

Strength

If your experiment needs statistics, you ought to have done a better experiment.
Ernest Rutherford 1871–1937 New Zealand physicist

Strength

The weak have one weapon: the errors of those who think they are strong.
Georges Bidault 1899–1983 French politician

You cannot strengthen the weak by weakening the strong.
William J. H. Boetcker 1873–1962 American Presbyterian minister, *often wrongly attributed to Abraham Lincoln*

It is the nature, and the advantage, of strong people that they can bring out the crucial questions and form a clear opinion about them. The weak always have to decide between alternatives that are not their own.
Dietrich Bonhoeffer 1906–45 German theologian

Toughness doesn't have to come in a pinstripe suit.
Dianne Feinstein 1933– American politician

A weak man has doubts before a decision; a strong man has them afterwards.
Karl Kraus 1874–1936 Austrian satirist

You are the weakest link…goodbye.
Anne Robinson 1944– English television presenter

A house built on granite and strong foundations, not even the onslaught of pouring rain, gushing torrents and strong winds will be able to pull down.
Haile Selassie 1892–1975 Ethiopian emperor

This is the law of the Yukon, that only the Strong shall thrive; That surely the Weak shall perish, and only the Fit survive.
Robert W. Service 1874–1958 Canadian poet

The gods are on the side of the stronger.

The gods are on the side of the stronger.
Tacitus c.AD 56–after 117 Roman historian

Style see also **Brevity**

Have something to say, and say it as clearly as you can. That is the only secret of style.
Matthew Arnold 1822–88 English poet

Style is the man.
Comte de Buffon 1707–88 French naturalist

Words easy to be understood do often hit the mark; when high and learned ones do only pierce the air.
John Bunyan 1628–88 English writer

I'm just trying to change the world one sequin at a time.
Lady Gaga 1986–   American singer

When we see a natural style, we are quite surprised and delighted, for we expected to see an author and we find a man.
Blaise Pascal 1623–62 French scientist and philosopher

Good design is intelligence made visible.
Frank Pick 1878–1941 British transport administrator

True wit is Nature to advantage dressed,
What oft was thought, but ne'er so well expressed.
Alexander Pope 1688–1744 English poet

Proper words in proper places, make the true definition of a style.
Jonathan Swift 1667–1745 Irish poet and satirist

'Feather-footed through the plashy fen passes the questing vole'…'Yes,' said the Managing Editor. 'That must be good style.'
Evelyn Waugh 1903–66 English novelist

391

Success

In matters of grave importance, style, not sincerity is the vital thing.
Oscar Wilde 1854–1900 Irish dramatist

 # Success see also **Failure**, **Winning**

'Tis not in mortals to command success,
But we'll do more, Sempronius; we'll deserve it.
Joseph Addison 1672–1719 English writer

For what shall it profit a man, if he shall gain the whole world, and lose his own soul?
Bible

Pourvu que ça dure!
Let's hope it lasts!
Laetitia Bonaparte 1750–1836, *on her son Napoleon becoming Emperor, 1804*

Veni, vidi, vici.
I came, I saw, I conquered.
Julius Caesar 100–44 BC Roman statesman

Success is not the key to happiness. Happiness is the key to success.
Herman Cain 1945– American businessman

I have climbed to the top of the greasy pole.
Benjamin Disraeli 1804–81 British statesman

If *A* is a success in life, then *A* equals *x* plus *y* plus *z*. Work is *x*; *y* is play; and *z* is keeping your mouth shut.
Albert Einstein 1879–1955 German-born theoretical physicist

Success is relative:
It is what we can make of the mess we have made of things.
T. S. Eliot 1888–1965 American-born British poet

Success is more dangerous than failure, the ripples break over a wider coastline.
Graham Greene 1904–91 English novelist

In most things success depends on knowing how long it takes to succeed.
Montesquieu 1689–1755 French political philosopher

Success makes life easier. It doesn't make *living* easier.
Bruce Springsteen 1949– American rock singer

He has achieved success who has lived well, laughed often, and loved much; who has enjoyed the trust of pure women, the respect of intelligent men, and the love of little children;…whose life was an inspiration, whose memory a benediction.
Bessie Anderson Stanley fl. 1905 American writer, *often wrongly attributed to Ralph Waldo Emerson or Robert Louis Stevenson*

All you need in this life is ignorance and confidence; then success is sure.
Mark Twain 1835–1910 American writer

It is not enough to succeed. Others must fail.
Gore Vidal 1925–2012 American writer

Suffering see also **Sympathy**

Justice inclines her scales so that wisdom comes at the price of suffering.
Aeschylus c.525–456 BC Greek tragedian

Children's talent to endure stems from their ignorance of alternatives.
Maya Angelou 1928–2014 American writer

Suffering

Even the dreadful martyrdom must run its course
Anyhow in a corner, some untidy spot
Where the dogs go on with their doggy life and the
   torturer's horse
Scratches its innocent behind on a tree.
     W. H. Auden 1907–73 English poet

Nothing happens to anybody which he is not fitted by
nature to bear.
     Marcus Aurelius AD 121–180 Roman emperor

The number of casualties will be more than any of us can
bear.
     Rudolph Giuliani 1944– American politician, *in the aftermath
of the terrorist attacks of 11 September 2001*

To each his suff'rings, all are men,
Condemned alike to groan;
The tender for another's pain,
Th' unfeeling for his own.
     Thomas Gray 1716–71 English poet

If suffer we must, let's suffer on the heights.
     Victor Hugo 1802–85 French writer

Scars have the strange power to remind us that our past
is real.
     Cormac McCarthy 1933– American novelist

It is not true that suffering ennobles the character;
happiness does that sometimes, but suffering, for the most
part, makes men petty and vindictive.
     W. Somerset Maugham 1874–1965 English novelist

A man who fears suffering is already suffering from what
he fears.
     Montaigne 1533–92 French moralist

What does not kill me makes me stronger.
Friedrich Nietzsche 1844–1900 German philosopher

Pain of mind is worse than pain of body.
Publilius Syrus fl. 1st century BC Roman writer

> The worst is not,
So long as we can say, 'This is the worst.'
William Shakespeare 1564–1616 English dramatist

He jests at scars, that never felt a wound.
William Shakespeare 1564–1616 English dramatist

> I am a man
More sinned against than sinning.
William Shakespeare 1564–1616 English dramatist

Nothing begins, and nothing ends,
That is not paid with moan;
For we are born in other's pain,
And perish in our own.
Francis Thompson 1859–1907 English poet

Those who have courage to love should have courage to suffer.
Anthony Trollope 1815–82 English novelist

Too long a sacrifice
Can make a stone of the heart.
W. B. Yeats 1865–1939 Irish poet

Summer

Sumer is icumen in,
Lhude sing cuccu!
Groweth sed, and bloweth med,
And springeth the wude nu.
Anonymous, 'Cuckoo Song' (c.1250)

The Supernatural

June is bustin' out all over.
Oscar Hammerstein II 1895–1960 American songwriter

Summer time an' the livin' is easy,
Fish are jumpin' an' the cotton is high.
Du Bose Heyward 1885–1940 and **Ira Gershwin** 1896–1983
American songwriters

Summer afternoon—summer afternoon…the two most
beautiful words in the English language.
Henry James 1843–1916 American novelist

The way to ensure summer in England is to have it framed
and glazed in a comfortable room.
Horace Walpole 1717–97 English connoisseur

 # The Supernatural

Up the airy mountain,
Down the rushy glen,
We daren't go a-hunting,
For fear of little men.
William Allingham 1824–89 Irish poet

From ghoulies and ghosties and long-leggety beasties
And things that go bump in the night,
Good Lord, deliver us!
Anonymous, *The Cornish or West Country Litany*

Then a spirit passed before my face; the hair of my flesh
stood up.
Bible

For we wrestle not against flesh and blood, but against
principalities, against powers, against the rulers of the darkness
of this world, against spiritual wickedness in high places.
Bible

The Supernatural

Black magic operates most effectively in preconscious, marginal areas. Casual curses are the most effective.

William S. Burroughs 1914–97 American novelist

THE FAT BOY: I wants to make your flesh creep.

Charles Dickens 1812–70 English novelist

There are fairies at the bottom of our garden!

Rose Fyleman 1877–1957 English writer

Superstition is the poetry of life.

Johann Wolfgang von Goethe 1749–1832 German writer

All argument is against it; but all belief is for it.

Samuel Johnson 1709–84 English lexicographer, *of the existence of ghosts*

If there's something strange in your neighbourhood, Who you gonna call? Ghostbusters.

Ray Parker Jr. 1954– American musician

Mr Geller may have psychic powers by means of which he can bend spoons; if so, he appears to be doing it the hard way.

James Randi 1928– Canadian-born American conjuror

Double, double toil and trouble; Fire burn and cauldron bubble.

William Shakespeare 1564–1616 English dramatist

There are more things in heaven and earth, Horatio, Than are dreamt of in your philosophy.

William Shakespeare 1564–1616 English dramatist

Superstition sets the whole world in flames; philosophy quenches them.

Voltaire 1694–1778 French writer

Sympathy

Nobody can tell what I suffer! But it is always so. Those who do not complain are never pitied.
Jane Austen 1775–1817 English novelist

O divine Master, grant that I may not so much seek
To be consoled as to console;
To be understood as to understand.
St Francis of Assisi 1181–1226 Italian monk

Our sympathy is cold to the relation of distant misery.
Edward Gibbon 1737–94 English historian

True kindness presupposes the faculty of imagining as one's own the sufferings and joys of others.
André Gide 1869–1951 French novelist

But yet the pity of it, Iago! O! Iago, the pity of it, Iago!
William Shakespeare 1564–1616 English dramatist

Honest plain words best pierce the ears of grief.
William Shakespeare 1564–1616 English dramatist

When times get rough,
And friends just can't be found
Like a bridge over troubled water
I will lay me down.
Paul Simon 1942– American singer

Taxes

To tax and to please, no more than to love and to be wise, is not given to men.
Edmund Burke 1729–97 Irish-born politician

Read my lips: no new taxes.
George Bush 1924– American statesman

The art of taxation consists in so plucking the goose as to obtain the largest possible amount of feathers with the smallest possible amount of hissing.

Jean-Baptiste Colbert 1619–83 French statesman

In this world nothing can be said to be certain, except death and taxes.

Benjamin Franklin 1706–90 American statesman and scientist

Only the little people pay taxes.

Leona Helmsley c.1920–2007 American hotelier, *reported at her trial for tax evasion*

Excise. A hateful tax levied upon commodities.

Samuel Johnson 1709–84 English lexicographer

Taxation without representation is tyranny.

James Otis 1725–83 American politician

Taxation is just a sophisticated way of demanding money with menaces.

Terry Pratchett 1948–2015 English novelist

Income Tax has made more Liars out of the American people than Golf.

Will Rogers 1879–1935 American actor

There is no art which one government sooner learns of another than that of draining money from the pockets of the people.

Adam Smith 1723–90 Scottish economist

Pecunia non olet.

Money has no smell.

Vespasian AD 9–79 Roman emperor, *quashing an objection to a tax on public lavatories*

The art of government is to make two-thirds of a nation pay all it possibly can pay for the benefit of the other third.

Voltaire 1694–1778 French writer

Teaching

Teaching see also **Education**

A teacher affects eternity; he can never tell where his influence stops.
  Henry Brooks Adams 1838–1918 American historian

There is no such whetstone, to sharpen a good wit and encourage a will to learning, as is praise.
  Roger Ascham 1515–68 English scholar

For precept must be upon precept, precept upon precept; line upon line, line upon line; here a little, and there a little.
  Bible

The task of the modern educator is not to cut down jungles but to irrigate deserts.
  C. S. Lewis 1898–1963 English literary scholar

We teachers can only help the work going on, as servants wait upon a master.
  Maria Montessori 1870–1952 Italian educationist

Men must be taught as if you taught them not,
And things unknown proposed as things forgot.
  Alexander Pope 1688–1744 English poet

For every person who wants to teach there are approximately thirty who don't want to learn—much.
  W. C. Sellar 1898–1951 and **R. J. Yeatman** 1898–1968 British writers

Even while they teach, men learn.
  Seneca ('the Younger') c.4 BC–AD 65 Roman philosopher

He who can, does. He who cannot, teaches.
  George Bernard Shaw 1856–1950 Irish dramatist

Technology

Give me a girl at an impressionable age, and she is mine for life.
Muriel Spark 1918–2006 British novelist

Delightful task! to rear the tender thought,
To teach the young idea how to shoot.
James Thomson 1700–48 Scottish poet

Technology see also Invention

Science finds, industry applies, man conforms.
Anonymous, *guidebook to 1933 Chicago World's Fair*

Give me but one firm spot on which to stand, and I will move the earth.
Archimedes c.287–212 BC Greek mathematician, *on the action of a lever*

I sell here, Sir, what all the world desires to have—POWER.
Matthew Boulton 1728–1809 British engineer, *speaking of his engineering works*

Any sufficiently advanced technology is indistinguishable from magic.
Arthur C. Clarke 1917–2008 English science fiction writer

For a successful technology, reality must take precedence over public relations, for nature cannot be fooled.
Richard Feynman 1918–88 American physicist

Technology happens. It's not good, it's not bad. Is steel good or bad?
Andrew Grove 1936–2016 American businessman

The thing with high-tech is that you always end up using scissors.
David Hockney 1937–   British artist

Technology

One machine can do the work of fifty ordinary men.
No machine can do the work of one extraordinary man.
Elbert Hubbard 1859–1915 American writer

Communism is Soviet power plus the electrification of the whole country.
Lenin 1870–1924 Russian revolutionary

The new electronic interdependence recreates the world in the image of a global village.
Marshall McLuhan 1911–80 Canadian communications scholar

The medium is the message.
Marshall McLuhan 1911–80 Canadian communications scholar

It is questionable if all the mechanical inventions yet made have lightened the day's toil of any human being.
John Stuart Mill 1806–73 English philosopher

When you see something that is technically sweet, you go ahead and do it and you argue about what to do about it only after you have had your technical success. That is the way it was with the atomic bomb.
J. Robert Oppenheimer 1904–67 American physicist

One of the universal rules of happiness is: always be wary of any helpful item that weighs less than its operating manual.
Terry Pratchett 1948–2015 English novelist

It has been said that an engineer is a man who can do for ten shillings what any fool can do for a pound.
Nevil Shute 1899–1960 British novelist

The Britain that is going to be forged in the white heat of this revolution will be no place for restrictive practices or for outdated methods on either side of industry.
Harold Wilson 1916–95 British statesman, *usually quoted as 'the white heat of the technological revolution'*

Television

Those who say they give the public what it wants begin by underestimating public taste, and end by debauching it.
   T. S. Eliot 1888–1965 American-born British poet

Television has brought back murder into the home—where it belongs.
   Alfred Hitchcock 1899–1980 British-born film director

Anyone afraid of what he thinks television does to the world is probably just afraid of the world.
   Clive James 1939– Australian critic

Television brought the brutality of war into the comfort of the living room. Vietnam was lost in the living rooms of America—not the battlefields of Vietnam.
   Marshall McLuhan 1911–80 Canadian communications scholar

Television is actually closer to reality than anything in books. The madness of TV is the madness of human life.
   Camille Paglia 1947– American writer

Television has made dictatorship impossible, but democracy unbearable.
   Shimon Peres 1923–2016 Israeli statesman

Nation shall speak peace unto nation.
   Montague John Rendall 1862–1950 English headmaster, *motto of the BBC*

It's just like having a licence to print your own money.
   Roy Thomson 1894–1976 Canadian-born British newspaper proprietor, *on the profitability of commercial television in Britain*

Never miss a chance to have sex or appear on television.
   Gore Vidal 1925–2012 American writer

Temptation

I hate television. I hate it as much as peanuts. But I can't stop eating peanuts.
Orson Welles 1915–85 American film director

Television contracts the imagination and radio expands it.
Terry Wogan 1938–2016 Irish broadcaster

 # Temptation

Watch and pray, that ye enter not into temptation: the spirit indeed is willing but the flesh is weak.
Bible

For the good that I would I do not: but the evil which I would not, that I do.
Bible

From all the deceits of the world, the flesh, and the devil, Good Lord, deliver us.
Book of Common Prayer 1662

What's done we partly may compute,
But know not what's resisted.
Robert Burns 1759–96 Scottish poet

The Lord above made liquor for temptation—but
With a little bit of luck…
When temptation comes you'll give right in!
Alan Jay Lerner 1918–86 American songwriter

If we are to be punished for the sins we have committed, at least we should be praised for our yearning for the sins we have not committed.
Jawaharlal Nehru 1889–1964 Indian statesman

Is this her fault or mine?
The tempter or the tempted, who sins most?
William Shakespeare 1564–1616 English dramatist

There are several good protections against temptations,
but the surest is cowardice.
Mark Twain 1835–1910 American writer

I can resist everything except temptation.
Oscar Wilde 1854–1900 Irish dramatist

Tennis

I call tennis the McDonald's of sport—you go in, they make
a quick buck out of you, and you're out.
Pat Cash 1965– Australian tennis player

New Yorkers love it when you spill your guts out there.
Spill your guts at Wimbledon and they make you stop and
clean it up.
Jimmy Connors 1952– American tennis player

You cannot be serious!
John McEnroe 1959– American tennis player, *said to tennis
umpire at Wimbledon*

I can cry like Roger, it's a shame I can't play like him.
Andy Murray 1987– Scottish tennis player, *after losing to
Roger Federer in the final of the Australian Open*

Do what you love and love what you do and everything else
is detail.
Martina Navratilova 1956– Czech-born American tennis
player

When we have matched our rackets to these balls,
We will in France, by God's grace, play a set
Shall strike his father's crown into the hazard.
William Shakespeare 1564–1616 English dramatist

Thanks

If you can keep playing tennis when somebody is shooting a gun down the street, that's concentration. I didn't grow up playing at the country club.
Serena Williams 1981– American tennis player

Thanks

No duty is more urgent than that of returning thanks.
St Ambrose c.339–397 French-born bishop of Milan

They say late thanks are ever best.
Francis Bacon 1561–1626 English courtier

A joyful and pleasant thing it is to be thankful.
Bible

When I'm not thanked at all, I'm thanked enough,
I've done my duty, and I've done no more.
Henry Fielding 1707–54 English novelist

For this relief much thanks.
William Shakespeare 1564–1616 English dramatist

The Theatre

I go to the theatre to be entertained, I want to be taken out of myself, I don't want to see lust and rape and incest and sodomy and so on, I can get all that at home.
Alan Bennett 1934– English writer

There's no business like show business.
Irving Berlin 1888–1989 American songwriter

Things on stage should be as complicated and as simple as in life. People dine, just dine, while their happiness is made

and their lives are smashed. If in Act 1 you have a pistol
hanging on the wall, then it must fire in the last act.
    Anton Chekhov 1860–1904 Russian writer

JOSEPHINE HULL: Shakespeare is so tiring. You never get a
chance to sit down unless you're a king.
    George S. Kaufman 1889–1961 and **Howard Teichmann**
    1916–87 American dramatists, *in the film* The Solid Gold
    Cadillac

O! for a Muse of fire, that would ascend
The brightest heaven of invention;
A kingdom for a stage, princes to act
And monarchs to behold the swelling scene.
    William Shakespeare 1564–1616 English dramatist

Four trestles, four boards, two actors, a passion.
    Lope de Vega 1562–1635 Spanish dramatist and poet, *on all he
    needed to create a play*

It's a sound you can't get in the movies or television…the
sound of a wonderful, deep silence that means you've hit
them where they live.
    Shelley Winters 1922–2006 American actress

Thinking *see also* **Ideas, Mind**

Think different.
    Anonymous, *advertising slogan for Apple Computers*

To change your mind and to follow him who sets you
right is to be nonetheless the free agent that you were
before.
    Marcus Aurelius AD 121–180 Roman emperor

Never express yourself more clearly than you think.
    Niels Bohr 1885–1962 Danish physicist

Thinking

Learning without thought is labour lost; thought without learning is perilous.

Confucius 551–479 BC Chinese philosopher

Cogito, ergo sum.

I think, therefore I am.

René Descartes 1596–1650 French philosopher

It is a capital mistake to theorize before you have all the evidence. It biases the judgement.

Arthur Conan Doyle 1859–1930 Scottish-born writer

What was once thought can never be unthought.

Friedrich Dürrenmatt 1921–90 Swiss writer

I'll not listen to reason…Reason always means what someone else has got to say.

Elizabeth Gaskell 1810–65 English novelist

Logical consequences are the scarecrows of fools and the beacons of wise men.

T. H. Huxley 1825–95 English biologist

Doublethink means the power of holding two contradictory beliefs in one's mind simultaneously, and accepting both of them.

George Orwell 1903–50 English novelist

I don't mind your thinking slowly: I mind your publishing faster than you think.

Wolfgang Pauli 1900–58 Austrian-born American physicist

Most people would sooner die than think—in fact they do so.

Bertrand Russell 1872–1970 British philosopher

Yond Cassius has a lean and hungry look;
He thinks too much: such men are dangerous.

William Shakespeare 1564–1616 English dramatist

The real question is not whether machines think but whether men do.

B. F. Skinner 1904–90 American psychologist

The important thing is not to think much but to love much.

St Teresa of Ávila 1512–82 Spanish mystic

Time

Time is an illusion. Lunchtime doubly so.

Douglas Adams 1952–2001 English science fiction writer

Every instant of time is a pinprick of eternity.

Marcus Aurelius AD 121–180 Roman emperor

VLADIMIR: That passed the time.
ESTRAGON: It would have passed in any case.
VLADIMIR: Yes, but not so rapidly.

Samuel Beckett 1906–89 Irish writer

Time is a great teacher but unfortunately it kills all its pupils.

Hector Berlioz 1803–69 French composer

I am Time grown old to destroy the world,
Embarked on the course of world annihilation.

Bhagavad Gita 250 BC–AD 250 Hindu poem

To every thing there is a season, and a time to every purpose under the heaven:
A time to be born, and a time to die…
A time to weep, and a time to laugh; a time to mourn, and a time to dance.

Bible

Men talk of killing time, while time quietly kills them.

Dion Boucicault 1820–90 Irish dramatist

Time

I recommend to you to take care of minutes: for hours will take care of themselves.
> **Lord Chesterfield** 1694–1773 English writer

I shall use the phrase 'time's arrow' to express this one-way property of time which has no analogue in space.
> **Arthur Eddington** 1882–1944 British astrophysicist

The distinction between past, present and future is only an illusion, however persistent.
> **Albert Einstein** 1879–1955 German-born theoretical physicist

Time is…Time was…Time is past.
> **Robert Greene** c.1560–92 English dramatist

In the long run we are all dead.
> **John Maynard Keynes** 1883–1946 English economist

Nothing puzzles me more than time and space; and yet nothing troubles me less, as I never think about them.
> **Charles Lamb** 1775–1834 English writer

But at my back I always hear
Time's wingèd chariot hurrying near:
And yonder all before us lie
Deserts of vast eternity.
> **Andrew Marvell** 1621–78 English poet

Time the devourer of everything.
> **Ovid** 43 BC–c.AD 17 Roman poet

Even such is Time, which takes in trust
Our youth, our joys, and all we have,
And pays us but with age and dust.
> **Walter Ralegh** c.1552–1618 English courtier

Half our life is spent trying to find something to do with the time we have rushed through life trying to save.
> **Will Rogers** 1879–1935 American actor

Three o'clock is always too late or too early for anything you want to do.
    Jean-Paul Sartre 1905–80 French philosopher

Ah! the clock is always slow;
It is later than you think.
    Robert W. Service 1874–1958 Canadian poet

To-morrow, and to-morrow, and to-morrow,
Creeps in this petty pace from day to day,
To the last syllable of recorded time;
And all our yesterdays have lighted fools
The way to dusty death.
    William Shakespeare 1564–1616 English dramatist

Time hath, my lord, a wallet at his back,
Wherein he puts alms for oblivion.
    William Shakespeare 1564–1616 English dramatist

As if you could kill time without injuring eternity.
    Henry David Thoreau 1817–62 American writer

Time is
Too slow for those who wait,
Too swift for those who fear,
Too long for those who grieve,
Too short for those who rejoice;
But for those who love,
Time is eternity.
    Henry Van Dyke 1852–1933 American minister

Sed fugit interea, fugit inreparabile tempus.
But meanwhile it is flying, irretrievable time is flying.
    Virgil 70–19 BC Roman poet

Time, like an ever-rolling stream,
Bears all its sons away.
    Isaac Watts 1674–1748 English hymn-writer

Toasts

Here's tae us; wha's like us?
Gey few, and they're a' deid.
Anonymous

HUMPHREY BOGART: Here's looking at you, kid.
Julius J. Epstein 1909–2001 and **others** American
screenwriters, *in the film* Casablanca

Lang may yer lum reek!
Scottish Proverb, *long may your chimney smoke*

May you live all the days of your life.
Jonathan Swift 1667–1745 Irish poet and satirist

 The Town see also **Country**

We do not look in great cities for our best morality.
Jane Austen 1775–1817 English novelist

If you would be known, and not know, vegetate in a village;
if you would know, and not be known, live in a city.
Charles Caleb Colton c.1780–1832 English clergyman

Slums may well be breeding-grounds of crime, but middle-
class suburbs are incubators of apathy and delirium.
Cyril Connolly 1903–74 English writer

The materials of city planning are sky, space, trees, steel and
cement in that order and in that hierarchy.
Le Corbusier 1887–1965 French architect

The fields and trees won't teach me anything, and the people
in the city do.
Socrates 469–399 BC Greek philosopher

There is no there there.

> **Gertrude Stein** 1874–1946 American writer, *on her hometown of Oakland, California, often misquoted as being said of Los Angeles*

Commuters give the city its tidal restlessness; natives give it solidity and continuity; but the settlers give it passion.

> **E. B. White** 1899–1985 American humorist

The modern city is a place for banking and prostitution and very little else.

> **Frank Lloyd Wright** 1867–1959 American architect

Transience

Sic transit gloria mundi.
Thus passes the glory of the world.

> **Anonymous**, *said at the coronation of a new Pope, while flax is burned*

All flesh is as grass, and all the glory of man as the flower of grass. The grass withereth, and the flower thereof falleth away.

> **Bible**

He who binds to himself a joy
Doth the winged life destroy
But he who kisses the joy as it flies
Lives in Eternity's sunrise.

> **William Blake** 1757–1827 English poet

Look thy last on all things lovely,
Every hour.

> **Walter de la Mare** 1873–1956 English poet

Gather ye rosebuds while ye may,
Old Time is still a-flying:

Travel

And this same flower that smiles to-day,
To-morrow will be dying.
Robert Herrick 1591–1674 English poet

Like that of leaves is a generation of men.
Homer fl. 8th century BC Greek poet

Ceaselessly the river flows, and yet the water is never the
same, while in the still pools the shifting foam gathers and
is gone, never staying for a moment. Even so is man and his
habitation.
Kamo no Chomei 1155–1216 Japanese poet

The butterfly counts not months but moments, and has time
enough.
Rabindranath Tagore 1861–1941 Bengali poet

 # Travel

Travel, in the younger sort, is a part of education; in the
elder, a part of experience. He that travelleth into a country
before he hath some entrance into the language, goeth to
school, and not to travel.
Francis Bacon 1561–1626 English courtier

See one promontory (said Socrates of old), one mountain,
one sea, one river, and see all.
Robert Burton 1577–1640 English clergyman

Men travel faster now, but I do not know if they go to better
things.
Willa Cather 1873–1947 American novelist

The whole object of travel is not to set foot on foreign land;
it is at last to set foot on one's own country as a foreign land.
G. K. Chesterton 1874–1936 English writer

Wherever you go, go with all your heart.
Confucius 551–479 BC Chinese philosopher

Like all great travellers, I have seen more than I remember, and remember more than I have seen.
Benjamin Disraeli 1804–81 British statesman

Worth seeing, yes; but not worth going to see.
Samuel Johnson 1709–84 English lexicographer, *of the Giant's Causeway*

A good traveller has no fixed plans.
Lao Tzu c.604–c.531 BC Chinese philosopher

A good traveller is one who does not know where he is going to, and a perfect traveller does not know where he came from.
Lin Yutang 1895–1976 Chinese writer

Traveller, there is no path. Paths are made by walking.
Antonio Machado 1875–1939 Spanish poet

I have not told even half of the things that I have seen.
Marco Polo c.1254–c.1324 Italian traveller, *when asked if he wished to deny any of his stories of his travels*

A man travels the world in search of what he needs and returns home to find it.
George Moore 1852–1933 Irish novelist

The real voyage of discovery…consists not in seeking new landscapes but in having new eyes.
Marcel Proust 1871–1922 French novelist

To travel hopefully is a better thing than to arrive, and the true success is to labour.
Robert Louis Stevenson 1850–94 Scottish novelist

Travel is fatal to prejudice, bigotry, and narrow-mindedness.
Mark Twain 1835–1910 American writer

Trust and Treachery

He that is surety for a stranger shall smart for it.
> **Bible**

Just for a handful of silver he left us,
Just for a riband to stick in his coat.
> **Robert Browning** 1812–89 English poet, *of Wordsworth accepting the Laureateship*

Anyone can rat, but it takes a certain amount of ingenuity to re-rat.
> **Winston Churchill** 1874–1965 British statesman, *on rejoining the Conservatives twenty years after leaving them for the Liberals*

I know what it is to be a subject, and what to be a Sovereign. Good neighbours I have had, and I have met with bad: and in trust I have found treason.
> **Elizabeth I** 1533–1603 English monarch

Anyone who hasn't experienced the ecstasy of betrayal knows nothing about ecstasy at all.
> **Jean Genet** 1910–86 French writer

Treason doth never prosper, what's the reason?
For if it prosper, none dare call it treason.
> **John Harington** 1561–1612 English courtier

And I said to the man who stood at the gate of the year:
'Give me a light that I may tread safely into the unknown.'
   And he replied:
   'Go out into the darkness and put your hand into the Hand of God. That shall be to you better than light and safer than a known way.'
> **Minnie Louise Haskins** 1875–1957 English writer, *quoted by George VI in his Christmas broadcast, 1939*

It is better to suffer wrong than to do it, and happier to be sometimes cheated than not to trust.
Samuel Johnson 1709–84 English lexicographer

Quis custodiet ipsos custodes?
Who is to guard the guards themselves?
Juvenal c.AD 60–c.140 Roman satirist

To betray, you must first belong.
Kim Philby 1912–88 British intelligence officer and Soviet spy

But I'm always true to you, darlin', in my fashion.
Yes I'm always true to you, darlin', in my way.
Cole Porter 1891–1964 American songwriter

I fear the Greeks even when they bring gifts.
Virgil 70–19 BC Roman poet

Truth see also **Lies**

The truth is often a terrible weapon of aggression. It is possible to lie, and even to murder, for the truth.
Alfred Adler 1870–1937 Austrian psychologist

The truth which makes men free is for the most part the truth which men prefer not to hear.
Herbert Agar 1897–1980 American writer

Plato is dear to me, but dearer still is truth.
Aristotle 384–322 BC Greek philosopher

It contains a misleading impression, not a lie. It was being economical with the truth.
Robert Armstrong 1927– British civil servant

What is truth? said jesting Pilate; and would not stay for an answer.
Francis Bacon 1561–1626 English courtier

Truth

And ye shall know the truth, and the truth shall make you free.
Bible

Great is Truth, and mighty above all things.
Bible (Apocrypha)

A truth that's told with bad intent
Beats all the lies you can invent.
William Blake 1757–1827 English poet

One of the favourite maxims of my father was the distinction between the two sorts of truths, profound truths recognized by the fact that the opposite is also a profound truth, in contrast to trivialities where opposites are obviously absurd.
Niels Bohr 1885–1962 Danish physicist

'Tis strange—but true; for truth is always strange; Stranger than fiction.
Lord Byron 1788–1824 English poet

What I tell you three times is true.
Lewis Carroll 1832–98 English writer

It is commonly said, and more particularly by Lord Shaftesbury, that ridicule is the best test of truth.
Lord Chesterfield 1694–1773 English writer

When you have eliminated the impossible, whatever remains, *however improbable*, must be the truth.
Arthur Conan Doyle 1859–1930 Scottish-born writer

A Hair perhaps divides the False and True.
Edward Fitzgerald 1809–83 English poet

An exaggeration is a truth that has lost its temper.
Kahlil Gibran 1883–1931 Lebanese-born American writer

Believe those who are seeking the truth; doubt those who find it.
André Gide 1869–1951 French novelist

True and False are attributes of speech, not of things. And where speech is not, there is neither Truth nor Falsehood.
Thomas Hobbes 1588–1679 English philosopher

It is the customary fate of new truths to begin as heresies and to end as superstitions.
T. H. Huxley 1825–95 English biologist

But, my dearest Agathon, it is truth which you cannot contradict; you can without any difficulty contradict Socrates.
Socrates 469–399 BC Greek philosopher

Rather than love, than money, than fame, give me truth.
Henry David Thoreau 1817–62 American writer

There was things which he stretched, but mainly he told the truth.
Mark Twain 1835–1910 American writer

I can't tell a lie, Pa; you know I can't tell a lie. I did cut it with my hatchet.
George Washington 1732–99 American statesman

The truth is rarely pure, and never simple.
Oscar Wilde 1854–1900 Irish dramatist

A thing is not necessarily true because a man dies for it.
Oscar Wilde 1854–1900 Irish dramatist

The Universe

Had I been present at the Creation, I would have given some useful hints for the better ordering of the universe.
Alfonso 'the Wise', King of Castile 1221–84, *on studying the Ptolemaic system*

The Universe

'Gad! she'd better!'
> **Thomas Carlyle** 1795–1881 Scottish historian, *on hearing that Margaret Fuller 'accept[ed] the universe'*

The eternal mystery of the world is its comprehensibility...
The fact that it is comprehensible is a miracle.
> **Albert Einstein** 1879–1955 German-born theoretical physicist, *usually quoted as 'The most incomprehensible fact about the universe is that it is comprehensible'*

Now, my own suspicion is that the universe is not only queerer than we suppose, but queerer than we *can* suppose.
> **J. B. S. Haldane** 1892–1964 Scottish mathematical biologist

If we find the answer to that [why it is that we and the universe exist], it would be the ultimate triumph of human reason—for then we would know the mind of God.
> **Stephen Hawking** 1942– English theoretical physicist

This, now, is the judgement of our scientific age—the third reaction of man upon the universe! This universe is not hostile, nor yet is it friendly. It is simply indifferent.
> **John H. Holmes** 1879–1964 American Unitarian minister

From the intrinsic evidence of his creation, the Great Architect of the Universe now begins to appear as a pure mathematician.
> **James Jeans** 1877–1946 Scottish astronomer

How is it that hardly any major religion has looked at science and concluded, 'This is better than we thought! The Universe is much bigger than our prophets said, grander, more subtle, more elegant'?
> **Carl Sagan** 1934–96 American astronomer

Sometimes I think the surest sign that intelligent life exists elsewhere in the universe is that none of it has tried to contact us.
> **Bill Watterson** 1958– American cartoonist

The world is everything that is the case.
Ludwig Wittgenstein 1889–1951 Austrian-born philosopher

Violence

Keep violence in the mind
Where it belongs.
Brian Aldiss 1925– English writer

Violence is the last refuge of the incompetent.
Isaac Asimov 1920–92 Russian-born science fiction writer

All they that take the sword shall perish with the sword.
Bible

I say violence is necessary. It is as American as cherry pie.
H. Rap Brown 1943– American Black Power leader

Victory attained by violence is tantamount to a defeat, for it
is momentary.
Mahatma Gandhi 1869–1948 Indian statesman

What has violence ever accomplished? What has it ever
created? No martyr's cause has ever been stilled by an
assassin's bullet.
Robert Kennedy 1925–68 American politician

　　Who overcomes
By force, hath overcome but half his foe.
John Milton 1608–74 English poet

If you strike a child take care that you strike it in anger,
even at the risk of maiming it for life. A blow in cold blood
neither can nor should be forgiven.
George Bernard Shaw 1856–1950 Irish dramatist

Where force is necessary, there it must be applied boldly,
decisively and completely. But one must know the

limitations of force; one must know when to blend force
with a manoeuvre, a blow with an agreement.
Leon Trotsky 1879–1940 Russian revolutionary

The quietly pacifist peaceful
always die
to make room for men
who shout.
Alice Walker 1944– American poet

 # Wales

It profits a man nothing to give his soul for the whole
world…But for Wales—!
Robert Bolt 1924–95 English dramatist

The English have forgot that they ever conquered the Welsh,
but some ages will elapse before the Welsh forget that the
English have conquered them.
George Borrow 1803–81 English writer

Who dare compare the English, the most degraded of all the
races under heaven, with the Welsh?
Giraldus Cambrensis 1146?–1220? Welsh historian

The land of my fathers, how fair is thy fame.
Evan James 1809–78 Welsh bard

Everyday when I wake up, I thank the Lord I'm Welsh.
Cerys Matthews 1969– Welsh singer

Though it appear a little out of fashion,
There is much care and valour in this Welshman.
William Shakespeare 1564–1616 English dramatist

The land of my fathers. My fathers can have it.
Dylan Thomas 1914–53 Welsh poet

War see also **Armed Forces**

We make war that we may live in peace.
> **Aristotle** 384–322 BC Greek philosopher

The bomber will always get through. The only defence is in offence, which means that you have to kill more women and children more quickly than the enemy if you want to save yourselves.
> **Stanley Baldwin** 1867–1947 British statesman

Not worth the healthy bones of a single Pomeranian grenadier.
> **Otto von Bismarck** 1815–98 German statesman, *of possible German involvement in the Balkans*

This policy cannot succeed through speeches, and shooting-matches, and songs; it can only be carried out through blood and iron.
> **Otto von Bismarck** 1815–98 German statesman

C'est magnifique, mais ce n'est pas la guerre.
It is magnificent, but it is not war.
> **Pierre Bosquet** 1810–61 French general, *on the charge of the Light Brigade at Balaclava, 1854*

As you know, God is usually on the side of the big squadrons against the small.
> **Comte de Bussy-Rabutin** 1618–93 French soldier and poet

In war, whichever side may call itself the victor, there are no winners, but all are losers.
> **Neville Chamberlain** 1869–1940 British statesman

War is a game that is played with a smile. If you can't smile grin. If you can't grin keep out of the way till you can.
> **Winston Churchill** 1874–1965 British statesman

War

We shall fight on the beaches, we shall fight on the landing grounds, we shall fight in the fields and in the streets, we shall fight in the hills; we shall never surrender.

Winston Churchill 1874–1965 British statesman

Let us therefore brace ourselves to our duty, and so bear ourselves that, if the British Empire and its Commonwealth lasts for a thousand years, men will still say, 'This was their finest hour.'

Winston Churchill 1874–1965 British statesman

Never in the field of human conflict was so much owed by so many to so few.

Winston Churchill 1874–1965 British statesman

Laws are silent in time of war.

Cicero 106–43 BC Roman statesman

War is nothing but a continuation of politics with the admixture of other means.

Karl von Clausewitz 1780–1831 Prussian military theorist, *commonly rendered 'War is the continuation of politics by other means'*

War is too serious a matter to entrust to military men.

Georges Clemenceau 1841–1929 French statesman

ROBERT DUVALL: I love the smell of napalm in the morning. It smells like victory.

Francis Ford Coppola 1939–   American film director, *in the film* Apocalypse Now

I am not only a pacifist but a militant pacifist. I am willing to fight for peace. Nothing will end war unless the people themselves refuse to go to war.

Albert Einstein 1879–1955 German-born theoretical physicist

There never was a good war, or a bad peace.

Benjamin Franklin 1706–90 American statesman and scientist

If we are attacked we can only defend ourselves with guns not with butter.
Joseph Goebbels 1897–1945 German Nazi leader

Would you rather have butter or guns?…preparedness makes us powerful. Butter merely makes us fat.
Hermann Goering 1893–1946 German Nazi leader

War is hell, and all that, but it has a good deal to recommend it. It wipes out all the small nuisances of peace-time.
Ian Hay 1876–1952 Scottish writer

War is the father of all and the king of all.
Heraclitus c.540–c.480 BC Greek philosopher

Always mystify, mislead, and surprise the enemy, if possible.
Thomas Jonathan 'Stonewall' Jackson 1824–63 American general, *his strategic motto during the Civil War*

Among the calamities of war may be jointly numbered the diminution of the love of truth, by the falsehoods which interest dictates and credulity encourages.
Samuel Johnson 1709–84 English lexicographer, *possibly the source of 'When war is declared, Truth is the first casualty'; attributed also to Hiram Johnson*

It is well that war is so terrible. We should grow too fond of it.
Robert E. Lee 1807–70 American general

Rule 1, on page 1 of the book of war, is: 'Do not march on Moscow'…[Rule 2] is: 'Do not go fighting with your land armies in China.'
Lord Montgomery of Alamein 1887–1976 British field marshal

War

Probably the battle of Waterloo *was* won on the playing-fields of Eton, but the opening battles of all subsequent wars have been lost there.
   George Orwell 1903–50 English novelist

My subject is War, and the pity of War.
The Poetry is in the pity.
   Wilfred Owen 1893–1918 English poet

Little girl…Sometime they'll give a war and nobody will come.
   Carl Sandburg 1878–1967 American poet

Once more unto the breach, dear friends, once more;
Or close the wall up with our English dead!
In peace there's nothing so becomes a man
As modest stillness and humility:
But when the blast of war blows in our ears,
Then imitate the action of the tiger.
   William Shakespeare 1564–1616 English dramatist

There is many a boy here to-day who looks on war as all glory, but, boys, it is all hell.
   William Tecumseh Sherman 1820–91 American general

War is capitalism with the gloves off.
   Tom Stoppard 1937– British dramatist

To win one hundred victories in one hundred battles is not the acme of skill. To subdue the enemy without fighting is the acme of skill.
   Sun Tzu fl. c.400–320 BC Chinese general

The battle of Waterloo was won on the playing fields of Eton.
   Duke of Wellington 1769–1852 British general

Next to a battle lost, the greatest misery is a battle gained.
   Duke of Wellington 1769–1852 British general

Wealth see also **Money**

It is easier for a camel to go through the eye of a needle, than for a rich man to enter into the kingdom of God.
> **Bible**

Greed is all right…Greed is healthy. You can be greedy and still feel good about yourself.
> **Ivan F. Boesky** 1937– American businessman

My riches consist, not in the extent of my possessions, but in the fewness of my wants.
> **Joseph Brotherton** 1783–1857 English politician, *responding to a slighting reference to the fortune that he had amassed in manufacturing*

A very rich person should leave his kids enough to do anything but not enough to do nothing.
> **Warren Buffett** 1930– American businessman

The man who dies…rich dies disgraced.
> **Andrew Carnegie** 1835–1919 American industrialist

Let me tell you about the very rich. They are different from you and me.
> **F. Scott Fitzgerald** 1896–1940 American novelist, *to which Ernest Hemingway replied, 'Yes, they have more money'*

In every well-governed state, wealth is a sacred thing; in democracies it is the only sacred thing.
> **Anatole France** 1844–1924 French man of letters

If you would be wealthy, think of saving as well as of getting.
> **Benjamin Franklin** 1706–90 American statesman and scientist

If you can actually count your money, then you are not really a rich man.
> **J. Paul Getty** 1892–1976 American industrialist

Wealth

We are not here to sell a parcel of boilers and vats, but the potentiality of growing rich, beyond the dreams of avarice.

Samuel Johnson 1709–84 English lexicographer, *at the sale of Thrale's brewery*

I've been rich and I've been poor: rich is better.

Beatrice Kaufman 1895–1945 American writer

Let us be frank about it: most of our people have never had it so good.

Harold Macmillan 1894–1986 British statesman

[New Labour] is intensely relaxed about people getting filthy rich.

Peter Mandelson 1953– British politician

A kiss on the hand may be quite continental,
But diamonds are a girl's best friend.

Leo Robin 1900–84 American songwriter

Wealth is like sea-water; the more we have, the thirstier we become, and the same is true of fame.

Arthur Schopenhauer 1788–1860 German philosopher

The chief enjoyment of riches consists in the parade of riches.

Adam Smith 1723–90 Scottish economist

How many things I can do without!

Socrates 469–399 BC Greek philosopher, *on looking at a multitude of goods exposed for sale*

The only way not to think about money is to have a great deal of it.

Edith Wharton 1862–1937 American novelist

I am grateful for the blessings of wealth, but it hasn't changed who I am. My feet are still on the ground. I'm just wearing better shoes.

Oprah Winfrey 1954– American talk show hostess

Weather ✳

What dreadful hot weather we have! It keeps one in a
continual state of inelegance.
  Jane Austen 1775–1817 English novelist

The rain, it raineth on the just
And also on the unjust fella:
But chiefly on the just, because
The unjust steals the just's umbrella.
  Lord Bowen 1835–94 English judge

Every time it rains, it rains
Pennies from heaven.
Don't you know each cloud contains
Pennies from heaven?
  Johnny Burke 1908–64 American songwriter

This is a London particular…A fog, miss.
  Charles Dickens 1812–70 English novelist

A woman rang to say she heard there was a hurricane on
the way. Well don't worry, there isn't.
  Michael Fish 1944– British weather forecaster, *weather
  forecast on the night before serious gales in southern England*

The weather is like the Government, always in the wrong.
  Jerome K. Jerome 1859–1927 English writer

When two Englishmen meet, their first talk is of the
weather.
  Samuel Johnson 1709–84 English lexicographer

No one can tell me,
Nobody knows,
Where the wind comes from,
Where the wind goes.
  A. A. Milne 1882–1956 English writer

Weddings

The first fall of snow is not only an event, but it is a magical event. You go to bed in one kind of world and wake up to find yourself in another quite different, and if this is not enchantment, then where is it to be found?
J. B. Priestley 1894–1984 English writer

The fog comes
on little cat feet.
Carl Sandburg 1878–1967 American poet

So foul and fair a day I have not seen.
William Shakespeare 1564–1616 English dramatist

There is no such thing as bad weather. All weather is good because it is God's.
St Teresa of Ávila 1512–82 Spanish mystic

Rain is grace; rain is the sky condescending to the earth; without rain, there would be no life.
John Updike 1932–2009 American writer

It was the wrong kind of snow.
Terry Worrall British railway spokesman, *popular summary of his explanation of disruption on British Rail*

 # Weddings

If it were not for the presents, an elopement would be preferable.
George Ade 1866–1944 American humorist

Now you will feel no rain, for each of you will be shelter for the other. Now you will feel no cold, for each of you will be warmth for the other.
Anonymous, *from the saying known as the 'Apache Blessing'*

As the bridegroom rejoiceth over the bride.
Bible

Wilt thou love her, comfort her, honour, and keep her in sickness and in health; and, forsaking all other, keep thee only unto her, so long as ye both shall live?

Book of Common Prayer 1662

Why am I always the bridesmaid,
Never the blushing bride?

Fred W. Leigh d. 1924 and **others** British songwriters

I'm getting married in the morning,
Ding dong! The bells are gonna chime.
Pull out the stopper;
Let's have a whopper;
But get me to the church on time!

Alan Jay Lerner 1918–86 American songwriter

Happy is the bride that the sun shines on.

Proverb

Winning

The race is not to the swift, nor the battle to the strong.

Bible

You ask, what is our aim? I can answer in one word: Victory, victory at all costs, victory in spite of all terror; victory, however long and hard the road may be; for without victory, there is no survival.

Winston Churchill 1874–1965 British statesman

Victory has a hundred fathers, but no-one wants to recognise defeat as his own.

Count Galeazzo Ciano 1903–44 Italian politician

STEERFORTH: Ride on! Rough-shod if need be, smooth-shod if that will do, but ride on! Ride on over all obstacles, and win the race!

Charles Dickens 1812–70 English novelist

Winter

Winning is everything. The only ones who remember you when you come second are your wife and your dog.
Damon Hill 1960– English motor-racing driver

The moment of victory is much too short to live for that and nothing else.
Martina Navratilova 1956– Czech-born American tennis player

We are not interested in the possibilities of defeat; they do not exist.
Queen Victoria 1819–1901 British monarch

 # Winter

The English winter—ending in July,
To recommence in August.
Lord Byron 1788–1824 English poet

Winter lies too long in country towns; hangs on until it is stale and shabby, old and sullen.
Willa Cather 1873–1947 American novelist

No shade, no shine, no butterflies, no bees,
No fruits, no flowers, no leaves, no birds,—
November!
Thomas Hood 1799–1845 English poet

The most serious charge which can be brought against New England is not Puritanism but February.
Joseph Wood Krutch 1893–1970 American critic and naturalist

Winter is icummen in,
Lhude sing Goddamm,
Raineth drop and staineth slop,
And how the wind doth ramm!
Ezra Pound 1885–1972 American poet

O, Wind,
If Winter comes, can Spring be far behind?
Percy Bysshe Shelley 1792–1822 English poet

Let no man boast himself that he has got through the perils
of winter till at least the seventh of May.
Anthony Trollope 1815–82 English novelist

Wisdom see also **Knowledge**

In our sleep, pain which cannot forget falls drop by drop
upon the heart until, in our own despair, against our will,
comes wisdom through the awful grace of God.
Aeschylus c.525–456 BC Greek tragedian, *quoted by Robert
Kennedy on the night of the assassination of Martin Luther King*

The price of wisdom is above rubies.
Bible

Authority without wisdom is like a heavy axe without an
edge, fitter to bruise than polish.
Anne Bradstreet c.1612–72 English-born American poet

The fool wonders, the wise man asks.
Benjamin Disraeli 1804–81 British statesman

Mere cleverness is not wisdom.
Euripides c.485–c.406 BC Greek dramatist

The art of being wise is the art of knowing what to
overlook.
William James 1842–1910 American philosopher

Wisdom is not the purchase of a day.
Thomas Paine 1737–1809 English political theorist

No man is wise at all times.
Pliny the Elder AD 23–79 Roman senator

Wit

One would need to be already wise, in order to love wisdom.
Friedrich von Schiller 1759–1805 German poet

 # Wit see also **Humour**

Wit is educated insolence.
Aristotle 384–322 BC Greek philosopher

A thing well said will be wit in all languages.
John Dryden 1631–1700 English poet

Wit is the salt of conversation, not the food.
William Hazlitt 1778–1830 English essayist

Wit is the epitaph of an emotion.
Friedrich Nietzsche 1844–1900 German philosopher

I am not only witty in myself, but the cause that wit is in other men.
William Shakespeare 1564–1616 English dramatist

Brevity is the soul of wit.
William Shakespeare 1564–1616 English dramatist

There's no possibility of being witty without a little ill-nature; the malice of a good thing is the barb that makes it stick.
Richard Brinsley Sheridan 1751–1816 Anglo-Irish dramatist

 # Woman's Role see also **Men and Women**

If all men are born free, how is it that all women are born slaves?
Mary Astell 1668–1731 English poet

The freedom women were supposed to have found in the Sixties largely boiled down to easy contraception and abortion: things to make life easier for men, in fact.
Julie Burchill 1960– English journalist

Woman's Role

I could have stayed home and baked cookies and had teas. But what I decided was to fulfil my profession, which I entered before my husband was in public life.
   Hillary Rodham Clinton 1947-   American lawyer

One is not born a woman: one becomes one.
   Simone de Beauvoir 1908-86 French novelist

Today the problem that has no name is how to juggle work, love, home and children.
   Betty Friedan 1921-2006 American feminist

I didn't fight to get women out from behind the vacuum cleaner to get them onto the board of Hoover.
   Germaine Greer 1939-   Australian feminist

My mother said it was simple to keep a man, you must be a maid in the living room, a cook in the kitchen and a whore in the bedroom. I said I'd hire the other two and take care of the bedroom bit.
   Jerry Hall 1956-   American model

A woman's preaching is like a dog's walking on his hinder legs. It is not done well; but you are surprised to find it done at all.
   Samuel Johnson 1709-84 English lexicographer

The first blast of the trumpet against the monstrous regiment of women.
   John Knox c.1505-72 Scottish Protestant reformer

But if God had wanted us to think just with our wombs, why did He give us a brain?
   Clare Booth Luce 1903-87 American writer and politician

Well-behaved women seldom make history.
   Laurel Thatcher Ulrich 1938-   American historian

Women

The Queen is most anxious to enlist every one who can speak or write to join in checking this mad, wicked folly of 'Woman's Rights', with all its attendant horrors, on which her poor feeble sex is bent, forgetting every sense of womanly feeling and propriety.
> **Queen Victoria** 1819–1901 British monarch

Womanist is to feminist as purple to lavender.
> **Alice Walker** 1944– American poet

I do not wish them [women] to have power over men; but over themselves.
> **Mary Wollstonecraft** 1759–97 English feminist

 # Women see also **Men and Women**

There's a special place in hell for women who don't help other women.
> **Madeleine Albright** 1937– American diplomat

The weaker sex, to piety more prone.
> **William Alexander, Earl of Stirling** c.1567–1640 Scottish poet

All the privilege I claim for my own sex…is that of loving longest, when existence or when hope is gone.
> **Jane Austen** 1775–1817 English novelist

Who can find a virtuous woman? for her price is far above rubies.
> **Bible**

Good women always think it is their fault when someone else is being offensive. Bad women never take the blame for anything.
> **Anita Brookner** 1928–2016 British novelist

Women

In her first passion woman loves her lover,
In all the others all she loves is love.
Lord Byron 1788–1824 English poet

The prime truth of woman, the universal mother…that if a
thing is worth doing, it is worth doing badly.
G. K. Chesterton 1874–1936 English writer

She knows her man, and when you rant and swear,
Can draw you to her *with a single hair*.
John Dryden 1631–1700 English poet

The happiest women, like the happiest nations, have no
history.
George Eliot 1819–80 English novelist

What does a woman want?
Sigmund Freud 1856–1939 Austrian psychoanalyst

Show me a woman who doesn't feel guilty and I'll show you
a man.
Erica Jong 1942– American novelist

Being a woman is of special interest only to aspiring male
transsexuals. To actual women, it is merely a good excuse
not to play football.
Fran Lebowitz 1950– American writer

She's the sort of woman who lives for others—you can
always tell the others by their hunted expression.
C. S. Lewis 1898–1963 English literary scholar

Woman was God's second blunder.
Friedrich Nietzsche 1844–1900 German philosopher

Woman is the nigger of the world.
Yoko Ono 1933– Japanese poet

Women

The greatest glory of a woman is to be least talked about by men.

Pericles c.495–429 BC Greek statesman

Every woman adores a Fascist,
The boot in the face, the brute
Brute heart of a brute like you.

Sylvia Plath 1932–63 American poet

She floats, she hesitates; in a word, she's a woman.

Jean Racine 1639–99 French tragedian

O Woman! in our hours of ease,
Uncertain, coy, and hard to please…
When pain and anguish wring the brow,
A ministering angel thou!

Sir Walter Scott 1771–1832 Scottish novelist

Frailty, thy name is woman!

William Shakespeare 1564–1616 English dramatist

Here's to the maiden of bashful fifteen
Here's to the widow of fifty
Here's to the flaunting, extravagant quean;
And here's to the housewife that's thrifty.

Richard Brinsley Sheridan 1751–1816 Irish dramatist

The great and almost only comfort about being a woman is that one can always pretend to be more stupid than one is and no one is surprised.

Freya Stark 1893–1993 English traveller

We are becoming the men we wanted to marry.

Gloria Steinem 1934– American journalist

From birth to 18 a girl needs good parents. From 18 to 35, she needs good looks. From 35 to 55, good personality. From 55 on, she needs good cash.

Sophie Tucker 1884–1966 American vaudeville artist

When once a woman has given you her heart, you can never get rid of the rest of her body.

John Vanbrugh 1664–1726 English architect and dramatist

Words see also **Language**, **Meaning**

The Greeks had a word for it.

Zoë Akins 1886–1958 American writer

'When *I* use a word,' Humpty Dumpty said in a rather scornful tone, 'it means just what I choose it to mean— neither more nor less.'

Lewis Carroll 1832–98 English writer

It cannot in the opinion of His Majesty's Government be classified as slavery in the extreme acceptance of the word without some risk of terminological inexactitude.

Winston Churchill 1874–1965 British statesman

A man who could make so vile a pun would not scruple to pick a pocket.

John Dennis 1657–1734 English writer

> Words strain,
> Crack and sometimes break, under the burden,
> Under the tension, slip, slide, perish,
> Decay with imprecision, will not stay in place,
> Will not stay still.

T. S. Eliot 1888–1965 American-born British poet

The chief merit of language is clearness, and we know that nothing detracts so much from this as do unfamiliar terms.

Galen AD 129–199 Greek physician

Words without actions are the assassins of idealism.

Herbert Hoover 1874–1964 American statesman

Work

And once sent out, a word takes wing beyond recall.
Horace 65–8 BC Roman poet

Lexicographer. A writer of dictionaries, a harmless drudge.
Samuel Johnson 1709–84 English lexicographer

I am not yet so lost in lexicography as to forget that words are the daughters of earth, and that things are the sons of heaven. Language is only the instrument of science, and words are but the signs of ideas.
Samuel Johnson 1709–84 English lexicographer

Words are, of course, the most powerful drug used by mankind.
Rudyard Kipling 1865–1936 English writer

Whatever we have words for, that we have already got beyond.
Friedrich Nietzsche 1844–1900 German philosopher

'Refudiate', 'misunderestimate', 'weewee'd up'. English is a living language. Shakespeare liked to coin words, too.
Sarah Palin 1964– American politician, *following controversy over her use of the word 'refudiate'*

Syllables govern the world.
John Selden 1584–1654 English historian

Was there anything so real as words?
Oscar Wilde 1854–1900 Irish dramatist

 # Work see also **Careers**

In the sweat of thy face shalt thou eat bread.
Bible

For the labourer is worthy of his hire.
Bible

Work is much more fun than fun.
Noël Coward 1899–1973 English dramatist

Work is love made visible.
Kahlil Gibran 1883–1931 Lebanese-born American writer

I have long been of the opinion that if work were such
a splendid thing the rich would have kept more of it for
themselves.
Bruce Grocott 1940– British politician

I like work: it fascinates me. I can sit and look at it for hours.
I love to keep it by me: the idea of getting rid of it nearly
breaks my heart.
Jerome K. Jerome 1859–1927 English writer

Why should I let the toad *work*
Squat on my life?
Can't I use my wit as a pitchfork
And drive the brute off?
Philip Larkin 1922–85 English poet

Blessèd are the horny hands of toil!
James Russell Lowell 1819–91 American poet

Work expands so as to fill the time available for its
completion.
C. Northcote Parkinson 1909–93 English writer

It's true hard work never killed anybody, but I figure why
take the chance?
Ronald Reagan 1911–2004 American statesman

If you have great talents, industry will improve them: if
you have but moderate abilities, industry will supply their
deficiency.
Joshua Reynolds 1723–92 English painter

Writing

Far and away the best prize that life offers is the chance to work hard at work worth doing.

Theodore Roosevelt 1858–1919 American statesman

Which of us…is to do the hard and dirty work for the rest—and for what pay? Who is to do the pleasant and clean work, and for what pay?

John Ruskin 1819–1900 English critic

One of the symptoms of approaching nervous breakdown is the belief that one's work is terribly important, and that to take a holiday would bring all kinds of disaster.

Bertrand Russell 1872–1970 British philosopher

The labour we delight in physics pain.

William Shakespeare 1564–1616 English dramatist

O God, give me work till the end of my life
And life till the end of my work.

Annie S. Swan 1859–1943 Scottish-born novelist

Work saves us from three great evils: boredom, vice and need.

Voltaire 1694–1778 French writer

 # Writing see also **Literature**, **Style**

Writers don't give prescriptions. They give headaches.

Chinua Achebe 1930–2013 Nigerian novelist

If you can't annoy somebody with what you write, I think there's little point in writing.

Kingsley Amis 1922–95 English novelist

Let other pens dwell on guilt and misery. I quit such odious subjects as soon as I can.

Jane Austen 1775–1817 English novelist

Writers, like teeth, are divided into incisors and grinders.
Walter Bagehot 1826–77 English economist

Manuscripts don't burn.
Mikhail Bulgakov 1891–1940 Russian writer

Beneath the rule of men entirely great
The pen is mightier than the sword.
Edward Bulwer-Lytton 1803–73 British novelist

When in doubt have a man come through the door with a gun in his hand.
Raymond Chandler 1888–1959 American writer

A writer must be as objective as a chemist: he must abandon the subjective line; he must know that dung-heaps play a very reasonable part in a landscape, and that evil passions are as inherent in life as good ones.
Anton Chekhov 1860–1904 Russian writer

We must beat the iron while it is hot, but we may polish it at leisure.
John Dryden 1631–1700 English poet

The writer's only responsibility is to his art. He will be completely ruthless if he is a good one…If a writer has to rob his mother, he will not hesitate; the *Ode on a Grecian Urn* is worth any number of old ladies.
William Faulkner 1897–1962 American novelist

Only connect!…Only connect the prose and the passion.
E. M. Forster 1879–1970 English novelist

The business of the poet and novelist is to show the sorriness underlying the grandest things, and the grandeur underlying the sorriest things.
Thomas Hardy 1840–1928 English novelist

Writing

The most essential gift for a good writer is a built-in, shock-proof shit detector. This is the writer's radar and all great writers have had it.
Ernest Hemingway 1899–1961 American novelist

No man but a blockhead ever wrote, except for money.
Samuel Johnson 1709–84 English lexicographer

Read over your compositions, and where ever you meet with a passage which you think is particularly fine, strike it out.
Samuel Johnson 1709–84 English lexicographer

When my sonnet was rejected, I exclaimed, 'Damn the age; I will write for Antiquity!'
Charles Lamb 1775–1834 English writer

> What in me is dark
> Illumine, what is low raise and support;
> That to the height of this great argument
> I may assert eternal providence,
> And justify the ways of God to men.
John Milton 1608–74 English poet

The last thing one knows in constructing a work is what to put first.
Blaise Pascal 1623–62 French scientist and philosopher

But those who cannot write, and those who can,
All rhyme, and scrawl, and scribble, to a man.
Alexander Pope 1688–1744 English poet

And, as imagination bodies forth
The forms of things unknown, the poet's pen
Turns them to shapes, and gives to airy nothing
A local habitation and a name.
William Shakespeare 1564–1616 English dramatist

Learn to write well, or not to write at all.
John Sheffield 1648–1721 English politician

Writing is not a profession but a vocation of unhappiness.
    Georges Simenon 1903–89 Belgian novelist

Not that the story need be long, but it will take a long while to make it short.
    Henry David Thoreau 1817–62 American writer

How vain it is to sit down to write when you have not stood up to live.
    Henry David Thoreau 1817–62 American writer

I have written my work, not as an essay which is to win the applause of the moment, but as a possession for all time.
    Thucydides c.455–c.400 BC Greek historian

Writing saved me from the sin and *inconvenience* of violence.
    Alice Walker 1944– American poet

A woman must have money and a room of her own if she is to write fiction.
    Virginia Woolf 1882–1941 English novelist

Never forget what I believe was observed to you by Coleridge, that every great and original writer, in proportion as he is great and original, must himself create the taste by which he is to be relished.
    William Wordsworth 1770–1850 English poet

Youth see also **Generation Gap**

I'm not young enough to know everything.
    J. M. Barrie 1860–1937 Scottish writer

Youth is something very new: twenty years ago no one mentioned it.
    Coco Chanel 1883–1971 French couturière

Youth

It is better to waste one's youth than to do nothing with it at all.
Georges Courteline 1858–1929 French writer

Youth is happy because it has the ability to see beauty.
Franz Kafka 1883–1924 Czech novelist

A boy's will is the wind's will
And the thoughts of youth are long, long thoughts.
Henry Wadsworth Longfellow 1807–82 American poet

Youth is vivid rather than happy, but memory always remembers the happy things.
Bernard Lovell 1913–2012 British astronomer

Whom the gods love dies young.
Menander 342–c.292 BC Greek comic dramatist

The atrocious crime of being a young man…I shall neither attempt to palliate nor deny.
William Pitt 1708–78 British statesman

My salad days,
When I was green in judgement.
William Shakespeare 1564–1616 English dramatist

Maturity is a high price to pay for growing up.
Tom Stoppard 1937– British dramatist

The force that through the green fuse drives the flower
Drives my green age.
Dylan Thomas 1914–53 Welsh poet

Make me young, make me young, make me young!
Kurt Vonnegut 1922–2007 American novelist

Youth is the one thing worth having.
Oscar Wilde 1854–1900 Irish dramatist

Heaven lies about us in our infancy!
Shades of the prison-house begin to close
Upon the growing boy.
      William Wordsworth 1770–1850 English poet

Index of Authors

Index of Authors

Index of Authors

Index of Authors

Index of Authors

Index of Authors

Index of Authors

Index of Authors

Index of Authors

Index of Authors

Index of Authors

Index of Authors

Index of Authors

Index of Authors

Index of Authors

Index of Authors

Index of Authors

Index of Authors

Index of Authors

Index of Authors

Index of Authors

Index of Authors

Index of Authors

Index of Authors

Index of Authors

Index of Authors

Index of Authors

Index of Authors

Index of Authors

Index of Authors

Index of Authors

Index of Authors

Index of Authors

Revolution,
Writing, Youth
Worrall, Terry
Weather
Wotton, Henry
Architecture,
Bereavement,
Diplomacy
Wright, Frank Lloyd
Architecture, Town
Yāqūt
Earth
Yeatman, R. J. *see*
Sellar, W. C. and
Yeatman, R. J.

Yeats, W. B.
Change, Death,
Heart, Idealism,
Indifference,
Ireland, Life, Love,
Old Age, Perfection,
Poetry, Suffering
Young, Edward
Foolishness,
Idleness,
Quotations,
Sickness, Sleep
Young, George W.
Drink
Young, Neil
Lifestyles

Zangwill, Israel
America
Zappa, Frank
Drugs, Journalism,
Progress
Zeno
Speechmaking
Zephaniah,
Benjamin
Christmas
Zobel, Hiller B.
Law
Zuckerberg, Mark
News